Fabulous Fanny Cradock

TV's Outrageous Queen of Cuisine

CLIVE ELLIS

FOREWORD BY

ANTONY WORRALL THOMPSON

SUTTON PUBLISHING

First published in the United Kingdom in 2007 by
Sutton Publishing Limited · NPI Business Park · Cirencester Road
Chalford · Stroud · Gloucestershire GL6 8PE

British Library Cataloguing in Publication Data
A catalogue record for this book is available from the British Library.

Hardback ISBN 978-0-7509-4545-5
Paperback ISBN 978-0-7509-4546-2

Picture credits: Every effort has been made to trace copyright holders. Sutton
Publishing apologises for any unintentional omissions and would be pleased, if
any case should arise, to add an appropriate acknowledgement in future additions.

Recipes: The recipes reproduced in this book have been selected to provide an
illustration of Fanny Cradock's style of cooking and have not been tested by Sutton
Publishing for use.

Line illustrations by Val Biro.

Typeset in 11/15pt Leawood Bk.
Typesetting and origination by
Sutton Publishing Limited.
Design by Glad Stockdale.
Printed and bound in Great Britain by
Oaklands Book Services Ltd
Stroud, Gloucestershire.

Contents

Foreword

BY ANTONY WORRALL THOMPSON

Fanny Cradock, a female colossus well before Germaine Greer, encouraged the female sex to burn their bras; there she was beating the insecurities out of middle England. She stood up for women's rights and it wasn't just a TV thing; I can't imagine that there were many men who weren't scared of this woman.

I met her aged seven – me that is not her – and her opening words directed about, not to, me were: 'Who does this ugly little runt belong to?' My mother was the floor manager for Fanny's TV show and there were times during my school holidays that I spent my time on the 'studio floor', with no childminder in sight. I thought she was a witch, a very scary witch.

Her sultry, booming voice would make everyone jump, her caked-on make-up and over-the-top dress sense reminded me of Cruella De Vil while I was one of the Hundred and One Dalmatians quivering behind my mother's apron strings; I could never feel at ease in her presence.

And yet, for some extraordinary reason, my mother had the ability to still the raging flames. Some of it undoubtedly was calculated on my mother's part; she plied Fanny with alcoholic drinks on her many dinner visits to our Putney house. And, as the alcohol flowed, so the pent-up liberationist anger was quelled and I saw a human side – not for long, but it was there.

On screen she was the same as she was in real life. Johnnie was there like a sponge absorbing the vitriol; he was Maggie to Dame Edna or perhaps Dennis to Maggie Thatcher. She didn't need to play herself – she was herself and she had ten million women domestic prisoners hooked. In Fanny they saw their kitchen freedom.

I soon worked out that as long as you agreed with Fanny, life could be smooth. She needed to be treated like royalty – no one else mattered. Her food was absurd over-the-top creations that middle Britain, for some extraordinary reason, warmed to. They were splashes of colour in an otherwise grey post-war Britain. And yet I felt privileged to have met her and I feel that I am now right in the centre of the spider's web she spun . . . she inspired me to cook.

Introduction

'Ah, Fanny, the Madonna of her day'

FAY MASCHLER

Fanny Cradock still raises a smile of recognition, wherever and whenever her name is mentioned. Hindsight has distorted the image, choosing to highlight her basic failings as a human being and lampooning her idiosyncrasies; but in the 1950s she was an empowering, if slightly scary-looking, Pied Piper to the nervous, L-plated housewife-cooks who approached their ovens with trepidation as Britain cast off the shackles of rationing. On live television, and even more vividly in ground-breaking stage shows which earned her rock-star-style adulation, she transformed the polite tedium of cooking demonstrations into an exotic playground.

T'adore: the photograph, signed to Johnnie under Fanny's pet name Jill, which accompanied her post-war books and articles. *(Lesley Studio)*

Monocle man: a studio shot of
Johnnie in the sixties.

Thirteen years after her death she is still a natural reference point for document-aries charting the rise and rise of the genre, and, without having much idea what she achieved or represented, a new generation finds her imprinted on its consciousness.

For fifteen years she monopolised the medium of TV cookery with her unique brand of glamour-encrusted infotain-ment. There was sound advice for the serious student and voyeuristic amusement for the culinary clueless, who tuned in as much to see her brandy-snapping at Johnnie as to crack the kitchen code. He was a monocled, moustached quasi-husband of a sidekick. In times of cooing harmony he was addressed by Fanny as 'darling' or 'my love'. As the heat rose he became the respected 'Major Cradock', the underling 'Cradock' and occasionally 'the silly old fool'.

Neither quite realised the career-enhancing significance of his decision to quit the family wool business in 1952 to work full time alongside Fanny, but the double act opened up whole new avenues of possibility. Johnnie was the Pavlovian nod to Fanny's assertion that women's cooking ambitions were held back by dictatorial husbands, blindly clinging to the drab food they had been brought up on. Johnnie was living proof that an ex-Army major could be taught the rudiments of cooking in a few weeks and volunteer to deputise for his wife at least once a week. Johnnie was the harangued underling who stood in permanent, quivering fear of his viper-tongued partner and allowed himself to be caricatured as a hapless drunk. Women dared to wonder if this striking example of role reversal had a future.

Fanny's overriding desire was to convey her love and knowledge of food to as wide a public as possible. In her eyes the rest was just garnish, but the fame and adulation had an aphrodisiac quality which she could not resist. She even enjoyed the mimicry and parody, most memorably Betty Marsden's radio take-off, and entered the lexicon of cockney rhyming slang (as haddock, of course).

She found that she could amuse in public and in her private life, though she wore the puzzled expression of someone uncertain what the joke was. The humour was frequently in the excess: in the ball gowns and tiara which Fanny donned to cook on stage and on television (this, to her, was just the natural extension of what she had been doing as a cook-hostess since the age of sixteen); in the multi-layered make-up; in the pencilled eyebrows which appeared to be on an independent journey north to meet her hairline; in the staring, unsynchronised eyes; in that husky, seductive voice honed on twenty-a-day and after-dinner Corona cigars (it was once compared to 'a circular saw going through a gin-soaked sheet'); and in the over-rolled Rs as she spat out the names of French dishes with an absurd flourish. In the BBC's top three of fast talkers she split astronomer Patrick Moore and racing commentator Peter O'Sullevan.

Fanny-watchers recruited in the early days were largely oblivious to, or uncaring about, her CV before *Kitchen Magic*. She was fortunate, too, that the press of the time did not regard celebrities' lives as ripe for intrusion. The skeletons would have been beating each other up in an effort to escape the cupboard and to curse and tell. It was said of Fanny that she could have hailed from another planet, an apt theory given her regard for the supernatural and her acknowledgement of previous lives. On Comet Cradock the maternal gene was suppressed, resulting in a shaming inability to bring up children or reconnect with them later in life. One husband had died, a second had been ditched and a third was on borrowed time by the time she met Johnnie in 1939. Twice she married bigamously, more

The entertainer: Fanny holds court at the Royal Albert Hall in 1956. *(North Thames Gas Board)*

Fanny as she appeared in her passport in 1946.

through administrative incompetence than amoral tendencies. Her
whirlwind of a temper sent casual acquaintances running for cover and
alienated family, friends and staff. Fanny's universe was a self-centred
monolith around which everyone else had to gather or be damned in their
disloyalty. Her opinions and prejudices were heavily glazed with snobbery.

On the credit side, there was a tireless vitality. She was described in the
fifties as having 'enough energy to drive a power station'. Her assistant at
the time, Wendy Colvin, asked why there was nowhere to sit down at the
Cradocks' South Kensington home. Fanny explained that chairs were things
they sat on only to eat (though she occasionally took root to play patience
and *Evening Standard* word games). She has been painted as an eccentric,
and was included by Christine Hamilton in her *Book of British Battleaxes*, but
Wendy Colvin has correctly pinned her down as a fanatic with an inflated ego.

When Fanny's first cookery book came out in 1949 – from the age of ten an
instinctive love of food had been nurtured by the smells, sights and sounds
of hotel kitchens in the south of France – she was already established as a
novelist and writer of quaint tales for children. She was a naturally
inquisitive journalist, but she pulled her own shutters down when asked the
most anodyne of questions by newspaper reporters. She gained the con-

fidence of the famous (notably the Duke and Duchess of Windsor, Somerset Maugham and Douglas Fairbanks Jnr). She wrote on food and travel for the *Daily Express*, *Daily Mail* and *Sunday Express*. She was an impressively versatile woman's editor for the *Sunday Graphic* in the early fifties, and she and Johnnie, under the pen name Bon Viveur, exuded authority and exerted influence for *The Daily Telegraph* for more than thirty years. Their restaurant and hotel reviews were pioneering and forthright – the good were praised and promoted, the indifferent and bad were ignored. Fanny helped to launch Egon Ronay, among others, to stardom when she extolled the virtues of his Knightsbridge restaurant, the Marquee. He regarded her more as an important ally than as a gifted cook.

She was a born campaigner. Immediately after the war she joined the British Housewives' League to bemoan the homemaker's over-rationed lot; she urged shoppers to complain about shoddy goods and services; she ridiculed restaurants that mixed menu-French with bill-of-fare English; she sounded an early warning over artificial foodstuffs and fertilisers. She terrorised builders, postmen, milkmen and local authorities.

The start of something: Fanny and Johnnie make their debut in the photographer's studio during the war.

Fanny in 1978: TV career all
but over, the Lormes saga in
full swing.

The massed ranks of today's TV chefs owe
Fanny Cradock a mighty debt, though it is
not one they are over-willing to voice. They
acknowledge her entertainment value, but
increasingly the retrospective stress is on
Fanny's irrelevance, as though her sell-by
date expired in 1959. Archive clips focus on
the green-dyed duchess potatoes, the overblown presentation, the Fanny look, the
ever-so-slightly ribald stream of consciousness, and Johnnie as resident punchbag.
Newspaper pundits' analysis concentrates
on the words she got wrong, the absurdly
strict amounts in her recipes, and the dishes that allegedly don't translate
from paper to plate.

Fanny Cradock was gloriously ahead of her time, a crusading cook who
sensed that television must seduce before it could instruct. Transposed to
2007, she would be competing for the
Ramsay millions; she would be intro-
ducing oyster appreciation classes to
the National Curriculum; she would
be more plain-speaking and outrageous than Anne Robinson and
Simon Cowell combined; and she
would be adopted as a national
treasure. Bring on the hors d'œuvres.

Dessert storm: as featured on the
cover of the Bon Viveur book *365
Puddings* in 1975. *(Michael Leale/BPC
Publishing)*

Beginnings

FROM BILLIARD TABLE TO BALLET

Fanny Cradock's loosely tethered childhood was defined by her change of ownership at the age of one. It was a story she retold a thousand times – in private, in public and in print – like a pop star regurgitating her first hit song. The most vivid rendition featured in Fanny's auto-biography, *Something's Burning*:

> I was a year old when Mother took me to see Gran on her birthday. We reached Apthorp at 11 a.m., the hour at which Gran trailed from bedroom to boudoir wrapped in a huge Turkish towel, cleaning her teeth with a dry toothbrush. Mother dumped me on the billiard table (why, we do not know) and, running upstairs to Gran, promptly forgot my existence.
>
> Some time later – and it must have been a considerable time, for Gran never dressed in a hurry – the two ladies descended the

> **'She was such a mixture of being an absolute slut, wandering round in grubby trousers, and then being very grand.'**
>
> *Alison Leach, Personal Assistant*

staircase and heard my hideous yells. Gran traced me and whipped me off the billiards table into her arms. 'Bijou,' she said furiously, 'you are not fit to have a child.' 'I brought her to you for a birthday present,' said Mum defensively. She had forgotten any more appropriate offering. Gran replied grimly, 'Thank you, I accept her.' Thus was my future determined. I stayed with Gran until I was sent off to school when I was ten.

Phyllis Nan Sortain Pechey (Fanny was a later acquisition) settled in at Apthorp, the imposing house in Leytonstone, east London, where she had been born on 26 February 1909, while her eighteen-year-old mother concentrated on her primary maternal purpose: producing a son and heir. Charles, a child she did care for in her own distracted way, was born in 1911.

Fanny, a 'bloody awful little girl' by her own admission, adapted without demur to the generation gap. Her grandparents took vague responsibility for her early education and her parents, who lived only a few miles away, were occasional visitors. In Fanny's eyes her grandmother, Emily Frances Hancock, vied with Johnnie for top billing as the most important figure in

Apthorp House: Fanny's birthplace, converted into drab flats after the death of her grandparents in the 1920s.

Fanny upbraided journalists and letter-writers who spelt her surname with two ds, so she would not have enjoyed the plaque outside Apthorp House, where she was born in 1909.

her life. She described her as 'the symbol of all that is cultivated and gracious, gentle and loving'. Both Fanny and she preferred an intelligent sinner to a foolish saint (of impeccable lineage of course).

'She made me translate a paragraph of *The Times* leader every morning into both French and German,' Fanny remembered. 'A delightful old Austrian was engaged to teach me the rudiments of violin-playing on a tiny fiddle when I was only five; he had a huge spade beard and smelled of garlic. My ballet training began with a curious old girl whose hair looked like a whipped cream walnut; she had a slight tic and throughout my bar-work sessions wore a hat which looked like a well-stocked aviary.'

Fanny's grandmother introduced her to colour-themed cookery, as well as the self-sufficient joys of bottling, potting, pickling and preserving. Her grandfather, Charles, who had been a surgeon-major in the Indian Army before returning to England in 1900, inadvertently fostered her love of cigars – she was rewarded with a weekly puff after filling his pipe – and an early appreciation of the grape. 'My wine was pale pink at five, deep pink by eight and often straight from the bottle by the time I went to school.'

'My wine was pale pink at five, deep pink by eight and often straight from the bottle by the time I went to school.'

SPOOKS AND SCHOOL

Fanny Cradock might have been more resentful of a chum-free early childhood if she hadn't discovered a psychic sensibility. It was largely a private world but one of PlayStation normality to her, until, that was, adults began to shriek in disapproval. She claimed to have a hotline to the court of Louis XIV of France and played levitation games with her brother Charles. 'If I had been handled differently,' she wrote, 'I would have continued to accept without question that what happened to me did not happen to everyone else and would have thought no more about it. But instead, when it came out later on and became a matter for the "gravest concern", I grew up to regard it as something shameful like bed-wetting and I developed the most painful complex about it.'

Fanny's spiritual guilt multiplied when she was bundled off to a 'distinguished' boarding school, the Downs, at the age of ten. 'I learned nothing, forgot all I knew and hourly hoped to die,' she recalled. A chance meeting with a fellow ex-pupil just before the Second World War brought the bitterness flooding back. 'Socking and being socked with mud from lacrosse sticks in a slippery field with a biting north wind howling up knee-length gym tunics. . . . Lesbian ties and lesbian matrons who wrenched those ties straight and only favoured little girls with pink cheeks and golden curls.' After five years of misery, Fanny was caught holding a séance in the school library. Further investigation revealed documents in her locker relating to past lives. She stirred the pot a little more urgently:

> About the same time I expressed my views with some force on the subject of unmarried women who chose child bullying as a career because no man would marry them and give them normal lives. It was also bad timing, which is inexcusable, that I chose this moment to resign publicly from the school's Girl Guide patrol for the – to me – perfectly valid reason that it was a bad thing for girls to dress up in uniforms and play soldiers.

She was expelled, then given a term's stay of execution when her parents mollified the headmistress. She was catapulted into adulthood at the age of fifteen.

FANNY'S FATHER

Tons of Money was the 1920s farce that made Archibald Thomas Pechey and indirectly dumped him, eight years later, in the quick sands of bankruptcy. The trouble, as it had been throughout his married life, was a wilful wife

Tons of Money was a temporary passport to wealth for Fanny's father, who co-wrote the 1922 farce as Valentine.

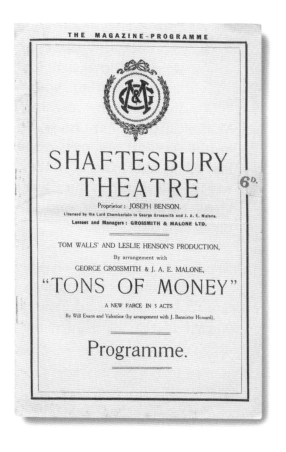

THE MAGAZINE-PROGRAMME

SHAFTESBURY THEATRE 6ᴰ·

Proprietor : JOSEPH BENSON.

Licensed by the Lord Chamberlain to George Grossmith and J. A. E. Malone.

Lessees and Managers : GROSSMITH & MALONE LTD.

TOM WALLS' AND LESLIE HENSON'S PRODUCTION,

By arrangement with

GEORGE GROSSMITH & J. A. E. MALONE,

"TONS OF MONEY"

A NEW FARCE IN 3 ACTS

By Will Evans and Valentine (by arrangement with J. Bannister Howard).

Programme.

who drained both his finances and emotions, and a gambler's double-or-quits mentality.

Fanny's father was a typical public-school-educated product of his time: polite, modest and understated. Less typically, he had a song (or at least a lyric) in his heart, and was part-credited for the words of 'A Bachelor Gay', one of the best-known tunes from the 1917 hit musical *The Maid of the Mountains*. He had turned his back on the corn merchants' business in 1910, the year after Fanny was born, and began writing verses for *The Winning Post*, a publication devoted to society gossip and horse-racing, and in particular horses owned by its charismatic editor-proprietor. Bob Sievier gambled his way from fortune to famine and back again, paying a world-record 10,000 guineas for the multi-Classic-winning Sceptre in 1901 and following Pechey into the bankruptcy courts in the 1930s.

Under the pen name Valentine, Fanny's father addressed such pressing topics as mixed bathing, a school for kissing and the perils of kilt-wearing. In 1913 he popped up as the briefly famous Jester of the *London Mail*, touring England's seaside hot spots to offer 2 guineas to anyone who could success-fully identify him as the Jester. Two years later he joined forces with Will Evans to write *Tons of Money* (comic chaos ensues when Aubrey Henry Maitland Allington, a heavily indebted inventor, inherits a fortune). Several years of painful rejection followed before it was taken on by producers Tom Walls and Leslie Henson, who were alerted to the script's potential by a chuckling office boy. *Tons of Money* opened at the Shaftesbury Theatre in April 1922, and graduated to the Aldwych later in the year, establishing both

'The pair of them were diametrically opposed on almost every subject except Mother, whom they both adored. Mother inspired him, believed in him, reviled him and gave him all his best plots, as well as every headache he ever knew. He adored her, and she drove him distracted.'

the acting team (led by Ralph Lynn) and the appetite for farce that sustained Ben Travers through nine sell-out productions. *Tons of Money* finally closed, 737 curtain-calls later, in February 1924 (it was revived by Alan Ayckbourn in the 1980s).

Archibald Pechey saw debts of £2,000 wiped out at a stroke. In 1922 alone he made an estimated £7,000 from the play (equivalent to more than £200,000 today), and he embarked on a peripatetic lifestyle befitting his new wealth. As if trying to keep one address ahead of the taxman, Fanny's family moved from Herne Bay in Kent to Swanage, to Bournemouth and finally to Wroxham in Norfolk. Fanny's mother persuaded her husband – Archibald preferred home

The men in her life: Fanny dining out in 1948 with her father, Johnnie and elder son Peter.

comforts – that winters in Nice were preferable to Norfolk. They stayed in the best hotels, headed for the casinos at night, and squandered a fortune. Warnings from the Inland Revenue went unheeded and Fanny's father was finally hauled before Norwich bankruptcy court in 1930, owing more than £3,500. He cited the 'drain imposed on him in helping relatives' and admitted: '*Tons of Money* changed my position once and I have been waiting for it to happen again.'

The film rights for *Tons of Money* were sold soon afterwards and another Valentine play, *Compromising Daphne*, was also adapted as an early talkie. However, disgruntled creditors – he owed a furniture company about £20,000 in current terms – had still not been appeased by the outbreak of the Second World War. All too predictably, Fanny's parents split up, though her father's devotion survived. After the war, he settled in Somerset and established a contented routine of prolific novel-writing in winter and butterfly-hunting in summer (he accumulated more than 6,000 specimens). The gentle romances were penned by Valentine, the crime-busting exploits of Daphne Wrayne and her Adjusters appeared under the pseudonym Mark Cross. His hundredth novel, and forty-sixth in the Adjuster series, was published just before he died in 1961.

FANNY'S MOTHER

Long after Fanny's mother had died, Johnnie Cradock was asked by the *Daily Mail* columnist Lynda Lee-Potter whether personality traits had been passed down:

'Oh she's just as mad,' he said reflectively.
'Like Mum?' blazed Fanny. 'Why she was round the twist.'
'Yes,' confirmed her husband. 'Just as mad.'

Mother and daughter both spoke in an intimidating growl – they were frequently mistaken for one another on the phone – but, to Fanny's mind anyway, the similarities ended there. The quaintly named Bijou ('like some damned Pekinese,' she complained) was as indolent and work-shy as Fanny was driven and industrious. 'Her singing voice was exceptional and she was the Invisible Voice in D.W. Griffiths' epic film *Intolerance*,' Fanny wrote. 'Offers for stage and films poured in, yet nothing tempted her away from her

Three of a kind: Fanny's mother and grandparents pictured at Apthorp House, *c.* 1908.

way of life. Anything that involved getting up at the same time every morning was impossible and unacceptable.'

Fanny's father, though already engaged to another, was no sooner introduced than smitten. He despatched a terse telegram from Henley post office to his fiancée which read: 'Engagement off – letter follows'. Archibald and Bijou married in 1908 and Fanny was born the following year, christened Phyllis in deference to the fact that her parents had met at Phyllis Court in Henley. It soon

'Daddy wanted peace and quiet and Dickens and entomology and watercolours. Mum wanted parties.'

became clear that the marriage was a loose alliance. Fanny later wrote wryly: 'The pair of them were diametrically opposed on almost every subject except Mother, whom they both adored.' She added: 'Mother inspired him, believed in him, reviled him and gave him all his best plots, as well as every headache he ever knew. He adored her, and she drove him distracted.'

Bijou was the soul of extravagance, champion of the snap purchase, and hopelessly addicted to sales. 'She once trundled up the drive towing a vast iron lawn roller which, she explained defensively, she had been forced to buy in order to obtain the dozen rose bushes which made up the Lot.' While her ideal start to the day was an 11 o'clock breakfast of a dozen oysters and half a pint of champagne, she resented every piece of toilet paper used by other members of the family.

Fanny's mother was an inadvertent aide to her husband's plays and lyrics, an effortless supplier of malapropisms. The Receiver in Bankruptcy became the Official Retriever; politician Anthony Eden's duodenal ulcer was translated as an *eau-de-nil* ulcer.

Archibald Pechey dubbed her, among other things, the 'oak-egger moth'. The female of the species, it is said, can, when feeling amorous, call on a natural radar system which summons males from 300 miles away. 'She was totally fantastic, totally inconsequential and illogical,' Fanny told the *Observer* in 1968, 'with no more idea of raising kids than a bull's foot.'

Mum's Tripe and Onions

Ingredients

2 lb double or honeycomb tripe
2½ lb best possible onions
½ pt double cream
1 pt milk

cold water
2 rounded tablespoons of *Fécule de Pommes* (potato flour packed by Groult)
salt and black pepper.

Method

Slice raw tripe as for English chips. Slice peeled onions as thinly as possible. Place both in a really roomy pan and cover liberally with cold water. Simmer steadily until tripe melts in the mouth and onions are correspondingly tender. Strain off all liquor. Place this in a clean pan and reduce by simmering hard to a mere ¼ pt of concentrated fluid. Stir in all but 1fl oz cold milk, then raise to boiling. Meanwhile mix potato flour with remaining 1fl oz milk. Stir into pot and stir fast as mixture will thicken instantly. Turn into tripe and onions, stir again until thoroughly blended, taste and correct seasoning with plenty of salt and pepper. Transfer to a casserole, stir in cream, leave until the next day and then reheat in the oven at Gas Mark 2 until bubbling and rather pale beige.

Time to Remember, 1981

Bijou, sixteen years younger than Archibald Pechey, was comfortably the senior partner in her second marriage, to a Berkshire estate agent. She died in 1949, though for months afterwards Fanny set a dinner place for her at the Cradock home in South Kensington.

FANNY'S BROTHER

If Fanny Cradock had an amoral streak, her brother Charles was positively anarchic, playing the part of misfit with greater success than any of the other roles into which he tumbled in adulthood. Fanny preferred to carry an untainted image of Charles as he was in early childhood. 'I remember him when he was five and quite ravishing. In my picture he wore a scarlet coat, bestrode an ancient mare and was borne like a baby Roman emperor, with his trophies (dead rabbits) slung from a stirrup and smothered in flies.'

The beautiful boy turned into a wayward youth – he was expelled from Cheltenham College after attending the school for only a year – and a feckless soldier. He was slung out of the Royal Berkshire Regiment in 1942, court-martialled and cashiered for trying to pay prostitutes with dud cheques. At various times he worked as an actor, rag-and-bone merchant and publican (a job for which his drink reliance made him madly unsuitable).

He was a serial sponger – Fanny's father told her in a post-war letter that despite Charles's suicide threats he would not 'lend' another penny – and was apt to phone his sister out of the blue, pleading for shelter after a midnight bunk from rented accommodation. For all that, there was a bond between Fanny (or Phatti as Charles affectionately knew her) and her brother. They shared the grimmest of times in the 1930s when they came to appreciate the subtle difference between bread and pepper and plain bread.

Charmer Charles: Fanny's brother, 'ravishing' at the age of five. *(H. Oscar Southgate)*

Fanny BY ANY OTHER NAME ———————

Phyllis Nan Sortain (Primrose) Pechey (Primrose = family name)
Phatti (brother's pet name for her)
Phyl (as known to friends)
Jill (Johnnie's pet name)
Phyllis Vernon Evans (first marriage)
Phyllis Chapman (second marriage)
Phyllis Holden-Dye (third marriage)
Phyllis Cradock (after changing name by deed poll)
Frances Dale (early novels and journalism)
Nan Sortain (beauty articles for *Daily Telegraph*)
Elsa Frances (fashion articles for *Daily Telegraph*)
Philip Essex (*Sunday Graphic* serial on lost continent of Atlantis)
Susan Leigh (children's book)
Phyllis Whitby-Cradock (incorporating Johnnie's second name)

Charles, more commonly known as John after the war, flitted in and out of Fanny's life. Ever charming, plausible and perpetually broke, his greatest talent was for answering crisis calls. He stepped in at the last minute to produce and direct Fanny and Johnnie in their most prestigious cooking show, at the Royal Albert Hall in December 1956, and a month later supervised the couple as they gave *Something's Burning* its test run at the Arts Theatre. Fanny recalled the television rehearsal for the Albert Hall show: ' "Lights," roared Charles. "Quiet everybody please. . . ." We looked at each other. "Bread and pepper," he said suddenly, and for a moment neither of us could speak.'

The concord never lasted for long, and Christopher Chapman, Fanny's son by her second husband, recalls a slightly surreal experience in the early sixties. 'I never ever spoke to him. I only once saw him in my life when I was going round the Ideal Home Exhibition with my mother and in the garden. She suddenly grabbed my elbow and said, "We're getting out of here quick. Look, there's your wicked uncle John." And she turned me round and marched me out.'

Rose Petal Jam
one of Fanny's grandmother's specialities

Method

Gather red roses while the dew is upon them, strip the petals down and wipe them carefully. It is necessary to remove the white or yellow centre pieces from the petals. Now spread them out loosely and rub them with powdered loaf sugar (folded in brown paper and well beaten and rolled with a wooden rolling-pin).

Using rain water only, measure 1½ pints water and 1½ lb of preserving or lump sugar. Dissolve slowly and bring to the boil. Boil till the edges begin to crystal. Remove from the fire, add the strained juice of a small lemon and enough rose petals to absorb the syrup to a thick pulp. Reboil, add 1oz unsalted butter to clear. Simmer very gently for 45 minutes, stirring occasionally. Pot immediately.

The Practical Cook, 1949

Alison Leach, Fanny's personal assistant, brought about a brief reunion in 1966, when Fanny still faced an uncertain prognosis after being operated on for bowel cancer:

I remember saying, 'Do you feel you'd really like to see your brother, who you're very fond of but who you've written out of your life.' She said, 'How extraordinary, I'd not thought of that. I don't know how to find him.' Somehow or other I found where his bank account was. The very next day he came rushing down to see her and they established this very warm relationship for two or three years.

Fanny and Family

STARVING FOR A LIVING

Spoiled, indulged and subsidised through her childhood and early teens, Fanny Cradock was suddenly sentenced to a subsistence lifestyle. As the 1920s bowed out she had just turned twenty. Widowed from her first husband, irretrievably separated from her second, she had a two-year-old son in bewildered tow. She wrote later:

> I came down to a hole-in-the-wall in West Kensington, where my son Peter and I led an existence that I am sure would have brought us before some authority or other in this era of Welfare State.
>
> The room was about eight by twelve. It had an ancient gas ring and a gas bracket which hissed malevolently. It looked out (from the basement) at a blank wall which was indescribably sooty. My first job (down to tuppence and the last bottle of milk for Peter) was in a Roman Catholic canteen in Lower Thames Street, where I washed up from 11 a.m. to 3 p.m. for half a crown and my luncheon. I walked there, walked back, unlocked Peter, cleaned up the mess, and nipped into Kensington Public Library to study the situations vacant.

Fanny before fame: Phyllis
Chapman in a photograph which
was taken just before the war.

Fanny's parents were about to
split up – her spendthrift mother
hustled her father towards bankruptcy and jumped ship when the
debts were finally called in. Fanny
was about to discover the fierce
determination and bloody-minded
persistence that sustained her
through the bad times and fired
her ambition when the dice began
to roll in her favour. In her later
accounts of this portion of her life
there is a self-parodying echo of
the Monty Python sketch 'We were so poor that . . .', but the truth cannot
have been too far removed.

Having already honed her cutting talents by improvising cardboard soles
for her shoes, she drew on her skills as a Vogue Pattern dressmaker
(another hobby-cum-money-saving activity to which she remained stoically
loyal) to start a business of sorts. A jilted, would-be boyfriend paid the
deposit on a sewing machine which Fanny bought on hire purchase, but an
early commission for an outsized garment went disastrously awry. 'After
calling with the dress and collecting a guinea, I received a card from the lady
on which was written, "I don't know whether you thought the dress was
intended for me or an elephant, but when I slipped it over my head it fell
straight down on to the floor." '

Fanny persuaded a semi-skilled dressmaker to work for her and found
temporary income in a variety of odd jobs. She worked in a grocer's shop in
Clapham, made and sold Swiss rolls at an Alexandra Palace exhibition,
hawked 3d cures for tired feet at the Ideal Home Exhibition, and helped out
in Selfridge's bargain basement during the Christmas rush. Her guiding text,
however, and the one that she expounded passionately from the pulpit at
St Mary Woolnoth in the East End of London almost forty years later, was

inspired by selling vacuum cleaners on a straight-commission basis. 'I learned *tout court* that if you knock on enough doors you sell a vacuum cleaner. It is just as simple as that. And when you have a small boy locked in a bedsitting room waiting to be fed and the only hope is a vacuum cleaner sale (twenty-five shillings!) you knock on doors and you go on knocking on doors. One way or another I have never stopped knocking on doors since.'

'When you have a small boy locked in a bedsitting room waiting to be fed and the only hope is a vacuum cleaner sale (twenty-five shillings!) you knock on doors and you go on knocking on doors. One way or another I have never stopped knocking on doors since.'

The slightly masochistic offshoot for Fanny was confirmation of her Conservative ideals. 'Yet even at the most disagreeable time of all it failed to colour my politics,' she wrote. 'I came down to starvation level of my own free will in a free country. The opportunity of climbing back was always there provided I was prepared to sweat, so I sweated. Most malcontents are bone idle.'

WEDDING BELLS I

Sidney Vernon Evans, 10 October 1926

Major and often traumatic chapters in Fanny Cradock's life were repackaged as anecdotal frippery; not just to please an impatient audience but to prove that her spirit was unbreakable. The first of three pre-war marriages was tossed on the emotional heap with a flip flourish: 'I married on Wednesday, settled his debts on Friday and he died on Sunday.' The truth, as with so many aspects of Fanny's life, was more complicated.

Though no classic beauty – Fanny lamented that her mother and brother had been more benevolently blessed in

Flying visit: Pilot Officer Sidney Vernon Evans (centre back) in a 56 Squadron picture at Biggin Hill in 1926.

that department – she appears to have been pursued by would-be suitors from her early teens. She boasted that she was first engaged, to a millionaire, when she was fourteen and returned to school sporting a square-cut emerald ring. A year later, in 1924, she met Sidney Vernon Evans, a public-school-educated, rugby-playing free spirit who had turned his back on the City to join the RAF.

Fanny's guiding light of a grandmother died at the end of September 1926 and a fortnight later she was circumventing parental permission (which would not have been granted) to marry Sidney, by then stationed with 56 Squadron at Biggin Hill in Kent. He was twenty-two; she was seventeen, though she claimed on the marriage certificate that she was twenty-one. Two of Sidney's fellow pilots were the sole witnesses to the wedding, which the couple celebrated by going sailing off Goodwin Sands. Fanny and Sidney were three weeks into married life when she thought she should break the news to her parents. She recalled, in her autobiography, that a telephone call brought a predictably dismissive response from her mother. '"No, you may not come home. I don't want any soiled doves in my house." I roared back down the telephone, "I'm not a soiled dove – I'm married," and then the row began.'

The couple established a pattern of conspicuous overspending and shared a growing sense of foreboding, which accelerated their baby-making plans (they had already decided that the child would be a son called Peter). 'On the first Wednesday in February, the station doctor confirmed that I was pregnant,' Fanny wrote:

> Two days later Sidney went off as usual. He flew over the house about eleven o'clock in the morning and waved to me. He failed to return to luncheon. Early in the afternoon, as I stood at the drawing-room windows, I saw a station tender pull up and the C.O. get out. I opened the door to him. I remember feeling desperately sorry for him – he looked so white and hopeless. I said, 'You needn't tell me, because I know' – and the only thing I can remember after that is wanting him to go quickly as possible and leave me by myself.

There was no heroism attached to Sidney's death on 4 February 1927: it was simply a routine map-reading exercise in a Gloucester Grebe which went horribly wrong in adverse weather. The *Evening Argus* reported:

He was coming from the direction of Brighton, and an eye-witness states that he, apparently, lost his bearings and, flying very low, narrowly missed hitting the Brighton Gas Works at Black Rock. He circled round several times, gradually flying lower, obviously with the intention of making a forced landing on the Downs.

When it seemed that he would not succeed in bringing his machine safely to ground, he was observed to release his parachute, but he had delayed too long for his machine crashed into a rising bank of Mr Filkins' field and turned a double somersault before bursting into flames.

The pilot, just before his machine smashed, is said to have tried to jump, but unhappily, his effort failed and he was killed instantaneously.

Strangely enough, within a few minutes of the accident the fog cleared and beautiful sunshine shone down on the debris of the ruined plane.

Fanny was left with a token service widow's pension of £24 a year, and in October gave birth to her first child, Peter.

Giant Sausage Roll

A perennial picnic dependable for Fanny's extended 'family'

Ingredients

THE FILLING

1lb sausage meat

3 hard-boiled eggs

1 finely chopped onion

1 teaspoon parsley

1 teaspoon mint, minced or finely chopped

3 tablespoons mayonnaise

THE PASTRY

4 oz sifted flour

1 teaspoon golden raising powder

1½ oz lard

1 oz margarine

cold water to mix

Method

Sift flour and golden raising powder together. Rub in fats, bind with cold water. Roll out on floured board into narrow strip 16 in long. Knead sausage meat with herbs and onion, roll out on floured board. Lay over the pastry. Cover with finely chopped eggs. Coat the top surface with mayonnaise. Wet pastry edges with cold water, roll into long sausage, brush the surface with milk or egg and milk. Bake in oven at Regulo 6, Thermostat 400.

Sunday Graphic, 1950

WEDDING BELLS II

Arthur Chapman, 23 July 1928

Arthur Chapman and Fanny Cradock were together for little more than a year, but effectively 'celebrated' their golden wedding anniversary just before he died in 1978. In the intervening period Fanny acquired two more husbands – she and Johnnie tied the knot in 1977 in the mistaken belief that Arthur Chapman had already passed on – and found fame and fortune.

Fanny was barely nineteen and her son Peter just six months old when she met civil engineer Arthur William Chapman early in 1928. Her parents' marriage was disintegrating; however, she had little option but to move back to the family home just outside Norwich when her first husband, Sidney, died. She eased herself back into the social whirl and conducted what her son Christopher described as 'a pretty short courtship by all accounts' with 22-year-old Arthur.

A less romantic, but probably accurate, interpretation is that Fanny was hustled into a face-saving wedding when she discovered she was pregnant in the summer of 1928. She and Arthur married on 23 July 1928; Christopher was born just over eight months later; and Fanny moved out in the summer of 1929, salvaging Peter from the wreck of the relationship. The marriage, from Fanny's perspective anyway, had no mileage, though Christopher later gathered that his father had been 'pretty devoted to her'. Arthur settled into a life of quiet simplicity, but his son gathered that there had been a wilful,

spontaneous streak which might have appealed to Fanny when they first met. 'He was a bit of a wild one and he was a little bit thirsty too at the time. He was also recovering from a badly broken leg which he carried with him for the rest of his life after a motorcycle accident. It meant he couldn't follow any athletic pursuits.' Arthur Chapman, who did his bit for the war effort by helping to build munitions factories, was spiritually battered by the winning and losing of Fanny. He converted to Catholicism – thus his refusal to give her a divorce – and saw out his final years in Hertfordshire.

A man and his pipe: Arthur Chapman.

When it came to writing her autobiography in 1960 it was pointed out to Fanny that she could not sensibly write about Christopher without reference, however elliptic, to his father. She delivered the cold epitaph: 'As my second marriage was not a happy one, Christopher, John and I have decided it shall have no place in this story.'

WEDDING BELLS III

Greg Holden-Dye, 26 September 1939

If Arthur Chapman was the husband written off in one dismissive sentence in Fanny Cradock's autobiography, Greg Holden-Dye was the spouse who never existed. He was still a non-person when she died in 1994 and it was only diligent digging for a 1998 Channel 4 documentary called *The Real Fanny Cradock* that brought Greg's brief part in her story to light.

On the face of it he was the ideal, fun-loving partner for Fanny as she emerged from hand-to-mouth penury in the early 1930s. He was handsome, had family money to subsidise his hedonistic urges and shared her love of spontaneity. He also had a daredevil streak: he played Captain Blood in a re-enactment of the stealing of the Crown Jewels from the Tower of London and leapt fearlessly from a tower window onto a horse below. He was also a motor racing driver of minor repute, attached to Woolf Barnato's stable of Bentleys, and drove regularly at the famous Brooklands track in Surrey. He did not always warm to the well-connected, arty social set with whom Fanny liked to mix, and a clash of personalities soon surfaced. Helen Davison, Greg's second wife, said: 'He had a third of Italian in him and had quite a temper, but she used to embarrass him terribly when they went into restaurants, always complaining in a loud voice.'

Greg also related an early example of Fanny's antipathy to authority figures. Helen Davison recounts: 'Greg and Fanny were stopped in his open sports car. She was terribly rude, calling [the policeman] Mr Plod and all sorts of things. He told me, "I thought

Young adventurer: Greg Holden-Dye at the age of twenty.

we were going to be put in jail or something." But then she charmed him.' On other occasions, Helen explains, Fanny's boundless self-confidence brought positive reward. 'Greg was mad keen on Louis Armstrong and they went to a concert of his before the war. They went backstage afterwards and, of course, Fanny was not backwards in coming forwards, so she invited him back with some of his band to their flat, where they played for them.'

In much the same way that Fanny rewrote personal history to assure Greg that Arthur Chapman had walked out on her and not vice versa, she told friends towards the end of her life that she agreed to marry Greg in 1939 as a personal favour. She claimed that he was gay, an absurd assertion shot down by his second marriage in 1954 and subsequent parenthood. Greg assured his new wife that he and Fanny had followed the correct procedure by advertising their intention to get married, heard nothing from Arthur Chapman and had been told that they were free to proceed; however, they were warned by the registrar that if Arthur subsequently surfaced any children Greg and Fanny had would be illegitimate. This was an irrelevant concern, Greg explained to Helen, because Fanny had already had a hysterectomy (though this does not tally with Fanny's later, cryptic assertion that she lost a third child in pregnancy).

Greg had been prevented from joining the RAF by deficient eyesight and opted for the Auxiliary Fire Service instead. Elsa Waters, whose dressmaking skills helped Fanny's business to flourish just before the war, remembered Greg ringing the bell madly as the fire engine passed the Kensington shop. In marrying Greg, Fanny acquired a hostile mother-in-law, who accused her of baby-snatching (though she was only two years older than Greg) and was re-invented as a deeply unsympathetic character in Fanny's first novel, *Scorpion's Suicide*.

Six weeks after Fanny and Greg were married she met Johnnie, and Greg was cast adrift early in 1940. Helen Davison explains: 'Everything seemed to be fine, but one evening she came in and said, "Sorry, I've met somebody else." He had no idea this was going on and he was totally broken and walked round South Kensington all night. He told me that in the morning he just went in and got all his things.'

Greg, who spoke fluent Malay on the strength of spending much of his childhood in the Far East, was recruited by British Intelligence towards the end of the war to interrogate alleged collaborators. Thinking he might be killed, he arranged to see Fanny. That was their last face-to-face encounter, though correspondence resumed in 1954. Helen Davison recalls:

IN RESIDENCE

1942–5	Wayfield Cottage, Snitterfield, near Stratford-upon-Avon
1945–58	29 South Terrace, South Kensington, London, SE7
1958–68	134 Shooters Hill Road, Blackheath, London, SE3
1968–74	Dower House, Watford, Herts.
1974–8	Doneraile, Co. Cork
1978–84	Villa Théoule, St Martin's, Guernsey
1984–7	Orchard House, Little Bentley, near Colchester, Essex
1987–8	Little Dean Court, Stockbridge, Hants
1988–91	Flat 2, Xavier House, Chichester, West Sussex
1991–4	Ersham House, Hailsham, East Sussex

We wanted to get married, but Greg said he didn't think he could because he was still married to Fanny. He wrote to her and said, 'Look I've met someone I want to marry. Can you tell me what the position is?' She wrote back and said, 'Don't worry. Everything's all right. I met Arthur in London. He's still alive so our marriage was null and void.'

When our son Jonathan was born she wrote and said, 'I'd very much like to be godmother.' I think she thought she was doing us an enormous favour because she was then quite famous. It must have been a bit of a slap in the face when Greg wrote back and said thanks very much but we've already chosen the godparents. She said she'd like to meet me but I said I wasn't really interested.

Greg Holden-Dye was diagnosed with pre-senile dementia in the early seventies and died in 1974.

PETER'S STORY

Peter Vernon Evans, mercifully, remembers nothing of the first four years of his life, a grim period in which Fanny was barely able to keep herself afloat, let alone attend to the basic needs of a small child. He was adopted by his paternal grandparents in 1932 – Peter's father Sidney had died before he was born – and given the kind of stable upbringing which would have been outside the range of Fanny's defective maternal radar, even in happier times. The terms of the adoption were that Fanny was barred contact until Peter turned twenty-one in 1948. In the event she was allowed to jump the gun by a few months; she kitted him out and launched him on London society like some male debutant.

Following a public school education at Wellington College, Peter had joined the Royal Marines in 1944, and after being demobbed he became a Lloyd's underwriter. The job bored him thoroughly and he was pleased to discover that there was one advantage, at least, in having Cradock connections: Johnnie fixed him up as a sous-chef at the Dorchester hotel.

Evangeline Banks, as next-door neighbour in South Terrace, daughter of the well-known actors Leslie and Gwen Banks, and an aspiring actress herself, was ideal daughter-in-law material in Fanny's eyes. Evangeline and Peter, three years her senior, dined, danced and partied, but the self-contained Peter was already uneasily aware that his mother was trying to mould and map out his future.

Disagreements were regular, but it took a chance meeting between Fanny and Peter's wife-to-be, Pam, to set off the chain of events that led to a permanent rift. Pam had been visiting relatives; Fanny and Johnnie were on a working holiday in Scandinavia; they met on a train traversing Finland in

1954. The Cradocks were still unknown faces, but the mention of Bon Viveur and *The Daily Telegraph* struck an instant chord. Pam also remembers being flattered with the observation that her nose was exactly the kind of delicate feature that Fanny cherished – and duly received when she went under the plastic surgeon's knife a few weeks later.

The Kenyan connection: Peter and Pam Vernon Evans with their three sons in 1968.

Pam was asked if she would like to work for Fanny and was soon a part of the Bon Viveur team. She helped out with stage shows, and was also involved in the preparation for their television début on *Kitchen Magic* in February 1955. Fanny, Pam and Peter combined forces to set up an outside catering business, Gourmet to Gourmet, which collapsed after a few months, condemned by Fanny's typically stingy refusal to put significant money into the venture. 'Everything went swimmingly until Peter and I started seeing each other,' Pam remembers. 'When we told her we were engaged she hit the roof and started to behave absolutely horrendously to both of us. She said that it would all end in tears and that she never wanted to see us again.'

Peter discovered that there was a sinister side-effect to Fanny's fury. The doors to catering jobs suddenly slammed shut en masse, and in April 1955, inspired by the free passage which went with the job, he joined the Kenyan police force. Pam followed a few months later and they were married in October of that year. Peter went on to become secretary of the Lake Naivasha Country Club, the hub of jealous intrigue in the film *White Mischief*. Apart from a few years spent in England while their three sons were being educated, Peter and Pam have remained in Kenya ever since, and they celebrated their golden wedding anniversary in October 2005.

Fanny's two sons, Peter and Christopher, were unaware of each other's existence until the early sixties, though they had spent the first few months of Christopher's life under the same roof. One reunion, thirty-five years ago, almost resulted in Peter's bizarre demise. He had arranged to stay at Christopher's pub in Axmouth, Devon, after rushing back from safari in Kenya when he heard that his step-grandmother had died. Exhausted and disorientated, Peter climbed out of a first-storey window in his sleep, fell heavily, and was found in a bloodied daze early the following morning, suffering from a cracked pelvis and shattered elbow.

He is too detached by the passage of time to harbour any lingering ill-feeling towards his mother, reasoning gently: 'Nothing should surprise you with a woman who deserts her children.'

CHRISTOPHER'S STORY

Even Fanny Cradock's closest friends were forced to live off cryptic scraps when the subject of her fractured family past was broached. Her next-door

Happy together: Christopher and Jane Chapman on their wedding day in 1966.

neighbour in South Terrace, Tenniel Evans, was told that her second son was 'conceived in hatred and born in fear'. Christopher Chapman was four months old when Fanny walked out on him and her second husband, Arthur, in 1929. Christopher's serene upbringing in Norfolk was supervised by a triumvirate of father, aunt and grandmother. Twenty-five years would pass before he discovered his mother's identity, though a vague channel of communication was maintained by Christopher's grandmother and his maternal grandfather, Archibald Pechey.

Christopher remembers being taken to see Fanny's father in London just before the outbreak of the Second World War, but he was given the general impression that 'mother was a subject to be avoided' and was only granted the password to re-enter Fanny's life when fame came knocking for her in the mid-fifties. Christopher, Harrow-educated in a chance echo of Johnnie Cradock's schooling, was now working at Marshall's Airport in Cambridge. He recalled: 'I was having a drink with my father on one occasion and he said, "By the way, I've found out what your mother's name is now. Her stage name is Bon Viveur." '

Then, in 1957, a half-interested glance at *The Daily Telegraph* brought the reconciliation a step closer. 'I happened to look at the personal column and I saw this advert: it was Bon Viveur looking to buy a house of a certain description within easy reach of central London. I wrote in and said, "Hello, this is me." I got quite a warm, though not ecstatic letter, saying we really must meet. I was asked to go and see them in South Terrace.'

Fanny discovered that she was acquiring not just a 28-year-old son, but a vivacious daughter-in-law, Nikki, and an angelic eighteen-month-old grandson, Julian (Fanny immediately dubbed herself 'Granny Fanny'). The outgoing Christopher adapted more comfortably to Fanny's high-octane world than his half-brother Peter, but soon got sucked into an all-encompassing game plan: one that could only end in tears.

The surname Chapman was an anomaly that Fanny did not fancy explaining to the press or her adoring public, so she persuaded Christopher to change his name by deed poll to De Peche Cradock, a grander and exaggeratedly French-sounding variant of Pechey. In return she agreed to put Julian through private education. The initial price for Christopher to pay was estrangement from his father, but the picture that Fanny presented in her autobiography, *Something's Burning*, in 1960 was of a family at peace with itself. She even dedicated the book 'To Christopher de Peche Cradock, though he is a lousy cook'.

The vague harmony was shattered in 1962. Christopher's marriage to Nikki was collapsing and when he switched his affections to Jane Cornelius, the sixteen-year-old daughter of Cornish friends of Fanny, the die was cast irretrievably. Jane Cornelius may have been consoled by an unusually sympathetic Fanny when her RAF fiancé was killed in a flying accident – Fanny

Eggspert: Fanny shows off the collection of Easter eggs which she made for her grandson Julian in 1958. *(Associated-Rediffusion)*

> **'She used to say I was the daughter which she always wished she'd had. But I wasn't welcome as a daughter-in-law. It was a complete mystery to me: anyone in their right mind would have been delighted.'**
>
> *Jane Chapman*

grimly recalled the services funeral which followed her first husband's death – but the drama which then unfolded at the Cradock home in Blackheath met with a less gentle response.

Fanny first accused Jane of trying to seduce Johnnie (her jealous interpretation of an innocent bedtime peck on the cheek), then resorted to poisonous rage when she found out that Christopher and Jane were romantically involved ('I think we lingered a little too long over a Christmas kiss,' Christopher recalled wryly). Fanny fired off a series of venomous letters to Jane's parents, guillotining a close friendship of ten years' standing, and lost her younger son for the second time in her life. He baled out to work at the hotel owned by the Cornelius family on the Cornish coast and married Jane in 1966. 'She used to say I was the daughter which she always wished she'd had,' recalls Jane. 'But I wasn't welcome as a daughter-in-law. It was a complete mystery to me: anyone in their right mind would have been delighted. As long as she was in control she was OK, but once she thought things were taking their own course she wasn't happy.'

Christopher and his father were reconciled – he changed his name back to Chapman – but the rift between Christopher and Fanny was never repaired. Their last, brief contact was at the end of 1966, soon after Fanny had been operated on for bowel cancer. Christopher remembers: 'Johnnie came on the telephone and said, "Your mother's had a very serious operation. She's not sure how she's going to be when it's all over, if indeed she's still with us. We would very much like you to come to see her." We agreed, but said we thought we ought to limit it to an hour. There were no dramatics, but we had no more contact with her after that.'

FANNY'S OTHER FAMILY

Family was a flexible concept in Fanny's lexicon, so after the blood relations fled she commandeered replacements. Staff, however fleetingly employed, qualified automatically, and her articles painted a picture of relaxed domestic harmony. 'Young people' wandered across the canvas, munching contentedly and mucking in without demur when Fanny, in her fantastic idyll, exhorted them to fill the picnic hamper.

Two special couples were at the heart of this new family, both recruited without ceremony in the mid-seventies. Sara and Paul Barker were referred to as the 'children'. Sara was a

'As my second marriage was not a happy one, Christopher, John and I have decided it shall have no place in this story.'

Daily Telegraph-reading newlywed who responded to Fanny's appeal for a young cook she could educate and mould in print. Sara was rewarded not only with a crash course in haute cuisine but a place in television folklore as one of Fanny's silent, downtrodden helpers. Wandering off with a spatula on one of the Christmas programmes in 1975, she was stopped in her tracks by

Tournedos Rossini

one of Phil Bradford's favourite Fanny Cradock dishes

Ingredients

three 1½ in minimum thickness fillet steaks
trimmed down into tournedos
3 matching rounds of ¼ in thick real *pâté de foie gras truffé* (if you have come into a fortune) or *le parfait pâté de foie truffé*
3 slices of truffle, optional
6 fl oz beef stock reduced by simmering to a syrup

2 fl oz Madeira
2 tablespoons brandy
2 oz butter
a little extra butter
three 3 in rounds of new white bread for croutons

Method

Heat the 2 oz butter until it sings and make and fry the croutons. Slip on a dish and keep warm. Then brown the tournedos on both sides over fairly strong heat, then on their sides and brown them too all round. Then reduce heat and cook on slowly; 1 minute on each side for blue, 2 minutes on each side for just pink in the middle and on and on for ruined. Place on the croutons and keep them warm. Step up the heat to full, pour the brandy into the pan residue, tip pan to flame to ignite and shake for as long as the flames will last to burn out every scrap of grease. Then add the syrupy stock and the Madeira, bubble again furiously and strain over the tournedos. Run a thin skin of extra butter over the well-wiped pan and over a mere thread of heat just heat the chosen pâté through. Lay one slice on each tournedos and surmount with the optional slices of truffle.

Fanny and Johnnie Cradock Cookery Programme, 1971

Sun-worshipping: Fanny in the south of France in the late seventies with, on the left, 'the boys', restaurateurs Terry Hibbert and Phil Bradford.

a booming 'No!' from the boss. Fanny formulated a scheme to adopt Sara and her husband Paul, and even proposed paying for the Barkers' son to go to Harrow, Johnnie's old school. Sara and Paul were executors for Johnnie's will when he died in 1987, but Fanny's exasperating behaviour both before and immediately after brought a terminal rift in the relationship.

She still had the 'boys', however. Phil Bradford and Terry Hibbert were a restaurant-running couple – Phil chef, Terry maître d' – whom she and Johnnie had met at a party in Ireland in 1974. Fanny gave them a till-clinking lift by showering praise on their restaurant, Guests in Hayes, Middlesex. They, in return, gave her the last enduring friendship of her life.

Fanny and Johnnie:
A Love Affair

WHEN JOHNNIE MET FANNY

Officially, Johnnie Cradock and Phyllis Holden-Dye met at a concert on 19 November 1939. Unofficially, their paths had crossed twice before (and frequently if previous lives are taken into account). Fanny claimed that their cars had been parked in snug proximity on a cross-Channel ferry two months before the concert, and also maintained that she had watched from the touchline as her first husband, Sidney Evans, and Johnnie played rugby for opposing club sides in the mid-twenties.

The fault-lines were already appearing in Fanny's two-month marriage to Greg Holden-Dye when she was asked to produce entertainment for the troops at Hackney Marshes in east London. An evening of what Fanny described as 'almost unrelieved gloom' took a fresh turn for the worse when members of the audience were invited by an artiste with

'Heads turned to a large fair man who was smoking a pipe and scowling. If there were two things I especially disliked they were large fair Englishmen and pipes.'

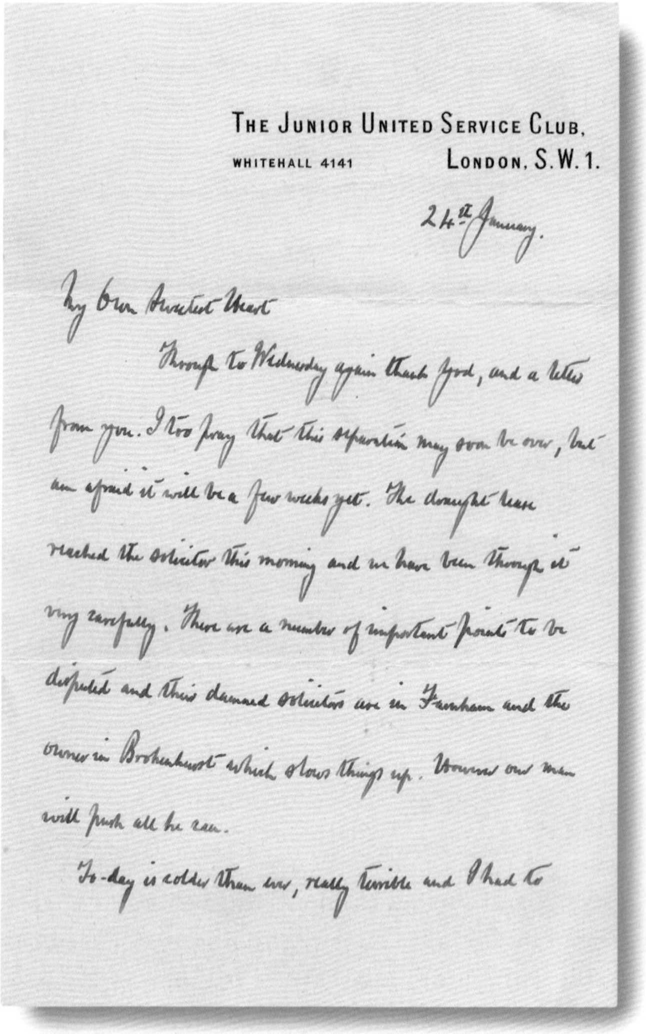
THE JUNIOR UNITED SERVICE CLUB,
WHITEHALL 4141 LONDON, S.W. 1.

24th January.

My Own Sweetest Heart

Through to Wednesday again thank God, and a letter from you. I too pray that this separation may soon be over, but am afraid it will be a few weeks yet. The draught lease reached the solicitor this morning and we have been through it very carefully. There are a number of important points to be disputed and their damned solicitors are in Farnham and the owner in Brockenhurst which slows things up. However our man will push all he can.

To-day is colder than ever, really terrible and I had to

Love letter straight from the heart: Johnnie to Fanny in their courting days at the start of the war.

'more courage than talent' to join her on stage as dance partners. A diffident Royal Artillery major, John Whitby Cradock, was beckoned. Fanny recalled: 'Heads turned to a large fair man who was smoking a pipe and scowling. If there were two things I especially disliked they were large fair Englishmen and pipes.'

They met in a post-concert dash for the bar, and Fanny's prejudices softened. The following morning the manageress at her dressmaking business announced: ' "There's a Major Cradock calling. Is this the latest?" I replied coldly, "It isn't. He's the sort of man who'll invite me to the Savoy, buy me champagne and give me a horrid mauve orchid with a pin in it." ' She was pleasantly surprised to find that a fashionable West End restaurant,

Luigi's, wines by Montrachet and Lafite, and usable orchids were Johnnie's alternative idea of sophistication. Lunch finished at 5.45 p.m.

Almost forty years later Johnnie was asked what his first impressions of Fanny had been. His reply, as so often, was ambushed by his partner. 'I'll tell you what he thought,' she said. 'Bad skin, good brains.'

THE LIFE JOHNNIE LEFT BEHIND

Once hypnotised, there was no way back for Johnnie Cradock: thirty-five years of middle-class normality were expunged from the records. The adrenalin rush of life with Fanny left little time for reflection, though there were gnawing regrets which Johnnie was as powerless to voice in private as he was in public.

Fanny Cradock shamelessly portrayed herself as the much-loved mother and doting grandmother, but four of the six children loosely referred to en masse were Johnnie's from his first marriage, as well as twelve of the eventual eighteen grandchildren. The pain for Johnnie was his almost

Fingers permitted: Peter West, TV commentator and occasional master of ceremonies for Bon Viveur Brains Trusts, enjoys Fanny's direct approach.

The perfect couple, 1959: Fanny wrote on the back, 'Us, together as always until Johnnie went to the other side'. (© *National Portrait Gallery*)

complete isolation from this family network: the flag of forgiveness was never flown. The hurt felt by his first wife, Ethel, never weakened, and her antipathy towards Fanny was acute.

Johnnie had been brought up to conform. He showed no great academic flair either at prep school or at Harrow, though he was an enthusiastic sportsman. He enjoyed cricket (Fanny hated the game), was a low-handicap golfer and immersed himself in the physical kinship of rugby. He was instrumental in re-forming the Beckenham club in the mid-twenties and boasted to the commentator Peter West: 'I had the reputation of being one of the dirtiest forwards in London.' Picnic-hamper-laden visits to internationals at Twickenham became one of Johnnie's few Fanny-free expeditions, prompting one of her favourite one-liners: 'The only things which keep us apart are rugby and the lavatory.' She wrote in her autobiography: 'Johnnie maintains that I do not know a goalpost from a grappling iron,' but pointed out that an uncle, Patrick Sortain Hancock, had played for England at the turn of the century.

After leaving school, Johnnie drifted unthinkingly into his father's wool merchants' business. His marriage to Ethel May Irvin in Aberdeen in 1928 was a major event on the social calendar – she was the daughter of Sir John and Lady Irvin – and between 1929 and 1934 the couple produced two sons and two daughters. The children Johnnie abandoned in 1940 were all between the ages of six and ten. He later told friends that the divorce settlement amounted to £75,000 (equivalent to more than £1 million in today's terms). The money offered no emotional compensation to his wife, and a near penniless Johnnie found that his relationship with his father, Henry, had been stretched to near breaking point.

Fanny invited even greater opprobrium when she wrote of Johnnie's first marriage: 'He cherished, with inexplicable unease, the conviction that there was another kind of marriage of which he knew nothing . . . a passionate, exhausting, demanding, satisfying relationship which could outweigh every other consideration and excel every other experience life could offer.'

SAUCEPAN LICKING AND CURRANT BUN SQUASHING

In Johnnie Cradock, Fanny saw the stiff-collared legacy of half a lifetime of middle-class propriety. She beckoned him, Pandora-like, into a world where hedonistic urges were the acceptable norm.

Johnnie was thirty-five, five years older than Fanny, when they met in 1939. She remembered the first time he came to dinner at her Kensington flat:

> I called to him from the kitchen to pour out a couple of sherries and bring them along. He stuck his face round the door. 'May I come in?' he asked.
>
> My maid and I stared, 'Well, of course,' said I and went on with my sauce. Tipping it from pan to tamis I was aware of a lustful sniffing – something like our boxer Pernod when he smells chocolate. I handed him the saucepan. 'Want to lick it out?' I asked.
>
> 'Oh can I?'
>
> 'Johnnie,' I demanded, fairly disconcerted at the sight of a large, fair, balding man licking with such excessive rapture, 'Don't you at home?'
>
> He shook his head. 'Not allowed in the kitchen,' he said between licks. This in my view is just asking for trouble.

Fanny's spontaneity was a pastime in which Johnnie, once converted, gleefully conspired. He even passed the currant bun test, a hangover from one of Fanny's favourite bedtime stories as a child. Edward the red teddy bear and his elephant chum spend their last sixpence on a bag containing thirteen currant buns. They consume twelve, find that they are still hungry and theorise that the last one will go further if the elephant sits on it. Major John Whitby Cradock, immaculate in his Royal Artillery uniform, delighted Fanny by sitting on his buns in a 'Ye Olde Willow Tree type of café' early in the war, and agreed that the taste was greatly enhanced. They maintained

Bite size: Fanny allows Johnnie to sample in the Dower House kitchen in 1970.
(© 2001 Topham Picturepoint)

the tradition in private and staged a public reprise while promoting their autobiography, *Something's Burning*, in 1960. Fanny wrote in her later memoirs, *Time to Remember*:

> We were invited to give a talk about it at teatime in Harrods Restaurant and of course to autograph copies of our book. Just before we went up to the restaurant Johnnie dashed through to the bakery department and returned with an enormous bag of new buns. . . . Women who were smothered in mink and wearing wildly expensive hats sat around sipping, nibbling, and listening to us. When Johnnie had told the story of Edward and the Elephant he marched off the rostrum and calmly went round asking these ladies to try for themselves. Believe it or not they all did.

ELBA EXILE: THE WAR YEARS

Johnnie Cradock's war finished ingloriously early. He was temporarily blinded in one eye by iritis and found that a magnifying glass of a monocle couldn't spare him the axe from the Royal Artillery. Fanny couldn't get a divorce from Arthur Chapman, was bigamously married to Greg Holden-Dye and, weighed down by wartime protocol, changed her name to Cradock by deed poll early in 1942.

Door-stepping: Fanny and friend outside the Cradocks' rented cottage near Stratford-upon-Avon in 1943.

Fanny later wrote: 'Johnnie obtained the world's most unsuitable job as an in-civil servant with the unflattering rank of "Temporary Principal" and instructions to proceed to Warwick Castle. We went into exile with a hundred pounds between us.' A rambling, rented, haunted house in Snitterfield, near Stratford-upon-Avon, became home for three years. They volunteered for revues at the village hall, offered rural respite to London-based friends (séances were a regular evening diversion), and improvised so successfully as hosts that they were presumed to be 'deep in the black market'. 'We simply used everything we could lay hands on legitimately and plundered the countryside to its uttermost. Johnnie says this "uttermost" was reached when I tried force feeding a Christmas draw goose in a savage craving for foie gras. The goose bit me which served me right.'

'I did not impress Johnnie in our walking-out days with any of my really elaborate dishes. But when I produced, on a gas ring, baby Brussels sprouts fast-fried (after steaming) with bits of tender chestnut; jacket-baked potatoes (foil-wrapped and cooked in the sitting room fire ashes); and a fat-featherweight beef-steak and kidney pudding, he ate himself into a coma and then proposed.'

They raised eighty-nine rabbits from an initial single doe in kindle; horse mushrooms were transformed into soups; bracken shoots were served as asparagus; hedgehogs were cooked in clay and tasted like frogs' legs; nasturtiums provided capers; acacia flowers were used for Escoffier's beignets; and Fanny's much-admired pastry was lubricated with liquid paraffin. Even rabbit skins came in handy for bedroom slippers and bathroom mats. From the want-for-nothing comfort of the late fifties,

Fanny reflected: 'We lived a very contented life in those lean days. People used to commiserate with me for having to work so hard without any servants in such a big house. I used to play up by begging everyone to let me know if they heard of any maids. I should have looked damn silly if any had appeared, because we could scarcely have raised their bus fares.'

A RECIPE FOR ROMANCE

Fanny Cradock painted a picture of well-matched mayhem when she quoted an anonymous close friend on her relationship with Johnnie: 'You two don't

A glass act: Johnnie's favourite picture of Fanny, taken in 1958. *(Behn)*

just scratch yourselves – you tear lumps out.' The truth was more one-sided: Fanny carped, cavilled, criticised and cajoled, while Johnnie desperately tried to dodge the bullets and ride the punches. Viewers may have doubted that the distorted dynamic of their on-screen relationship could be reproduced in private, but it was. Fanny's interpretation, shaped by her devotion to astrology, was that they were a classic example of a creative, wild Piscean locking horns with dependable Taurus.

'In the intimate, sweet hurly-burly of the double bed, I've been an utterly faithful wife. I think promiscuity is unbelievably messy. Our marriage is the golden thing in both our lives.'

If Johnnie was not actively scared of Fanny, he made a bad job of concealing it from friends and staff. Wendy Colvin, who helped the Cradocks put together their stage shows in the 1950s, recalls a general willingness on Johnnie's part to divert blame to others rather than field Fanny's fury. On one occasion Wendy saw Johnnie drop some dry cleaning as he got out of the Rolls-Royce. Rather than own up, he pinned the offence on the cleaners, who were promptly stung by an outraged telephone call from Fanny. 'I never heard him answer her back except once,' said Wendy,

> We were driving in the south of France and she was really nagging him because the route was not right, he hadn't put the right things in the car. He turned round to her and said, 'Shut up!' And she blew her top and that was when I heard a lot about what she had done for Cradock. She said, 'If it hadn't been for me you'd still be doing this, this and this and don't you ever speak to me like that again or you will be back where you came from so fast you won't know what's hit you. You're not indispensable to me. I am Fanny Cradock and don't you forget that.'

Just occasionally he would stand up and be counted. The *Daily Mail* columnist Lynda Lee-Potter wrote in 1976: 'Fanny tells marvellous stories about how Johnnie pushed a man into the Mediterranean because he'd been rude, and once sorted Fanny out by stuffing gooseberry tarts in her face. He then stalked off in a fury and his wife says that she followed meekly behind like a little squaw.'

The chemistry was self-evident to Fanny Cradock – 'our insane enjoyment of life together results from one being an extrovert and the other an introvert' – but it didn't stop everyone else being puzzled and perplexed by this uneven alliance. She elaborated in a radio interview:

> FANNY. 'Domineering female; gentle, compliant husband. Now the plain facts are these: Johnnie gives me my own way on absolutely everything of no importance whatsoever. But when it comes to the major decisions one of my dearest friends described it best of all. She said a mule is capricious in comparison to Cradock. And I maintain that if it wasn't that way I wouldn't love him and respect him and stay with him. It's so simple. For us it's heaven. Check?'
> JOHNNIE. 'Check.'

Almost forty years after they met (though before they were actually married), Fanny was still serving up casseroles of sickly sentimentalism. 'My darling is the most faithful, loving husband,' she told Lynda Lee-Potter. 'In

Major Cradock requests: Johnnie sent Fanny a formal invitation to coincide with her birthday each year.

the intimate, sweet hurly-burly of the double bed, I've been an utterly faithful wife. I think promiscuity is unbelievably messy. Our marriage is the golden thing in both our lives.'

By way of keeping the magic alive, Johnnie would mark Fanny's birthday each February by sending her a formal invitation. She would then find herself whisked off by plane, train or boat to some exotic, mystery location. The 1973 version, written when they were still happily ensconced in Watford, read: 'Mr John Whitby Cradock requests the pleasure of Mrs John Whitby Cradock in the drawing room at 6.30pm on Monday 26th February 1973 and also at 6.15pm on Wednesday 28th February 1973. Destinations to be disclosed at the appropriate times. RSVP to above address. Dress Monday: informal. Dress Wednesday: Cocktail dress.'

SPIRITS AND STARS: FANNY'S FAITH

Mainstream religion may not have appealed to Fanny Cradock – she did express the belief that 'being dull is an insult to God' – but she had no such

'My first snapshot of Johnnie: carried in my cigarette case from November 1939 throughout the War.'

Baked Hedgehog *(2–3 persons)*

Method

Clean the hedgehog and roll in thick moist clay. Stand on a baking sheet and leave in a medium oven until the clay is hard and cracking. Break away the crust and the skin and the bristles will come away cleanly. Place the flesh in a baking tin and continue baking in a medium oven, at Regulo 5, in hot fat, basting frequently until the flesh is tender. Serve with thick brown gravy and small boiled onions.

The Practical Cook, 1949

doubts about the spiritual world. Johnnie, whether brainwashed or converted, tapped into the same ethereal supply. They tempted the *People* into the exclusive revelation in 1975 that they were about to turn their backs on television and set up as faith healers.

An embittered Fanny was convinced that this cavalier interpretation of their plans – the 'yellow press' at its most vindictive, to her mind – had effectively killed off their prospects of further cookery programmes on TV, but there was some substance in the story. Fanny's initial scepticism about the power of faith healing vanished in the face of personal experience. She claimed that she was cured of bowel cancer in 1967 by the laying on of hands – after being given 'six months to live' – and attributed another startling recovery to the healing powers of Ted Fricker. She said that when she visited him she had a steel collar round her neck and had been warned by an osteopath that she would have to give up cooking, gardening and typing, and might even lose the use of her legs. Fanny told the *TV Times* in 1970: 'I had no faith in Ted Fricker when I first saw him, but when he put his hands on me I seemed to accelerate when standing still. I had gone in crying with pain and after 20 minutes I came out crying with happiness.'

She told a radio documentary, on which the *People* based its story: 'Johnnie is a superb healer and has healed a lot of sick people.' Maintaining that they were empowered by 'higher beings of higher intelligence', Johnnie explained: 'We do not do the healing. We are merely the instruments – like the machine that transmits the power.'

Val Biro, who illustrated a number of Fanny's books and became friendly with her and Johnnie in the 1950s, remembers two examples of the spiritual awareness that guided the Cradocks:

> She invited my wife and I to go down with them to the south of France in their old Vauxhall. She drove all the way. Although we were very young and eager we were very frightened. She said, 'There's nothing to worry about: Nubian [the great cosmic mother] is sitting on the car and looking after us.'
>
> The other experience which sticks in my mind is when we invited Fanny and Johnnie for dinner at our house in Surbiton. I remember that immediately she came through the door our cats bristled and ran out of the French windows and stayed at the bottom of the garden. It got to 9 p.m. and they suddenly said, 'We must go to a quiet room because we have to meditate on behalf of a patient of ours.'

HERE TODAY, HERE TOMORROW

Fanny Cradock was convinced that she had lived previous lives and equally certain that she would be recycled in the future. She also believed that she had brought knowledge with her from the past and claimed that she could prepare dishes automatically, without having to learn them first, because she already knew them.

Johnnie sang from the same hymn sheet. When he and Fanny appeared on *Desert Island Discs* in 1962 he was asked by Roy Plomley why he had chosen Chopin's *Les Sylphides* as his first record: 'Because I will then have the opportunity to practise my ballet. You see, I am a frustrated ballet dancer. I'm quite convinced that in a previous incarnation I was a female ballet dancer. In this incarnation, unfortunately, my shape and figure is wrong for it, but I still have the inclination.' Fanny weighed in: 'Well, darling, you must admit you still do rise to your pretty toes, in spite of your six feet, and bald pate, round the domestic house and dry us all up, don't you?'

Doris Collins, the clairvoyant, recalled that Fanny could hardly contain herself when they first met. 'She saw me walk into a party and she immediately rushed over and sat on the floor at my feet. I thought, that's odd, and she said, "Doris, you're my long-lost sister in a previous incarnation. I can feel it, I know."' Collins confessed that she felt an 'at-oneness' with Fanny, but also detected a lost, troubled soul.

Wendy Colvin, who began working for Fanny in the mid-fifties, remembers some unnerving experiences. 'She was a bit spooky, because she used to give me instructions without even talking to me. I became aware that I used to get messages from her, almost like a hypnotist.' Fanny also shocked dinner guests on one occasion by exclaiming out of the blue: 'My god, I'm going to live long after the rest of you are dead.'

Wendy also witnessed seemingly transcendental exchanges between the Cradocks:

Every so often there would be a conversation between Fanny and Johnnie. Johnnie would say, 'What we really need at this point, we can't ring so and so, he's got to ring us, then we'll be in a very strong position.' Then Fanny would take Johnnie's hand and say, 'We'll have to ask HIM.' Then the pair of them would concentrate like hypnotists and suddenly she'd say, 'It's all right.'

MARRIED AT LAST

Alison Leach, Fanny's long-serving personal assistant and manager, had suspected that something was missing in the Cradock relationship. There was no wedding anniversary to celebrate and she also recalled seeing a wartime press cutting from a court case in which Fanny had been

Fanny AND JOHNNIE'S GASTRONOMIC AWARDS —

Chevalier et Grande Dame des Chevaliers du Tastevin
Commandant et Grande Dame de la Chaîne des Rôtisseurs
Compagnons du Beaujolais
Membres du Club Prosper Montagne (*en raison de leur haute
connaissance gastronomique et culinaire*)
Officier et Grande Dame de l'Ordre de St Fortunat
Membres Honoraires du Club des Becs de Cannes
Honorary Members of the Worshipful Company of Meadmakers
Honorary Members of the Order of King Christian IV of
Denmark
Diplôme de Médaille Vermeil de la Société des Arts, Science
et Lettres (Fanny)
Chevalier de l'Ordre de la Courtoisie Française (Johnnie)
Grand Mousquetaire d'Armagnac (Johnnie)
Chevalier et Grande Dame de la Tripière d'Or
Chevalier et Grande Dame de la Gastronomie Normande
Membres de la Jurade de St Emilion
Compagnons du Bon Temps du Médoc

prosecuted for her bigamous marriage to her third husband, Greg Holden-Dye. Alison finally discovered the whole truth at her St John's Wood flat in 1977, when Fanny, in a bizarrely matter-of-fact way, invited her to the couple's wedding. The catalyst was a death notice for Arthur Chapman, Fanny's second husband, which Johnnie had spotted in *The Times*. The silent embargo had been lifted; after thirty-eight years of quasi-married life Fanny and Johnnie were finally free to get married for real.

Alison and Johnnie's sister Dorothy Findlay agreed to be witnesses for the lowest key and most secret of register office ceremonies in Guildford on 7 May 1977. Fanny reverted to her pre-war identity of Phyllis Chapman on a marriage certificate festooned with fibs and coy omissions. She trimmed her age from sixty-eight to fifty-five and amalgamated her father's real name, Archibald Pechey, and pen name, Arthur Valentine, to produce Arthur Pechey.

Johnnie's age was given as sixty-five rather than seventy-two. Fanny confessed to no 'rank or profession' and Johnnie was 'Major, R.A. (retired)'.

The marriage was blessed at nearby Chiddingfold the following day by the Reverend John Nicholls, a forceful character who had seen the Cradocks as a source of charitable bounty in the 1960s when he was both Vicar of St Mary Woolnoth and Chaplain to the Tower of London. They provided flowers on demand at Easter, and Fanny and Johnnie established a Christmas routine in which they attended the Reverend Nicholls's midnight service and then paid a Christmas morning visit, weighed down with mince pies and sweet meats, to the severely disabled 'Ladies of Love Walk' in Camberwell.

Unwittingly, however, Johnnie had landed Fanny in a bigamous state for the second time in her life by getting his Arthur Chapmans mixed up. The man Fanny married almost fifty years earlier was still alive. By the time the *Daily Express* exposed the confusion two years later – Arthur had, by then, died – there were no careers or reputation to ruin, but the Reverend Nicholls was understandably distressed by his unwitting role in the farce.

Alison Leach said Dorothy Findlay had been 'totally mystified by the whole thing'. She herself has tried hard to avoid revisiting the experience: 'It was such a very, very odd day. It's something I've really tried hard not to think about ever since.'

Johnnie's Simplest Mulled Wine

'Nose-tingling and tum-warming on a cold night'

Ingredients

1 bottle red 'plonk' wine
14 lumps sugar
1 thin-skinned orange stuck with 6 cloves
1 flat eggspoon (2.5 ml spoon) each of
powdered cinnamon and of powdered ginger
1 torn bay leaf
strained juice of half a lemon and the other half
very thinly sliced

Method

Place all ingredients in a thick pan over a low heat and raise slowly to just below boiling point. On no account allow the mixture to boil. Stir well and pour into warmed, napkin-wrapped glasses, remembering to immerse a spoon into each.

A Lifetime in the Kitchen, vol. I, 1985

Feeding time: Fanny broke down the barriers of kitchen etiquette for Johnnie.

THE WAY TO A MAN'S HEART . . .

Cooking was much more than a functional skill to Fanny Cradock. She saw it as a guarantee of marital longevity (frequently claiming that she had never met a good cook who was divorced), an aid to seduction, and the magic dust that transformed conversational stodge into wit and wisdom. Simplicity, as she explained to *Home* magazine in 1960, was often the key to romantic success:

> I did not impress Johnnie in our walking-out days with any of my really elaborate dishes. He took those for granted with my cooking background; but when I produced, on a gas ring, baby Brussels sprouts fast-fried (after steaming) with bits of tender chestnut; jacket-baked potatoes (foil-wrapped and cooked in the sitting room fire ashes); and a fat-featherweight beefsteak and kidney pudding, he ate himself into a coma and then proposed.

Fanny offered ancillary tips: 'Don't give him small plates to balance on large knees before a fire which scorches him on one side and makes him twitch. Sit him up properly at a table the way Mum did when she tied his bib.' And, of course: 'Don't forget to ask him if he'd like to smoke his pipe after the meal, even if you hate it.'

A decade later there was still marital magic in the air. Novelist Maeve Binchy, then a journalist on the *Irish Times*, captured one of those vaguely surreal exchanges in which Johnnie's role was just to nod and agree. Fanny said: 'We have a blissful marriage. I cook lovely things for him because I still regard him as my boyfriend, you know, and I love his palate. We never have a fight about anything, do we darling?'

'Never, dear,' said Johnnie.

'It's all great fun, darling, isn't it?'

'Great fun,' said Johnnie.

FAREWELL JOHNNIE

Illness and Johnnie Cradock were inseparable throughout his adult life. His colds and catarrh were hardy perennials. He nearly died when he had his tonsils removed, was almost blinded by iritis, required critical surgery at the base of his spine; and all before the age of fifty. Seemingly a prime candidate for a premature death, he bounced back with stoic resilience before being diagnosed with lung cancer in 1986 at the age of eighty-two.

Johnnie died at Basingstoke General Hospital on 30 January 1987, a half-drunk bottle of claret at his bedside. In Fanny's romanticised reconstruction

Parting words: the card which accompanied the flowers sent to Johnnie's funeral. It is signed 'Jill', Johnnie's pet name for Fanny.

of his final moments she would have proffered the glass to his lips for one last sip. He might have stirred briefly from his deepening coma, forced his eyes half-open and mouthed: 'Thank you, darling. It's all been enormous fun. See you on the other side.' Fanny would then have felt the last life drain from the hands she gripped tightly before kissing him gently on the forehead.

Fanny was not at the hospital, however. The wine was a surgeon-approved gift from friends, Tony and Yvonne Norris, who had helped to fill the void left by Fanny's apparently callous absence over the past few weeks. Yvonne remembered:

> She wouldn't visit him. It was so sad because I walked in one day and Johnnie said, 'Thank God you've come. She's abandoned me, hasn't she?' I didn't know what to say. The surgeon went berserk. He said, 'Why hasn't she visited?' I said, 'She doesn't like death, she's frightened of illness.' He was on the phone immediately and said to her, 'Mrs Cradock, if you do not come and see your husband you will not see him alive again in a few days.' She did turn up in a great kerfuffle. She arrived in a wheelchair which she didn't really need. I offered to leave the room, but Fanny said, 'Don't go, I'm only going to be five minutes.'

She had already antagonised the hospital authorities by instructing them haughtily: 'Whatever happens, when Johnnie's sons come, do not allow them to see their father.' Fanny's PA, Alison Leach, told her: 'I think he would be terribly upset if his sons came and he didn't see them,' the more so because in the twenty years that Alison had known the Cradocks she was only aware of one meeting between Johnnie and his younger son, Richard.

Fanny's bizarre behaviour continued. She rang up her literary agent, Rosemary Bromley, to report incorrectly that Johnnie had already expired, and on the day before his actual death she stormed out of a guest appearance on Pamela Armstrong's afternoon programme on the BBC when the hostess wandered innocently on to the set to wish her good luck. After Johnnie's death, she marched into the hospital and demanded to be given his greatcoat. By then nurses who had launched a panicky search for his signet ring had been informed by Tony Norris that Fanny had removed it on her previous visit.

She refused to attend the funeral, claiming that women in her family were spared the pain, though that did not prevent her trying to inconvenience mourners by having the ceremony delayed.

4

Bon Viveur

THE 'INN-SIDE STORY'

Fanny Cradock always knew that she would be somebody, but it took time to build up a head of self-promotional steam. The 1930s brought odd jobs and a pauper's income; the war years were spent trying to forge a reputation as a novelist; and it was only after she passed forty in 1949 that she began to convince others of her employability. The publication of her first cookery book, *The Practical Cook*, was a hugely significant addition to her CV; in October 1949 she began a short-lived 'My Kitchen' column in the *Daily Express*, under the byline Frances Dale, and suddenly she was a journalist in demand.

Fanny was running out of pseudonyms when *The Daily Telegraph*'s woman's editor, Evelyn Garrett, dreamt up an innovative column that would propel her to newspaper stardom. She had already appeared in the *Telegraph* as fashion writer Elsa Frances, showing how to make a trendy long-quilled cap, and beauty consultant Nan Sortain – 'all acne, leaking scalps and very curious enquiries always made on behalf of some very mysterious "friend" and never for the writer'.

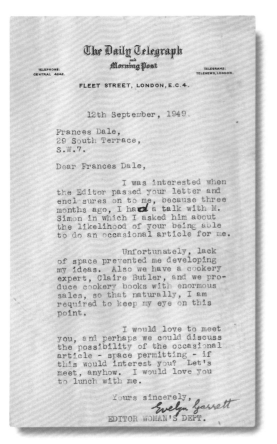

The Daily Telegraph
and
Morning Post

TELEPHONE:
CENTRAL 4842.

TELEGRAMS:
TELENEWS, LONDON.

FLEET STREET, LONDON, E.C.4.

12th September, 1949.

Frances Dale,
29 South Terrace,
S.W.7.

Dear Frances Dale,

I was interested when
the Editor passed your letter and
enclosures on to me, because three
months ago, I had a talk with M.
Simon in which I asked him about
the likelihood of your being able
to do an occasional article for me.

Unfortunately, lack
of space prevented me developing
my ideas. Also we have a cookery
expert, Claire Butler, and we produce cookery books with enormous
sales, so that naturally, I am
required to keep my eye on this
point.

I would love to meet
you, and perhaps we could discuss
the possibility of the occasional
article - space permitting - if
this would interest you? Let's
meet, anyhow. I would love you
to lunch with me.

Yours sincerely,
Evelyn Garrett
EDITOR WOMAN'S DEPT.

Stars are born: the letter from *The Daily Telegraph*'s woman's editor, Evelyn Garrett, which heralded Fanny and Johnnie's thirty-year relationship with the paper.

Evelyn Garrett was the strong-minded, unflappable mentor Fanny needed but rarely encountered. She was more used to men who cowered and gave way, or ran for cover. Garrett had rejected an early, ill-disciplined attempt at travel writing with the clipped critique: 'Muddled thinking, wordy, pointless. Remember the story of creation was written in seven words.'

In her autobiography, *Something's Burning*, Fanny recreated the conversation that led to Johnnie and her taking the Dover Road in October 1950. Various roads led to an estimated 10,000 hotels and restaurants, home and abroad, over the next five years.

EVELYN. Fanny, how would you and Johnnie like to go away for a half a dozen weekends into the country?

ME. *(disbelievingly)* Doing what?

EVELYN. Now don't run away with the idea this is something big. It's simply a series I think might hold up for six weeks. I should want you both to go. We'd pay expenses, of course, I want you to try to find out if there is anything left that is worth while in the inns of England.

ME. What sort of anything?

EVELYN. A warm welcome, honest fare, *integrity*, Fanny, if it still survives. But first of all we'll have to decide what name you could use.

ME. For God's sake, not another name! [There were six at the moment.]

EVELYN. It's not going to last, remember, Fanny – almost any name would do.

ME. All right, then, if it's just for six weeks, why not let us sign ourselves Bon Viveur? It's sexless and it's right, because Bon Viveur covers food, wine *and* travel, whereas Bon Vivant deals solely with the table. Besides [I added crossly] it'll keep them guessing.

The six articles, at 8 guineas apiece, expanded into a thrilling voyage of discovery for the Cradocks, in the course of which Johnnie turned his back on £3,500 a year with the family business to climb aboard the charabanc full time. They outlined their modus operandi in the book *Around Britain with Bon Viveur*:

In order to find three or four hotels or restaurants to praise we visited up-wards of twenty every weekend. . . . In short we go in unheralded, eat what is offered to the public, sleep a night and take breakfast, and thereafter, when the bill is paid and in John's pocket, disclose ourselves by handing over a card marked: 'Bon Viveur, *Daily Telegraph*'. And this last we only do if we intend to mention the hotel or restaurant favourably in the following Friday's article.

They were offered and resisted bribes, they discovered the con-straining effect of the Catering Wages Act, and they witnessed the good, bad and indifferent:

There is the delicious scent which is a compound of willing service, well-cooked food – however simple – friendliness, comfort and cleanliness. There is the shameful scent of stale beer and unclean chambers, bad food, grudging service, and a suspicious watchful treatment which suggests that every traveller is potentially under the caption 'wanted'.

*Fali w/wto 15/gus siewl equally
with elsa d Frd. vet 14th 1949*

Daily Telegraph Exclusive Design, No. 30

How To Make Smart Long-Quilled Cap

By ELSA FRANCES

AUTUMN fashion's darling is undoubtedly the cap, often feathered. It can be in velvet or velveteen, satin or faille, fine woollen or jersey fabric.

Many women who are clever with their hands would love to make a successful one themselves. It is easy if you have a basic design. You can then make the long-quilled style on left or a number of variations.

Such an opportunity is provided here by DAILY TELEGRAPH Exclusive Pattern No. 30. You probably have already ¼ yard of suitable material, so that it would cost you only 8s 6½d. to make. made up as follows:

¼ yard book muslin ..	10½d.
¾ yard petersham ribbon	3d.
¼ yard lining	1s. 6d.
Feather mount	5s. 11d.
	8s. 6½d.

LONG quill is firmly fixed into cap by opening side seam, tucking it in, sewing over. Model above is in black velvet and pink moss crêpe.

You obtain Exclusive Pattern No. 30 by sending 3d. (postage free) to Cap Feature. Daily Telegraph, E.C.4.

Fanny's first column in *The Daily Telegraph*, in 1949.

BON VIVEUR: A CLEVER MISTAKE?

Fanny Cradock was rather proud of her choice of Bon Viveur as a *nom de plume*, but pedants disapproved. A letter from a French reader to the *Observer*, though not specifically directed at the Cradocks, found its way into their cuttings album for 1960: 'A *viveur* is a debauchee, a libertine, and can in no circumstances be considered a good man; therefore *bon viveur* is a contradiction in terms. What the English writers mean is *bon vivant*. A *bon vivant* is a genial and pleasant man who enjoys all the good things of life. A *viveur* can never be *bon*.'

Even if she had betrayed what she frequently liked to portray as her mother tongue, Fanny was unrepentant. It gave her the crucial upper hand in a civilised copyright dispute: 'Nothing is more eloquent of *The Daily Telegraph*'s principles and standards than what followed a year later [in 1951] when they wholly and completely ceded copyright to us for what seemed to them the unassailable reason that I first spoke the words over the telephone.' The *Telegraph* showed the same gentlemanly good manners when the Bon Viveur team (and imprint) marched off to the *Daily Mail* and Associated-Rediffusion, the fledgling commercial TV channel, in 1955. Fanny and Johnnie were welcomed back into the *Telegraph* fold three years

Escoffier's Pêche Melba

Escoffier's Pêche Melba – 'The definitive one, which we dedicated to him on the night we made it at the Royal Albert Hall, was as follows . . .'

Method

A dozen peeled, stoned, halved fresh peaches were poached in 5 fl oz (150 ml) stock sugar syrup with an extra ½ pt (300 ml) water and a split vanilla pod, until just tender and well infused. These were then laid over an 8 in (20 cm) diameter block of real vanilla cream ice, which was in turn lowered into a hollowed-out giant swan in ice, sculpted in the Savoy kitchens and wearing a small garland of roses around its neck. Its dish was also encircled with more roses and maidenhair fern. Finally 1lb (450g) of fresh raspberries were rubbed through a large sieve so that they fell over the peaches and down onto the cream ice below. And that is the real *Pêche Melba*.

A Lifetime in the Kitchen, vol. III, 1985

What we cannot comprehend is how our criticism of poor cooks and ineffective management can possibly denigrate gas. Even we could burn toast under a gas grill – and if we did so would you not say that the fault was in our foolishness and not in our gas grill?

Are we to be divorced by gas if we do not confine our journalistic activities to comments dictated by the gas industry?

later, and their weekly food and travel columns, still mostly under the anonymous cloak of Bon Viveur, survived until the mid-eighties, largely thanks to Win Frizell's championing diplomacy.

Win, who had succeeded Evelyn Garrett as woman's editor, asked Fanny to be godmother to her daughter Amy in 1970. Fanny played bulldozing dictator at the christening and further alienated Win's mother by dipping four-month-old Amy's finger in champagne and encouraging her to suck it. The animosity extended to the then *Telegraph* editor, Bill Deedes, when Fanny upset a friend of his by claiming on a television programme that a Chinese restaurant of her acquaintance was serving up cat and dog meat, producing a carcass from her bag to give the allegation gruesome emphasis.

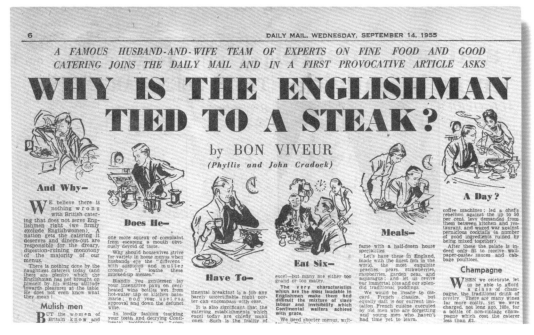

Bon Viveur make their debut for the *Daily Mail* in 1955.

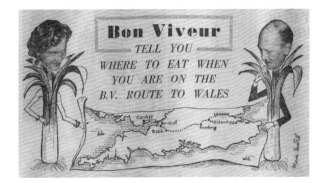

Leek motif: Fanny and Johnnie go west in 1956.

'FANNY CRADOCK'S SCAMPI RECIPE UPSETS FISHERMEN'

Fanny Cradock turned fish detective in 1974 after learning that a restaurant in Devon was offering a three-course meal for 75p, including scampi and chips as one of its main-course dishes. Having established that *real* prawn scampi retailed for not less than £2 per lb, Fanny discovered that monkfish (35p to 40p a pound) was being widely used as a cut-price and scarcely detectable substitute.

She unveiled recipes for monkfish sauté and monkfish steaks in her Bon Viveur column in *The Daily Telegraph*, and the power and influence of the Cradocks took over. Three months later the *Telegraph* carried a news story highlighting the crisis facing the Ayr fleet: prawn prices had halved and skippers who had seen their costs double over the previous twelve months were forced to adopt a quota system.

TODAY LUNCHEON CLUBS, TOMORROW THE WORLD

From modest beginnings – a princely £25 for addressing clubs and flower societies – the Cradock empire expanded into a 1950s phenomenon. Fanny and Johnnie began cooking on stage in 1953 and in the spring of 1954 *The Daily Telegraph* had the bright idea of complementing their *Kitchen Magic* extravaganzas with a Food and Wine Brains Trust, for which experts such as Constance Spry and a pre-guide Egon Ronay were recruited. The questions covered the gamut of domesticity. Johnnie was asked at a show in Blackpool if he had any tips for low-budget decoration of a dining room. 'In a seaside place an effective yet cheap décor is fishing and shrimp net curtaining as wall draperies,' he replied.

Win Frizell, who reported on the shows for the *Telegraph*, recalls that there was a simmering tension between Fanny and Ronay. 'He was a bit tart with her. One day she was going on about making this stockpot, how every kitchen should have one. Everything goes into it, she said: scraps of meat, bones. And Egon piped up, "I'd hate to be a dog in Fanny's kitchen." She turned on him like a tiger and said, "I wouldn't have you in my kitchen."

> **'She might make a point of impressing a young mother with a child or an old woman in a wheelchair. She recognised they were wildly important to her, her fans, that they were the ones who created these extraordinary sales for her books.'**
>
> *Alison Leach, Personal Assistant*

Fanny and Johnnie showed extraordinary stamina by laying on matinées and evening performances, up to 2½ hours apiece, at every venue. Chiffon dress and lounge suit were the afternoon attire of choice. Then Johnnie's top hat and tails would complement Fanny's full-length ball gown and tiara for the evening show. She had presumed that stores would be of a size appropriate to the level of interest, but the *Telegraph* promotions team booked the biggest halls instead, and their confidence was rewarded: the sold-out signs went up everywhere. In November 1954 the paper could report, with a hint of smugness, that 'over 20,000 women in Manchester, Sheffield, Harrogate, Scarborough, Leicester, Bournemouth and Bristol, have been helped and entertained at these stimulating gatherings'.

The female-exclusive reference was telling, but Johnnie's involvement, however peripheral and put-upon, began to alter the make-up of the audiences. It was estimated that women outnumbered men twenty to one at the first Gas Board-sponsored show, at the Kursaal, Southend, in February 1955, but Fanny reckoned that by the early sixties the crowds were almost equally divided between men and women.

FANNY IN PERFORMANCE

The early TV cookery programmes were billed as demonstrations. Fanny Cradock rebelled against the description, both on screen and on stage. In 1960 she complained: 'It sounds too much like white overalls, clinics and "I'm-telling-you".' By 1971 she had honed her dissent: 'Demonstration is a dirty word. It is what is applied to making horrible little savouries for distribution to

THE FOOD & COOKERY BRAINS TRUST

MABEL PICKLES   EGON RONAY   CONSTANCE SPRY   R.L.C

Panel power: the Food and Cookery Brains Trust, including a youthful Egon Ronay, in action in Manchester. *(Wilson)*

Any questions: Fanny and Johnnie with Brains Trust regular Isobel Barnett in Blackpool. *(Studio Rex)*

THE CHARACTER OF HERBS – ACCORDING TO *Fanny*

Angelica – an old, old lady in the herb galaxy
Basil – a treasure
Bay – the handmaiden of the rest
Borage – the beauty of the family
Dill – a pretty creature, a temperamental animal
Fennel – is important and knows it
Garlic – the lady of easy virtue
Mint – invasive, perilous in the kitchen
Parsley – bad-tempered, secretive and choosy
Rosemary – a stickly, prickly customer
Sage – rather common
Sorrel – lusty and well bred
Tarragon – an aristocrat

Getting the bird:
A glamorously
gowned Fanny
takes delivery of a
pheasant on
stage in Norwich.
(Coe)

bored, middle-aged housewives with nothing better to do than while away an afternoon in a department store.' Fanny, in case anyone didn't know by now, was a performer, an entertainer, a communicator.

On television she never lost sight of the primary duty to impart information; on stage the canvas had to be more expansive. The angled mirrors above the gas cookers could only illuminate so much: the basic truth was that Fanny and Johnnie were distant figures to the majority of the punters who packed out some of the biggest indoor arenas in Britain. Cue the patter, cue the pseudo-theatrical tableaux, cue audience involvement.

Johnnie would launch proceedings by cracking open a bottle of champagne and picking out a lady in the seventh row for a complimentary glass, duly delivered by a home service girl (hearty round of applause guaranteed). Fanny would issue the apron-free battle cry, 'Cooking is a cleanly art, not a grubby chore', and, when the mood took her, would spit, 'Only a slut gets in a mess in the kitchen.' She would then try to convince even the most timid housewife that cooking was easy, fulfilling and fun, and give the first of frequent name checks to Escoffier. 'The great importance of French cooking is profound economy and practical good sense, not just the oh-la-las and the frivolity,' she told the assembled masses at the Weston-super-Mare Winter Gardens in 1953.

For all the genial, mildly ribald ad-libbing, there were solid ingredients to Fanny's stage presentation. Her zealous insistence on precise quantities was offset by the indulgent observation: 'There is a lot of bungling and sloshing in good cooking.' At various stages audience members would be invited to join the Cradocks on stage; they were required, of course, to confirm that the food tasted as good as it looked. Any reluctance would be overcome with a hint of self-deprecation: 'We've never lost a member of the audience yet.' Once hooked, they were told: 'You can say anything you like provided you use one of two words – "delicious" or "disgusting"!'

'Whatever your way of life, you have only one responsibility. To make sure your daughters never come within shouting distance of dirty little clubs, wide boys, latchkeys, unchaperoned late night careening, or any of the grubby forerunners to 20th century tragedies.'

As if by magic: cardboard cut-outs of Fanny and Johnnie are used to advertise a show in Bournemouth. *(Kitchenham)*

ACCIDENTS WILL HAPPEN

Reading was a regular port of call for the Cradock roadshow. It also left a stain (or two) on Fanny's spotless reputation. She was five minutes from a perfect ten at the Town Hall in 1956 when Johnnie, upset after jabbing his finger with a trussing needle, forgot to remove a chocolate pan from behind the preparation table. Fanny emerged with a large dollop of chocolate on her dress. She draped a towel over the offending patch and laughed off the mishap afterwards: 'This Balenciaga dress has already had a pot of hot water down it, and the hotel will be able to get the chocolate off, I'm sure.' The curse of Reading returned in 1964 when Fanny spilt milk down the front

Evening Performance

'KITCHEN MAGIC'

FANNY AND JOHNNIE CRADOCK

" Bon Viveur "

in an entirely new presentation of their famous,
high-speed and exciting stage cookery show

at the

Town Hall, Reading at 7.30 p.m.
on Thursday, 13th April, 1967

To ensure seats it is essential that you arrive at the hall as early as possible before the
performance. Doors will be open at 6.30 p.m.

ADMIT ONE

A ticket for a Bon Viveur
show of *Kitchen Magic*
at Reading in 1967.

of her vivid red evening gown. She carried on without breaking stride,
showing the same single-minded sangfroid which often prevented the seeds
of drama turning into full-blown crisis.

Peter Botterill, one of Fanny's longer-serving student cooks, remembered:

On one occasion we were in Edinburgh doing a show and the poor old
lighting man wasn't doing her spot correctly, so she tore him off a strip
really quite badly and he collapsed and he had a minor heart attack.
Whether the rowing brought it on or not I don't know, but he was carried
off to hospital and all she said was, 'Get somebody else quickly. We've got
to get the show on tonight.' And that night we did the show and there
were four big lights over her demonstration table, and one of them just
happened very strangely to miss her by two inches as it came crashing to
the stage floor, and like a true professional she just carried on and told
me to sweep it up.

BEHIND THE SCENES

The glad-handing and diplomacy did not come easily to Fanny Cradock. On
a good day she could muster an outpouring of unctuous gratitude to her
devoted public; on a bad day she wanted nothing to do with fans, sponsors

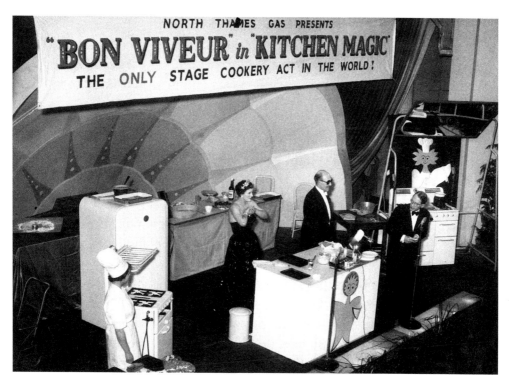

Another night, another stage: Fanny and Johnnie are introduced for an evening of *Kitchen Magic. (A. Dawson)*

or the local press, all of whom powered the Cradock bandwagon. Wendy Colvin and Alison Leach were the tactful tour manager-arbitrators who smoothed on-the-road relations.

Alison recalls that there were countless ways to displease Fanny:

If they couldn't park their car in exactly the position which they wished to park it, if they didn't have the right sort of dressing room, if the lights weren't quite right, if anything was the slightest bit wrong or hadn't been completed by the deadline. The crew had to be off stage and I had to be there smiling and welcoming.

Sometimes, if she met her fans, which often happened of course, she'd say, 'Darling, get me out of here. I can't stand these bloody women.' The 'blasted press' were close to her face and she'd rush out. Other times she'd say, 'How marvellous. Well, of course we depend on you. How lovely . . . and you watched that programme? Well, we're back on next week.' She could be super charming.

The press were left in no doubt that there were many subjects (anything of a vaguely personal nature) that were off limits. Here again Alison Leach filled in the gaps: 'Of course she would have to have good coverage in the paper, so I would have to feed stuff to the journalists which would be acceptable to back up the rather cursory interview that she would give.'

I THINK I WANT TO BE ALONE, DARLING

Fanny Cradock recalled sitting on a crowded bus before the war, unknown and anonymous, and thinking, 'One day all these people will know who I am.' Once she had achieved that level of celebrity, however, she loved and loathed it in equal measure.

Alison Leach, Fanny's personal assistant at the height of her fame, remembers: 'If she was in M&S and she was recognised she'd want to get out, but at the same time she was pleased she'd been recognised.' Wendy Colvin, who worked with Fanny in the fifties and early sixties, witnessed the same love-hate relationship with her public. Having announced that she wanted to preserve her anonymity at the theatre in Chester one night, Fanny flounced in late, conspicuous in furs and dark glasses, then feigned amazement that her cover had been blown.

Feeding time: audience members sample the fruits of Fanny's labours on stage in Reading. (Walton Adams)

It has been assumed that Fanny took an automatic dislike to any new acquaintance who used her first name. In truth she was playing a more subtle game, one in which she could reward a stranger who made a positive first impression with a conspiratorial, 'You can call me Fanny.' Her sense of humour could easily lapse if she felt slighted. 'One time when we were in the south of France we were in a loo together,' Wendy recalls. 'There was a woman in there and she kept looking at Fanny and she suddenly turned round and said, "Excuse me, I hope you won't be insulted if you're not, but are you Fanny Cradock?" Fanny just looked at her and swept out. Of course I was hysterical with laughter. She looked at me and said, "It wasn't funny, it was insulting." '

'WEDDED TO GAS'

Fanny and Johnnie Cradock found themselves in the dock in 1957, accused of biting the hand that fed them. Broad brush-stroke criticisms of Britain's catering industry were interpreted as a thinly veiled attack on the Gas Council, which had sponsored the Cradocks' stage shows since the start of 1955. They were by now committed to a show a year in each of the council's twelve regional boards.

They had been reluctant converts to electricity in 1953 – in deference to the fact that their early appearances were underwritten by the Electricity Board – and were genuinely relieved to be back on familiar ground. 'We are not "linked to gas", *we are wedded to gas*,' Fanny wrote in an impassioned defence to *Gas Journal*. She went on:

Wedded to gas: Fanny and Johnnie hand out the goodies at their first Gas Board-sponsored show, at Southend, in 1955. *(A. Dawson)*

Mr. Therm and Bon Viveur

make light work

of Christmas

What a combination: Fanny and Johnnie were committed to gas cookers and Mr Therm.

What we cannot comprehend is how our criticism of poor cooks and ineffective management can possibly denigrate gas. Even we could burn toast under a gas grill – and if we did so would you not say that the fault was in our foolishness and not in our gas grill?

Are we to be divorced by gas if we do not confine our journalistic activities to comments dictated by the gas industry? If this were so, we should lose the entire reputation we have built up over the past nine years and instead of being looked up to by the public as incorruptible we should rightly be made useless to the gas industry or anyone else.

The gas authorities, for the most part, saw immense value in the partnership, and were more likely to be criticised by the paying public than their star turns. A request for 130 VIPs to turn up in 'evening or dinner dress' at Liverpool's Philharmonic Hall in 1955 was received with astonishment. However, D.P. Wellman, chairman of North Western Gas Board, responded: 'I think it is only common sense. After all, this is rather more than a mere cookery demonstration. The Cradocks put over quite a show and as it is an evening performance, I cannot seen why people cannot dress for it. I think it would be a good thing if people took a little more care how they dressed, anyway.'

ROYAL APPOINTMENTS

Nothing convinced Fanny Cradock more certainly that she had arrived than her audiences with the royal family in the mid-fifties. It was an unfamiliar sensation for her to feel, on these isolated occasions, that she was in the presence of her social superiors.

A brief conversation with the Queen Mother during the International Kitchen extravaganza at the Royal Festival Hall also provided unscripted confirmation that the Bon Viveur message was being received in palaces and pubs alike. Fanny recalled:

After chatting for several minutes, the Queen Mother said to us, 'I read you, you know' (we were then writing the original Bon Viveur column in *The Daily Telegraph*), and added with a twinkle, 'But not always'. The Queen Mother went on more seriously to Johnnie, 'Do you consider that catering standards have improved in the last three years?' Johnnie replied, 'Indeed we do, ma'am. There has been a marked improvement.' The Queen Mother nodded, 'We agree,' she said smiling, 'and in our opinion you two are largely responsible.'

Fanny was so shaken by the compliment that she forgot to curtsey.

Fanny and Johnnie (left) show the Queen their elaborate *table d'honneur* at the *Daily Mail* Ideal Home Exhibition in 1957. *(Ideal Home Exhibition)*

Coffee sir? Fanny
satisfies the Duke of
Edinburgh's curiosity
at the *Daily Mail*
Ideal Home
Exhibition in 1957.
*(Ideal Home
Exhibition)*

There was also a surprise element to Fanny and Johnnie's introduction to the Queen and Prince Philip at the Ideal Home Exhibition in 1957. In a grandiose display of culinary overkill the Cradocks were debating where to place their new £6 10s toy, a spit, when the playing of the national anthem announced the arrival of the royal couple. Johnnie had set the spit to work by the time the entourage – 'and seemingly every camera in Christendom' – arrived at the *table d'honneur*.

When we reached the farther, stage-end of the table, the Queen bent over our lagoon. 'Are those edible?' asked the Duke. I picked up a tiny crab. 'Yes sir,' I replied, 'even for children,' at which moment out of the corner of his eye he spotted the turning spit. He did not say a word. He just vanished up the steps, on to the stage and towards the spit. Johnnie and I were left standing with the Queen and not knowing what the devil to do next. The Queen simply nodded, 'Go on,' she said smilingly, 'follow him,' so I did. I showed the Duke how it worked and then asked him to stand back while I threw a ladleful of butter into the burners to prove they would not clog. One must prove things, not just make statements, to the

Duke of Edinburgh. Then he said, 'We have an electric spit in our kitchen,' and so saying turned. There in all its shambles was the inside of our cooking table.

'Ah, ha!' said he, grinning, 'that's what I like to see.' 'I'm very sorry, sir,' I apologised. 'You were not supposed to look under there.' Again he laughed and again he turned. This time he crossed to examine a rather special Breton coffee-pot Johnnie and I had brought back from Quimper. Finally, having kept everyone waiting, the Duke turned away and went back down the steps. Below stood Johnnie, talking to the Queen. The Duke leaned over, slung one arm across Johnnie's shoulder and said to the Queen with a grin, 'Isn't it nice, darling, to find the experts are messy cooks too?'

AN ALBERT HALL EPIC

The Bon Viveur International Christmas Cookery show at the Royal Albert Hall in 1956 was the Cradocks' answer to Ten Commandments: a quasi-religious epic. It boasted two superstars, the Elizabeth Taylor and Richard Burton of the high-speed gas generation; a celebrity panel of tasters; a battalion of helpers; and 6,500 extras, occupying every seat in the famous arena. The text was taken from *Guide Escoffier*, Fanny's culinary bible.

The show had been months in the planning. How, for instance, would Fanny and Johnnie, from a space in the middle of the hall normally reserved for title fights,

Bon Viveur, aka Fanny and Johnnie Cradock, made history with their International Christmas Cookery show at the Royal Albert Hall in 1956.

La Gougère Bourguignonne

La Gougère Bourguignonne – 'The origin of Yorkshire pudding'

Ingredients

7½ fl oz milk

2 oz butter

1 flat teaspoon salt

5 oz self-raising flour

4 No. 2 eggs

2 oz diced Gruyère

1 small, raw beaten egg

Method

Place milk, butter and salt in a small thick pan and bring to the boil by the time butter has melted. Toss in the flour, turn out the gas and beat well. Then beat eggs in singly. Stir in 1½ oz Gruyère. Spread into a well-buttered, flute-edged flan dish. Brush surface with beaten raw egg, sprinkle with remaining diced Gruyère. Bake in pre-heated oven at Gas Mark 8 for 25 minutes and it will rise hugely, like a golden brown feather bed.

Time to Remember, 1981

contrive to face and cook in four directions at the same time? Their producer jumped ship at the eleventh hour and Fanny persuaded her brother Charles to take over. As an occasional actor-director he was vaguely qualified and, more importantly, he had the immunity to crisis of someone who hobbled helplessly from one personal drama to the next. He surrounded himself with beer bottles and explained to a bemused North Thames Gas Board dignitary that Guinness and Benzedrine formed his staple diet.

Rehearsals dragged on until 4 a.m. on the day of the show, 11 December. Fanny visited her hairdresser, still felt sick with nerves, and asked her taxi driver to stop off at a church en route to the Albert Hall. 'As I pushed open the doors,' she remembered, 'a pure clear stream of Bach flowed out. I assume the organist was practising. Whoever he was, I sat for half an hour listening and he drowned my fears in Bach.'

At 7.30 p.m. in South Kensington a fanfare cued in master of ceremonies Leslie Hardern. 'The roll of great names which have filled the Albert Hall is probably the longest in the world, but never before, I think, have two people attempted to hold your attention with a frying pan and a spit. . . .'

A spotlight picked out a 12ft high photograph of Georges Auguste Escoffier as Johnnie's voice rose from the darkness: 'Once upon a time in a little Provençal village called Villeneuve-Loubet, there lived . . .'. Fanny took up the story, finishing: 'And so with great pride and humility we dedicate this programme to Georges Auguste Escoffier.'

Thirty-six Gas Board girls followed a complex card index system of exits, entrances and stage crosses to relay and remove materials and equipment while Fanny, resplendent in what the programme acknowledgements referred to as 'silicone stain-resisting satin by Madame Cordeau', floated efficiently between three cookers and a spit. Her brief was not just to entertain the live audience but to link to BBC coverage of the show at $8.32\frac{1}{2}$ precisely. Fanny's hand was on the cooker door as she said: 'Hello, viewers. Here we are in the thick of it at the Albert Hall.' She produced a magnificently inflated Burgundian *gougère* and started to enjoy herself.

Fanny and Johnnie's most prestigious show, in front of 6,500 people, celebrity guests and the TV cameras, at the Royal Albert Hall in 1956. *(North Thames Gas Board)*

The iced swan containing Escoffier's Pêche Melba makes its entrance at the Royal Albert Hall in 1956. *(North Thames Gas Board)*

Part one of the show finished with the wheeling-on of Fanny's Escoffier Pêche Melba, showcased in an 80lb sculpted ice swan. Part two, in which the Cradocks reprised a *Chez Bon Viveur* programme originally shown on Associated-Rediffusion, was going swimmingly until they discovered that the gas had gone out. Cue 10 minutes of relighting, furious ad-libbing and a 'wobbly golden mushroom' of a soufflé to bring the metaphorical curtain down.

Fanny's brother was asked afterwards about the raw material he inherited. 'They gave me a scrap of paper. I asked, "What the hell is this supposed to be?" And they said, "The script." On that tatty sheet was written, "Fanfare. Spotlight on Leslie Hardern. Les does his deathless. Spotlight on F. and J. Enter F. and J. They ad-lib. Running time 2½ hours. God save the Queen".'

On the Box

TV CHEFS BEFORE FANNY

There is a casual assumption that Fanny Cradock was the Adam and Eve of TV cooking, but chefs had been passing on tips of the trade for almost twenty years when Fanny made her television debut. Programme makers were quick to anticipate the demand, but it was only when Fanny flounced on screen in 1955 that the mass-market potential of the genre was realised.

Moira Meighn: This authority on medieval cuisine became British television's first cooking demonstrator on 9 December 1936, five weeks after the BBC's launch. Meighn, real name Phyllis Twigg, offered tips on how to prepare quick snacks to the few hundred viewers who then comprised the BBC's localised audience. After her audition she had been described as suffering from 'social inflections – Lady Bountiful opening the village fête'.

Marcel Boulestin: An impeccably qualified Frenchman who launched the BBC's first regular cooking slot in January 1937 with the fluffiest of plain

omelettes, he had opened his own restaurant, Le Boulestin – a sub-
terranean, art-deco-influenced haven – in London's Covent Garden in 1926.
The eatery of choice for MPs, aristocrats and royalty, it was advertised
during the war as a 'perfect air-raid shelter'.

The practical difficulties involved in putting out early cookery
programmes were indicated by an internal BBC memo in May 1939: 'Camera
2 streaked rather badly from the splash plate of M Boulestin's gas cooker.
This could be prevented by toning the white enamel down a little. The stove
is very noisy.'

Philip Harben: The French-looking, French-sounding but thoroughly
British Harben headed the team of post-war cooks when the BBC resumed
normal service in 1946. Bearded and rotund, Harben sported a distinctive
striped apron and performed with the elan of someone whose parents,
Hubert Harben and Mary Jerrold, were both stage and film actors.

Philip Harben and his wife watch Fanny and Johnnie in action at the Royal
Albert Hall in 1956. *'We do not think they were amused,'* was Fanny's
caption. *(North Thames Gas Board)*

When Harben died in 1970, Fanny wrote: 'We feuded over cookery with Philip Harben, yet he was always the first with congratulations on any good fortune which blessed us as cooks. . . . For who but he could hold us riveted for 20 minutes over boiling a kipper which we would have preferred grilled, and making a pot of English tea, which we abhor.'

Marguerite Patten: This out-of-work actress who tried to convince housewives that they needed refrigerators immediately before the Second World War was a Ministry of Food employee during hostilities. She advised families how to manage rations and was charged with 'inspiring people' into believing that raw, grated turnip, an adult vitamin replacement for orange juice and other foodstuffs permitted for children, was nutritional nectar. She championed Spam and was casually billed as the 'queen of ration book cuisine' before converting her newspaper and magazine work into a cookery book empire of Delia Smith proportions long before Delia was making a fortune out of commonsense cuisine.

Marguerite Patten described her and Harben's approach as 'making the best use of what was available and making rather dull food more interesting. Then suddenly the emphasis changed: everybody was longing to go back and be gracious hostesses and have cocktail parties and cheese and wine.' Fanny Cradock fitted the bill, even if the garb grated with traditionalists. 'It was very evening dressy, spangles and sequins,' remembered Patten. 'What a way to approach cooking, looking like that!' She also became aware, when fulfilling engagements around the country, of the trail of trauma that Fanny could leave in her fiery wake. She recalled the frosty reception at one venue: 'All the young home economists were cowering in corners and they didn't seem to want to come near me. I knew their senior very well and I said, "What's the matter with your girls, has something awful happened?" She said, "No, but Fanny Cradock was here last week and she threw knives at them." '

THE NAME'S THE SAME

Frances Dale was more than an alter ego for Fanny Cradock: she was the author of the early novels and children's books, the up-and-coming cookery demonstrator engaged by the BBC for her first radio assignments in the early fifties, and the conduit from Phyllis to Fanny.

Radio times: Fanny's invitations to the National Radio Awards in 1954, where the panel programme on which she appeared, *The Name's the Same*, was among the winners.

The BBC had begun to scent a star in the making when it gave Fanny a voice test in 1952. Grizel Paterson, the deputy editor on *Woman's Hour*, wrote in a memo: 'She had a pleasant, mature, rather husky voice. She read very badly at first but responded instantly to production – and though she is extremely conceited and very hard, I am certain I could work with her and shape her into a good broadcaster.'

The panel show *The Name's the Same* represented Fanny's highest-profile radio gig to date – she was paid 10 guineas per edition – though in her case the name could not be the same. The producer, Mike Meehan, had already booked the comedy writers Frank Muir and Denis Norden and the actress Frances Day, and pointed out that there was a potential for high confusion with both Frances Day and Frances Dale on the panel. 'Could he bill me as Phyllis Cradock? This was then quite unknown, as any publicity I had had was given to Frances Dale. After discussing it we finally agreed to my own name being used.' The programme was extremely popular, picking up a coveted National Radio Award in 1954, but Fanny found herself embroiled in a curious controversy when viewers claimed that she had been fed the answers in advance. Fanny's plea of innocence to Meehan was couched in bizarre terms: 'As Mr Hitler demonstrated with such ability, there is a form of mass telepathy where you seem to tune in and are, as it were, on the beam. Then an answer arrives with no trouble. On other occasions you are way off the mark and you never get in contact – that at least is how it has been to me.'

KITCHEN MAGIC, 17 FEBRUARY 1955

As a firm believer in the galvanising effect of good food and good company, Fanny cherished the flash of inspiration that launched the chain of events leading to the Cradocks' TV debut. The guest list for a typical dinner party at their South Terrace home, attended by the usual mix of artistic achievers

On a roll: Fanny and Johnnie show the fruits of their labours on *Kitchen Magic*, their first BBC TV appearance, in February 1955.
(© BBC/Corbis)

and well-connected social animals, included the television producer-director Henry Caldwell. Fanny, elegant and sophisticated in white chiffon, was cooking a course or two in the dining room and scooped a soufflé from the oven. She recalled that Caldwell's response was: 'That's kitchen magic, that is. Why don't you two do it on the stage?'

Fanny pointed out that Johnnie could not cook and that she wanted no truck with 'a profession which makes civilised entertaining an impossibility'; but Caldwell persisted, offering a tempting scenario which Fanny recounted in her autobiography:

> 'It's new,' he was clearly thinking aloud, 'it's a fabulous gimmick – cooking in evening dress. You haven't got a mark on that frock, have you?'
> 'I never do.' I was most offended.
> 'Exactly. Tell you what, Fanny. I'll produce you for free! Invite the press. Call it Kitchen Magic. Wear a dress from somebody like Hartnell. . . .'

Johnnie, she remembered, gave her 'the old, familiar twinkle' and, in the space of a few minutes, the idea had been planted, all but aborted and hatched. Fanny taught Johnnie a dish a day for the next week, starting with four variants of the soufflé and progressing to choux paste and finally spaghetti. She fed him the chant, 'eight and a half minutes for true *al dente*, eleven minutes for average English palate, twenty minutes for "stewed knitting".'

At 4 a.m. on 17 February 1955 rehearsals were already underway at the Empire, Shepherds Bush, for the Cradocks' biggest pay day. A 10-guinea bonus had been added to their 40-guinea fee to take account of the longer-than-expected rehearsal time and the fact that Fanny and Johnnie had supplied their own 'heavy equipment', in the shape of cookers and refrigerator. The BBC they joined was a one-channel, monochrome enterprise; programmes began at 3 p.m. and ended at 10.45 p.m. The number of TV licence holders had just broken through the 4 million barrier. *Kitchen Magic* had been slotted in, almost apologetically, at 10.15 p.m., billed with restraint in the *Radio Times* as: 'John and Phyllis Cradock, the Bon Viveur husband and wife cookery team, present an unusual style of cookery to a studio audience at the Television Theatre.'

The behind-the-scenes tension communicated itself to the 500-strong audience as Fanny and Johnnie prepared to meet their ascetic brief of showing how three party dishes, a Swiss roll, éclairs and soufflé *en surprise*,

Homard Mélanie

Ingredients

1 lobster weighing approx 1–1¼ lb
4 tablespoon dry white wine (ideally Chablis)
2 teaspoon brandy

2 rounded teaspoon milled, fresh parsley
2 level dessertspoon grated Parmesan
2 pinches milled black pepper
6 tablespoon single or coffee cream

Method

Take lobster and split lengthwise. Remove the pouch (which is inedible), take out all the flesh from the shell, remove claws, crack and take out all this flesh too. Dice lobster meat neatly and return it to the shells. Lift into buttered baking tin, head to tail. Moisten each with half wine, add to each half parsley, half brandy, half pepper and half cheese and spoon half the cream overall, not minding if some of these ingredients fall into pan. If resting, place uncovered in mild refrigeration. For cooking, cover loosely with foil and bake at Gas Mark 4 for 25–30 minutes, one shelf above centre. Serve with plenty of bread, preferably French, with which you unashamedly soak up the juices.

Ten Classic Dishes (BBC), 1967

Cheers: Fanny at a post-show celebration dinner after her triumphant TV debut in 1955. *(Photopost)*

could be prepared for eight people at a total cost of 6s 2¼d (31p). Fanny recalled in her autobiography: 'I wonder if anyone else can truthfully claim to have been kicked on to television. Johnnie was so appallingly egg-bound with stage fright that, when he was cued on, he couldn't move. A shocked technician, seeing the state he was in, simply gave him a flying kick up the back side and, to the exhortation, "Go on, Johnnie, you're on you silly sod, you're on", Johnnie lurched on to the screen.'

At the start of the routine Johnnie proffered Fanny a bought Swiss roll, which had been christened 'Little Willie' earlier in the day. Fanny scoffed and rejected it on the grounds that at 1s 7½d (8p) it was absurdly expensive. Johnnie explained to the audience that he would keep the manufacturers' Swiss roll at hand so that it could be compared, with an unfavourable flourish, to the Cradocks' special-formula masterpiece. When the time came to produce the evidence, however, the shop roll had disappeared. 'Where's Little Willie?' Johnnie whispered in a panicky aside. 'Who the hell's Little Willie?' responded a prop man – their regular assistant had caught his foot in a grating. The roll was retrieved moments before the camera tracked back on to Johnnie.

Surprisingly, perhaps, it was Fanny who, in a rare show of vulnerability, dissolved into make-up-streaking tears after the programme. Johnnie tried to convince her that they had pulled it off. 'Don't talk nonsense,' she snapped. 'We were only on about five minutes. We left out every damn thing, excepting the beginning and the end.'

The viewing figures were impressive – 73 per cent of the potential audience delayed their bedtime to tune in – and Fanny was consoled by a positive postbag of 'several hundred' letters. One woman wrote: 'Your demonstration on TV was superb and was responsible for two big decisions in my life – A, to keep my TV set after all – B, to go right out and buy a 10" x 14" tin and have a go.' The one cautionary note was sounded by Doreen Stephens, who as Women's Programme editor was to be become Fanny's main point of contact with the BBC. 'I think the highly-strung nervousness of Mrs Cradock which resulted in one or two rather irritating mannerisms can be avoided if they come on again,' she wrote.

10.15 **The Cradocks with**
KITCHEN MAGIC
John and Phyllis Cradock, the Bon Viveur husband and wife cookery team, present an unusual style of cookery to a studio audience at the Television Theatre
Produced by Alan Sleath

The *Radio Times* billing for Fanny's BBC TV debut on 17 February 1955.

Talking tactics: Fanny and Johnnie discuss the script for one of their early Associated-Rediffusion programmes with director Christopher Mercer. (*Associated-Rediffusion*)

Fanny and Johnnie turned down the offer of three fifteen-minute programmes in the summer of 1955 – they wanted half-hour slots – and felt perennially undervalued by the BBC. By the time *Frying Tonight* was aired in November 1955 they had also been wooed by the newly established commercial channel, Associated-Rediffusion.

WINKLES ON THE MOVE

The writer Daniel Farson got more than he bargained for when he interviewed the Cradocks for the TV programme *Success Story* in 1959: wriggling winkles for instance. A less poised performer than Fanny might have wriggled in embarrassment, but she just laughed off the rogue presence in the *fruits de mer*. After speculating that they were 'resuscitated', she said to the vaguely horrified Farson: 'What are you going to eat? Live ones?'

Hunter's Pot

Ingredients

1lb 7oz onions
1lb least expensive Cheddar cheese
salt and freshly milled black peppercorns
   mixed in proportions 4 salt to 1 pepper

softened butter (approx 4 oz by my method)
14 slices from a thin-cut standard sandwich
   loaf
7½ pts water or stock

Method

Slice cheese thinly with knife or Danish-type cheese slice. Slice onions as thinly as possible. Melt butter in shallow heat-resistant flat dish or Victoria sponge tin in oven, if in use, or over lowest possible heat top burner. Slap each bread slice over melted butter surface, scrape surplus back into container and repeat with all slices. Place 2 whole slices, butter side downwards, on base of chosen container and fill in gaps with one halved slice; cover with a quarter of the onions; season lightly with mixed salt and pepper; cover with quarter of the cheese and repeat three times more, pressing each layer down very firmly as you work. Finish with a fifth 'lid' layer of buttered bread slices; two whole, one halved and one quartered. Press this final layer down very firmly indeed and with wooden handle of knife or spoon make a hole in the centre. Boil the water or stock in a kettle and holding kettle high above the container, pour the liquid into the central hole. This will cause the 'island' of bread, cheese and onions to rise up the container until it forms a central, edible 'lid'. Cover with an ordinary lid or two thicknesses of kitchen foil and cook at Gas Mark 3 (325°F), lowest shelf, for 3½ hours. Remove coverings, step up heat to Gas Mark 6 (400°F) and leave for 10 minutes to develop a golden brown crust. Serve in heated soup bowls.

Colourful Cookery (BBC), 1968

Farson's scepticism was deftly deflected by Fanny and Johnnie. When he suggested that they were guilty of over-gilding their food, and that simple was best, they said in telepathic unison: 'You're absolutely right!' His contention that every Cradock dish was automatically subjected to sickly adornment brought the patronising retort from Fanny: 'We don't have to doll *everything* up, ducky.' Their stage show, Farson suggested, was little more than a circus act. 'I don't have any clowns or elephants . . . except Cradock,' countered Fanny.

CHATTERBOX FANNY

The pots, pans and pingers remained silent on 13 April 1960 as Fanny Cradock poured herself into an exciting new venture, as chat-show hostess on ITV's *Late Extra*. 'I would loathe the idea of doing any cooking in that programme,' she told the *TV Times*. 'I enjoy leaving my kitchen behind for a while.' She reasoned that it was a bit like being at home and a bit different to boot. 'I don't pretend that I am inviting guests into my drawing-room because there are times when I have to put the pointed question. For instance, I may have to ask a man how much money he has made. I would never do that in my own drawing-room.'

Douglas Keay, the programme editor, remembers having severe reservations about the choice of Fanny. He told her as much. She fluttered her false eyelashes and suggested that with a little help she would prove him wrong. 'I'll be Trilby to your Svengali,' she said. She also promised that she would use her celebrity connections to attract the best guests in town, though the policy of recruiting on the day created further tension among the production team.

'She plays herself, warts and all, and you can get as bugged as you like by the ribbon in her hair, her sultry voice, her maddening assumption that every viewer is like herself and holds Sunday brunches and has garden secateurs to divide their duck with, but she's got an honesty and real personality which you don't see much of on the small screen.'

Virginia Ironside, Daily Mail

Unobtrusively elegant in a full-length gown (but 'no dangling earrings or flash jewellery to distract attention'), she eased herself into the role with a chummy chat to a friend, Douglas Fairbanks Jnr. But she was also to discover that familiarity did not necessarily make for a happy and relaxed guest. Fanny and Johnnie had previously entertained Sir Gerald Kelly, President of the Royal Academy, but Fanny found to her horror that the promise of a meal did not guarantee a garrulous interviewee. Sir Gerald gave a series of one-word answers to Fanny's carefully crafted questions before she said, in near despair, 'Is there anything else you'd like to say?' 'Yes. Good night,' he replied. 'Silly old fool,' she complained the following day to her personal assistant, Alison Leach.

At the end of a ten-week stint, in which her more forthcoming guests included actors Edith Evans and Ian Carmichael, writer Arthur Hailey and theatre critic Kenneth Tynan, opinion was divided. The *Daily Mail* likened it

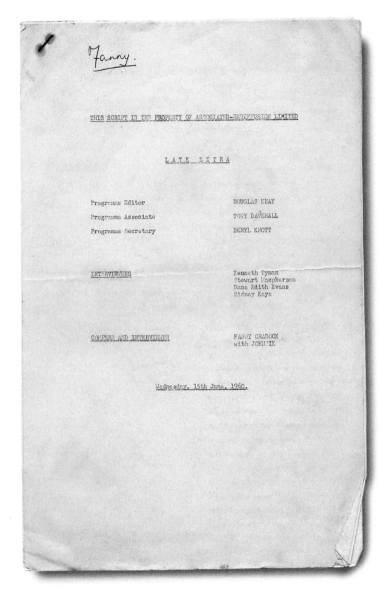

Fanny.

THIS SCRIPT IS THE PROPERTY OF ASSOCIATED-REDIFFUSION LIMITED

L A T E   E X T R A

Programme Editor	DOUGLAS KEAY
Programme Associate	TONY DAVENALL
Programme Secretary	BERYL KNOTT

INTERVIEWEES	Kenneth Tynan
	Stewart Macpherson
	Dame Edith Evans
	Sidney Kaye

COMPERE AND INTERVIEWER	FANNY CRADOCK
	with JOHNNIE

Wednesday, 15th June, 1960.

The queen of chat: a script from the 1960 show *Late Extra,* which gave Fanny a short-lived stint as a chat show hostess.

to 'watching someone who had come from another planet', and concerned correspondents worried about Johnnie's eerily mute involvement. 'Her interviews,' the *Mail* continued, 'were intelligently conducted and held, often, a pleasing note of mockery of the guest, the programme, television. The reviewer suggested, too, that this mockery was only checked by the producer from becoming Rabelaisian. 'Even so, I always felt that one night she would come out with something that would cause terrified engineers to pull the master switch.'

To Fanny with love: a signed photograph from Douglas Fairbanks Jnr and family.

THE DOUGH THAT WOULD NOT BUDGE

Fanny and Johnnie Cradock may have looked like an accident for ever waiting to happen on television – that was part of the attraction – but they were also adept at the cover-up and the ad-libbed escape. They worked with two invisible safety nets. One was Fanny's ability to create on auto-pilot: 'My hands do the cooking. You mustn't think about the cooking while you're performing. You have to think about your voice, your timing, your words. I've never used a script in my life.' The other she could only express in French: *mise en place*, a lifelong insistence on having ingredients and utensils to hand at every stage of the cooking process.

There were occasions when neither instinct nor preparation could come to the rescue. Fanny recalled an early programme for the BBC, *We're Frying*

Tonight, which was to feature a sequence of Johnnie deftly filleting sole. The fish, however, was still in the hands of a panic-stricken assistant who at the last second hurled it in his general direction. 'By some million to one chance,' Fanny wrote, 'that whole, raw sole sailed through the air and landed in exactly the right position at the exact moment that Johnnie picked up his knife and said, with outward tranquillity, "And now to fillet my sole." '

The *Chez Bon Viveur* programmes for Associated-Rediffusion had their sticky moments, too. Johnnie left behind part of his thumb on a white-hot dish, and had a scar to remind him for the rest of his life. Fanny's horror story centred on raw dough which, when cooked, trapped the lid of a pot:

I heard myself saying, 'It seems to be a little stubborn. . . .' The seconds fled by as I prodded and prodded. Finally I said, after what seemed about ten years, 'I've dreamed of something like this happening' – at which

Tart work: Fanny and Johnnie show viewers that small can be beautiful. (© *BBC*)

moment I became quite insane with panic. Gripping the knife with the four fingers of my right hand, I gave one almighty shove. The lid came off, I beamed and on we went. But I had cut all four fingers in that last desperate shove.

Cradock continental: Fanny (as Françoise) and Johnnie bring a touch of Brittany to TV in the fifties. (*Associated Newspapers*)

FOR SALE: THE CRADOCKS. PRICE: £200 A MINUTE

Forget bold dramas, laugh-a-second comedies and campaigning journalism. The cutting-edge entertainment on commercial television in the autumn of 1957 was the ad mag, a drab hybrid of conventional programming and advertising that today would have regulators snorting in censorious indignation. Who better to present the acceptable face of the hard sell than those darlings of the TV kitchen, Fanny and Johnnie Cradock?

For between £200 and £400 a minute advertisers could pitch their tent in various fields: there was 'Flair' for the fashion-conscious; the music-loving 'Please Note' for the young and glamorous; and 'Store Gazing' which reached out to the dedicated shopper. The Cradocks were signed up to write and present 'It's the Tops', with the accent on class and distinction. This was their first gainful freelance employment after being released from the exclusive contract which had tied them to the *Daily Mail* since 1955.

If the money's right: Fanny and Johnnie helped to promote Kelvinator fridges and freezers on commercial TV in the mid-fifties.

The face of Fairy: Fanny could be found 'selling' soap on ITV in the 1960s.

Fanny and Johnnie always protested that their services could be bought but never their principles. They refused to endorse malt vinegar (except when used to clean out fridges and polish furniture), bottled sauces, butter substitutes and pressure cookers; but they were ever alive to the little earner. Though prevented by BBC regulations from mentioning products, Fanny did her best to bring manufacturers' names into view. She and Johnnie were the TV faces of Fropax frozen foods in the late fifties, *Advertisers' Weekly* observing that Fanny, 'looking very much like a pantomime "dame", delivers her spiel with a face as frozen as the product'. Her commercials for Fairy Liquid in the sixties – featuring the immortal line, 'You should not have kissed me, darling, there is lipstick on my collar' – were greeted with equal derision.

'I'll never digest her sour sarcasm, her snide aside glances to the camera, and the way she tried to fillet Mrs Troake's feelings, while they were still moving, in front of 10 million viewers.'

Jean Rook, Daily Express

CATERING FOR SMALL FRY

In the absence of a maternal gene, Fanny Cradock adopted the half-baked theory that grandparents were better suited to the job of raising their children's children. In the late 1950s much of her domestic contentment centred around her grandchild, Julian, and the discovery that, Pied Piper-like, she could lead a whole generation of 'small fry' into her culinary Disneyland of sponge hedgehogs, edible clowns and carrot girls. The proof was in the *Lucky Dip* postbag which deluged Associated-Rediffusion. One of the Cradocks' earliest programmes for children generated 9,000 letters within twenty-four hours; two eight-minute slots in 1960 drew a staggering 40,000 letters. Programme Promotions Ltd, urging the BBC to catch the mood of the nation, wrote: 'When Fanny and Johnnie show the children how to make "toys" i.e. lemon pigs and marzipan rabbits asleep, the figures

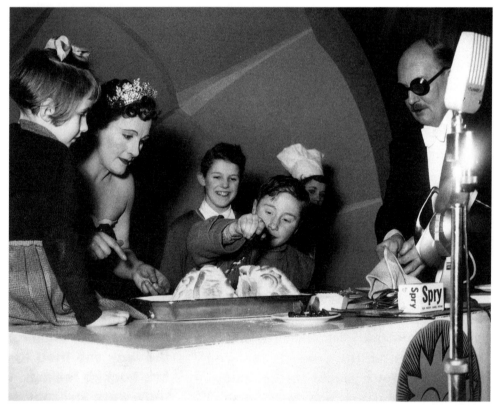

Catering for small fry: Fanny and Johnnie discovered a new captive audience in the late fifties. *(A. Dawson)*

DESERT ISLAND DISCS
(1962) ————————— *Fanny's* CHOICE

Franck, String Quartet in D (Prague City Quartet)
Beethoven, Symphony No. 5 (NBC Symphony/Toscanini)
Mozart, Oboe Concerto in C Major, K314 (Leon Goossens/Sinfonia
    of London/Kostelanetz)
Tchaikovsky, 'None But The Lonely Heart' (NY Philarmonic/
    Kostelanetz)
Her luxury: typewriter and paper
Her book: Smith's *Dictionary of Greek and Roman Biography and
    Mythology*

ON JOHNNIE'S BEST QUALITY ————————————

'Utter reliability'.

DESERT ISLAND DISCS
(1962) ————————— *Johnnie's* CHOICE

Chopin/Douglas, Les Sylphides (Paris Conservatoire Orch/Maag)
Dvorak, Slavonic Dance in C Major, Op. 67 (Bamberg SO/Keilberth)
Debussy, *Claire de Lune* (Gieseking)
Rimsky-Korsakov, *Scheherazade* (RPO/Beecham)
His luxury: golf clubs and balls
His book: Churchill's *History of the English-Speaking Peoples*

ON FANNY'S BEST QUALITY ————————————

'Well, a rude word, perhaps, but guts. . . . Because of her
utter refusal to recognise the possibility of defeat in any
circumstances, and also her immense capacity for work,
which I wish I could equal.'

shoot up whereas plainer things like making their own bread don't have such appeal. The overall picture is that their viewing public consists of 60% girls, 40% boys, including children of four and five years old whose parents write in for them.'

The Cradocks had to tread carefully in this catering minefield, adopting a four-part plan based on these bywords: safe, clean, professional and amusing. Their rationale was explained in the *TV Times* in 1959:

> Safety they put first. 'Who would dream of asking the tiny ones to cook?' says Fanny. 'No real cooking until 10, I say. No fat frying until they are at least 13. Knives? We like knives with sharp points. But a cork on the end saves cuts.'
>
> Says Johnnie: 'Little ones get along nicely with blunt-edged scissors.'
>
> 'We never tell the children to do anything,' says Fanny. 'Ask a grown-up before you start out is our advice. After all, we're not in charge of the children.'
>
> 'Wash your hands before you start' is the Cradocks' first rule in hygiene.

If Fanny had been totally up-front about her attitude to cleanliness in the kitchen the message would have been: 'Do as I say, not as I always do.' Instead, she deflected and defused the whinges of cover-up dissenters. A fifteen-year-old girl wrote to the *TV Times* in 1958: 'I think the Lucky Dip cookery demonstrators Fanny and Johnnie would look much nicer in white overalls, or aprons. It would also show an example to us younger ones following them.' Fanny proposed, with matronising overtones: 'You wear aprons long enough to prove to yourself they never get marked. Then you throw them away and wear your party clothes.'

Fanny and Johnnie cashed in with a bevy of slim books for their new audience, and Fanny had no qualms about setting herself up as instant guru on child behaviour. She dealt with manners in *Happy Cooking Children*:

> 'Frilly' manners are bad manners. If you have beautiful manners and you make a little hiccoughing noise at the table, you never say anything. If your grown-ups have beautiful manners, too, they will not say anything either, because it would be drawing attention to an accident.
>
> People with best manners never allow themselves to do anything which might make someone else feel uncomfortable.

'TV COOK IN HOT WATER'

Fanny Cradock could dodge the bullets of the individual snipers, but when a whole battalion of protesters took aim it was time to fire back. This was no petition of influence in *The Times* letter page, but a councillor's call for action in the backwaters of Lincolnshire.

The *Lincolnshire Echo* reported on 10 March 1961, under the headline 'TV cook in hot water':

Television cookery experts should set a good example to schoolgirl cooks and wear hygienic caps, Kesteven Education Committee will be told when they meet at Grantham next week.

Behind a move to get the committee to tell the BBC they are wrong in allowing Mrs Cradock, of Cookery Club, for instance to appear with nothing on her hair is Coun John H. Lewis.

Coun Lewis, a Cambridge MA, who farms at Birkholm Manor, Corby Glen, said yesterday: 'Under the Food Hygiene Regulations, workers are supposed to wear head coverings.

'Our girls wear caps in their cookery classes and the school canteen staff stick to the rules. Yet when the girls look at television they can see Mrs Cradock wearing evening dress with nothing on her hair.

'It is against all we are trying to teach about cleanliness and I hope to get things altered pretty soon.

'The resolution the committee will consider is: "That the Director of Education, Dr T.W.P. Golby, be instructed to write to the BBC pointing out that in the interests of hygiene and as an example to children, cookery demonstrators should wear head coverings."'

As my husband and partner is practically bald, the onus of defence seems to rest on me.

Fanny's response:

I was most amused to read this, and somewhat startled that Councillor Lewis is so oddly out of touch with hair hygiene whilst babbling in defence of food hygiene requirements. . . . Nothing would induce me ever to degrade the culinary art by appearing on Stage or Television as if I was assisting at an operation; to those who know their subject, cookery is a cleanly and creative art, and not a grubby chore. To those who wash and

Home service: Fanny faces the photographer for a *Radio Times* shoot in 1968. *(© BBC)*

tend their hair properly, there is no possibility of short, well-groomed heads causing unhygienic conditions during the pursuance of this art.

We feel that the Councillor would be far better to strive for women to wash and brush their hair more frequently. As my husband and partner is practically bald, the onus of defence seems to rest on me. My hair, as my hairdresser's accounts can prove, is shampooed and set twice weekly. It is then lacquered with what my Mayfair hairdresser gives me authority to state is a disinfectant lacquer, which keeps every hair in place, even in the torrid heat in our theatre of Kitchen Magic, currently presenting two shows daily at the Ideal Home Exhibition. In fact, during this run, not only my hair but that of my assistants, is shampooed three times per week.

They follow the same hair routine as I have pursued since instructed by my grandmother when I was a small girl. If every head were brushed, as mine is, night and morning for 100 strokes and washed, as I have said, (which can always be done at home) then no-one need go around in disfiguring caps. Moreover, the modern nylon hairbrush (I have two, and both are washed by my personal maid daily) if used with a few scraps of cotton-wool on the bristles for the afore-mentioned brushing, gives an automatic twice-daily washing and, surprising as it may sound, the cotton-wool does not remain on the head.

Perhaps I am treating the Councillor with more gravity than his rather frivolous remarks merit; this, I feel, you are more expert to judge than we – we leave the final assessment, with the utmost confidence, in your hands.

COLOURFUL COOKERY: A BBC PIONEER

If snooker was made for colour television, so too was Fanny Cradock. Haute cuisine was released from its monochrome straitjacket at 8.50 p.m. on 26 September 1968. Fanny had said the series was 'about cooking for everyone – from the girl living in the bed sitter to the harassed housewife with little time to spare'. But the whiff of a mixed message was in the air. One viewer wrote to the *Radio Times*: 'Although I very much enjoy Fanny Cradock's cookery programmes I am at a loss to understand at whom this new series, Colourful Cookery, is aimed. The emphasis in the first pro-gramme was on an economy-satisfying soup at *5d* per bowl. Mrs Cradock mentions that this new series is aimed at the hard-up housewife. May I ask how many of these hard-up housewives can afford £300 for a colour television set?'

Such qualms apart, this was Fanny basking in her natural habitat. At the end of the series David Wainwright gushed with admiration in the *Evening News*:

> Colour even adds a new dimension to Fanny Cradock. We know her as the Boadicea of the Boeuf Bourgogne [sic] – but in colour she is Wellington fighting Waterloo again in a picture by David, as with harassed determination she rides her electric mixer like a snorting charger.
>
> The moment when she makes with the Parma violets around a golden soufflé newly drawn from her turquoise oven – it's ecstasy.

FANNY CRADOCK INVITES

Fanny Cradock was accustomed to her domestic kitchens being recreated in a studio environment. Finally, in 1970, outside broadcast facilities gave her the opportunity to show off her magnificent Dower House kitchen to the

Great British public in a thirteen-part cookery series, *Fanny Cradock Invites*. The one worry for Fanny was the prospect of heavy-booted BBC technicians trampling on her parquet floor in the hall, en route to the downstairs toilet; she asked the Corporation to bring in a portable loo. The *Daily Mail* reported: 'The floor remained unmarked, but bringing in the loo the BBC crashed into the gate post and knocked it down.'

The *Radio Times* was given exclusive access to the recording of the final programme in the series, and Denis Curtis offered a vivid impression of Fanny's precision and attention to detail, not to mention the constant haranguing of her apprentices, even under extreme pressure:

'OK everybody, programme 13, run VT for clock.' And, while the countdown continued Fanny's voice could be heard: 'Where's my swabs? No dear, I had them here, one, two and three. Thank you Peter (star pupil) but how are you going to run a restaurant of your own if you always forget? Now who is going to hand me the cooked puff-pastry if Peter is over there? Why in hell can't you do it Frank? (Frank's learning about wines from Johnnie and looking after Fanny's garden) . . . Shut up Peter, we're almost on. . . .'

Frying tonight: home doubled as studio for *Fanny Cradock Invites* in 1970. (© BBC)

LADY MACBETH AS LADY MACBETH

A reader wrote in to the long-running radio programme *Woman's Hour* in 1950 to exclaim: 'I never thought I would hear Lady Macbeth reciting a recipe.' The nickname stuck – Fanny rather liked it – and twenty years later she was given the chance to play the villainous role for real on television.

The rationale behind the late-night show *Whatever Next* was to present celebrities in the Shakespearian guises of their choice: Spike Milligan played Shylock, TV reporter Julian Pettifer was Hamlet, and singers Paul Jones and Julie Felix duetted as Romeo and Juliet. Fanny threatened to pull the plug on her performance, relented and transformed *Macbeth* into a tragic-comic masterpiece. She fumed to the *Daily Express*: 'It was the first time I'd done any acting, and I took it very seriously. There was no guidance or help at all.'

'SO, LIKE TINY TIM, I SAY GOD BLESS YOU ALL.'

The Fanny Cradock who presented a series of short Christmas-themed programmes for the BBC in 1975 was a fading flambé, overtaken by age, a quirkily apocalyptic vision of the world and the Delia Smith generation. It was a wistful nostalgia trip for viewers who had been educated, entertained or enraged over the twenty years of Queen Fanny's TV reign. She tried to trick time – she was now an unacknowledged sixty-six – by wearing ribbons in her hair, rosettes and buckled belts.

The tried-and-tested themes were hauled out of the rusting vaults, dusted down and recycled in 13½ minutes of cooking cabaret. 'It's all so gloriously easy when you know how'; 'Men are responsible for the low cooking esteem and lower ambition of their wives'; and that illusion of a humble, coy paragon of femininity, desperate to establish personal rapport with each viewer – 'It isn't easy trying to hide the fact that I'm scared stiff to meet you at the beginning of a programme.'

Minutes later the love-in had been transformed into a scene of sadistic slaughter as Fanny turned demented proctologist to stuff a turkey with a swollen nylon bag, dismantled the bird with garden secateurs, then stabbed a goose into submission. A thrilling undercurrent of domestic violence was never far away. Fanny's test for a good rolling pin, frequently articulated on stage and on screen, was 'to slosh father or husband over the head with it. If he falls unconscious it's all right for cooking.'

She had also learned from bitter experience that the hygiene-conscious had to be appeased rather than resisted. 'I have scrubbed and scrubbed downstairs in the make-up room and got my fingernails and my hands spotless, and of course there's no nail varnish on them, and I'm going to use them unashamedly because that's the best way to make a good cake.'

There was a quasi-regal tone to her treacly sign-off, delivered with a wooing smile and unintentionally comic tilt at sincerity: 'May I say how much I admire the housewives of Britain in these appalling present conditions for their courage in trying to give their families another super Christmas. So, like Tiny Tim, I say God bless you all.'

THE BIG TIME: 'MY BIGGEST MISTAKE'

Fanny Cradock called it her 'biggest mistake', one final controlled explosion of withering honesty that snuffed out the weak flame of her television career. Yet even in the immediate, self-critical aftermath of her spat with an unassuming Devon housewife, Fanny felt that she was essentially right in her criticism: the error was tactical not actual.

In 1976 the BBC dreamt up a documentary series called *The Big Time* in which gifted amateurs crossed over into the world of the professional. Gwen Troake, who had won the Cook of the Realm title four years earlier, was asked by the programme's producer, Esther Rantzen, to lay on a banquet for the former Prime Minister, Edward Heath, at the Dorchester Hotel; Fanny was engaged as culinary adviser. Esther Rantzen remembered:

> Viewers watched Fanny smile at Gwen with venomous sweetness and ask what menu she had planned. Gwen, dimpled and sweet as custard, said in her soft Devon voice, 'I was thinking of duck with bramble.'
>
> Fanny's voice squawked like an outraged parrot. 'Bramble? What, may I ask, is bramble?' Had she really never seen an English hedgerow? Gwen explained the sauce was made out of blackberries. Fanny's lips puckered with disgust. Dave [the cameraman] zoomed in tight, and stayed there. 'A blackberry?' she oozed sarcasm, a Bakewell tart overflowing with treacle. 'No, dear. Blackberries may do in Devon, but you're among professionals now.' 'And the pudding?'

As Gwen falteringly described the ingredients of her coffee pudding, Fanny pretended to retch. 'Coffee essence' – heave – 'cream' pretend belch – 'sugar' – Fanny hawked and spat. At each heave and gulp, the camera zoomed in tighter and tighter, on her.

Fanny persuaded Gwen Troake to substitute pastry boats – clever yachting reference she thought – but the public were already swearing at their televisions, reaching for their phones, putting pen to indignant paper. Esther Rantzen described it as 'Cruella De Vil meets Bambi'. The *Radio Times* received 600 letters of complaint. Fanny was variously condemned as self-centred, condescending, insulting, patronising, rude, tactless, pathetic and offensive; she could not even sound the appropriate note of damage-limiting contrition in her defence to the magazine:

To be truthful, I was genuinely astonished that the programme compilers showed someone who seemed to me to have no concept of making a menu and whose palate was so extraordinary that she seemed incapable of appreciating what a sorry combination her rich duck dish and the subsequently very sickly pudding would be.

If my inward bewilderment registered as condescension I am very cross with myself. What I was feeling was genuine pity for an obviously very nice person who was clearly out of her depth.

Daily Express columnist Jean Rook wrote:

I could forgive Fanny her dramatics – it's her style to go on like a boiling-over panful of spuds. I could just stomach the French with which she annoyingly ices her conversation. I could even excuse the pink hair ribbons which make her look as sickly as a soft centre round a very hard nut.

But I'll never digest her sour sarcasm, her snide aside glances to the camera, and the way she tried to fillet Mrs Troake's feelings, while they were still moving, in front of 10 million viewers.

Gwen Troake soon discovered that she had not only the sympathy of the nation but a consoling book deal. *Gwen Troake's Country Cookbook* was published the following year, 1977, and included the coffee cream dessert that Fanny had ordered off the menu.

CELEBRITY AT LARGE

Fanny Cradock's fame could not be confined to the TV kitchen, and – when the money was right – she popped up on everything from *Jukebox Jury* to *The Generation Game*. She almost came to blows with the comedian Jimmy Edwards on *The Auction Game* in 1968, and she was a pulse-racing challenge for chat-show hosts.

She was bracketed with the historian A.J.P. Taylor and comedian Bernard Manning on *Parkinson* in 1972. The host recalls: 'She frightened the life out of me. I remember thinking, "I'm glad you're not *my* mother." She was loud and aggressive and I can still picture the fierce eyes and hear that rasping voice.'

Nervously playing with a handkerchief throughout, Fanny revealed a little of her spiritual philosophy: 'You can never be sorry for yourself because you can believe implicitly that you asked for it somewhere before and if you don't face up to it you'll get it again later on. This to me is the important thing about it. It totally eliminates what I regard as man's second disease: self-pity. The first, of course, being fear.' Fanny was more comfortable playing off her co-guests, all contemptuous sideways glances and eyelashes fluttering wildly as she sighed, sneered silently and puffed her cheeks out in derision. She dug her claws into Alan Taylor for his political outlook – 'party politics stinks', she said – and his attitude to the French. She responded to Manning's bigoted brand of humour with a regurgitated soundbite: 'I'm only intolerant of two things: racial intolerance and margarine.' Perversely, Fanny decided that there was 'an element of sympathy' in Manning's gags and offered to put him on a diet which would enable him to shed 2½ stone in two months.

Terry Wogan was hauled up for the seemingly innocuous observation that Fanny and Johnnie had been together for fifty years. Fanny interpreted this as a sneaky way of trying to establish her age and boomed: 'That's a very rude, English-type question which I will not answer.' Despite plying a bizarrely fair-headed Fanny with champagne, a callow Jonathan Ross was treated like a schoolboy heading for detention as he tried to interview her on Channel 4's *The Last Resort* in 1987. The plug was pulled prematurely, much to Fanny's disgust.

She and Johnnie appeared on Bruce Forsyth's *Generation Game* in 1973, entering stage left with a large, white teddy bear which they cryptically described as their eighteenth grandchild. Johnnie took the chance to ham it

Hats off: Fanny resting from the strain of the 7½lb headgear she wore as the Duchess in the all-star production of *Alice in Wonderland* on ITV in 1960.

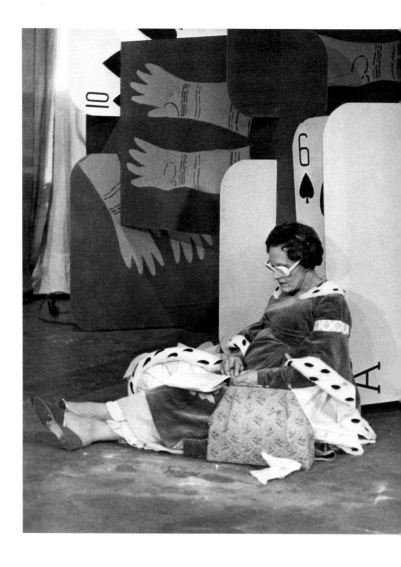

up as he and Fanny demonstrated the art of mince-pie making: 'You take this rolling pin. It has to be heavy enough to knock me out and I've been knocked out hundreds of times in my life. In fact, when I go to the barber's now, if I haven't got a mark on my head, he says, "What's wrong with the old woman, is she ill?" '

A few weeks later Fanny was the mystery celebrity on *What's My Line?*. More importantly, at a time when she was starting to feel insecure about her prospects of further employment on TV, the ebullient Kenneth Williams gave a tribute to cherish. 'I sit there enthralled and I can't stand cooking: a boiled egg drives me up the wall. You give it to us totally directly, without any hint of pretension.'

6

At Home... <u>and</u> Abroad

29 SOUTH TERRACE

A blitz-battered house in South Kensington (Fanny upgraded it to Knightsbridge when she was feeling socially insecure) was all that the Cradocks could aspire to when they returned to London at the end of the Second World War. Fifty-seven panes of glass needed replacing, two ceilings were down, and multi-layered grime had claimed squatters' rights. Once salvaged, however, this six-floor, fourteen-room property became the nerve centre for a networking campaign of military precision. Here, in 'the most burgled street in London' according to Fanny, she was first dubbed a cordon bleu cook by the influential gastronome André Simon; here she entertained publishers, editors, TV producers, minor aristocracy, and even the occasional friend; and here the idea was hatched for *Kitchen Magic*, her first television programme.

When the *Daily Mail* came visiting in 1955 – Fanny and Johnnie had just transferred the Bon Viveur imprint from *The Daily Telegraph* – she boasted that they churned out anything from 250 to 800 meals a week in their cosy, idiosyncratic basement kitchen. 'They have aimed for gaiety ("A kitchen is a

At home with the Cradocks: Fanny and Johnnie in their bustling South Terrace kitchen in the fifties.

place to cook in, not perform surgical operations"), efficiency ("Three cookers are more efficient than one range – we want lots and lots of burners"), plenty of working surfaces ("Detachable heat- and stain-resisting plastic covers fit over the gas stoves when not in use and all working surfaces are covered in the same way").' They had even invested £11 12s in a home canning machine. Posters of their best-loved foreign haunts covered the ceiling, from which hung herbs, seaweed, garlic, dried octopus, squid and an Ardennes smoked ham.

Fanny was regarded as a *nouveau riche* nuisance by longer-established residents of South Terrace, and was threatened with legal action by their landlords after illuminating the entrance with a wrought-iron lamp which she likened to 'a big meat dish supporting lily leaves and a crane'. 'They'll move it over our dead bodies,' she told the *Daily Sketch* defiantly. 'The only other one in the world like it stands in the dining-room of the Duke of Windsor's converted mill near Paris. So it must be in good taste.'

Even the ceiling played its part in storage at the Cradocks' South Terrace kitchen in the 1950s. *(Associated-Rediffusion)*

Ringing endorsement: Fanny forges another deal at South Terrace in the fifties.

By the time the lease expired in the late fifties, Fanny had further aggravated her neighbours by insisting on parking their newly acquired Rolls-Royce outside the house.

134 SHOOTERS HILL ROAD

Fanny Cradock knew the move from South Kensington to Blackheath had been justified when her vegetable supplier said he was 'glad the carriage folk were back'. She was just another jumped-up celebrity in South Terrace, but in SE3 she was the closest thing to royalty.

There was more room to entertain, though Tenniel and Evangeline Evans, their next-door neighbours in South Terrace, still had the impression that they were the lone constants in the Cradocks' social set. The TV personality turned Tory MP Gyles Brandreth, who was a later addition to the invited list, saw parallels with functions laid on by Robert Maxwell and Jeffrey Archer. His diary verdict was: 'Whenever the host is out of the room, the guests talk about him – not as a proper friend, but as a kind of oddball curiosity.'

The kitchen conversion alone cost £5,000 (multiply by ten for a modern equivalent) and gave Fanny more breathing space (33ft 6in by 15ft) and more cookers (five) than before. She was so proud of it that she arranged guided tours for the locals and joked that Langton House was Blackheath's answer (albeit within hailing distance of the 89 bus) to Woburn Abbey.

She switched on the Christmas lights, opened fêtes and fairs, supported the local Conservative Association and exuded regal munificence at the fifth annual dinner and dance of the Kidbrooke House Community Centre in 1960. 'My fellow villagers,' she told her loyal subjects, 'you represent the most important structure of this great nation. We think you are the most valuable people for three reasons – for your family life, your friendship and

Charity begins at home: Fanny and Johnnie enter into the spirit for an Oxfam benefit in Blackheath.

Account master: Johnnie meticulously recorded all the incomings and outgoings in the Cradock household.

			1975		10.
		brot forwd		7316	14
JULY	12	Yellow Broom	Dinner for D.T.	17	07
	14	Kildwick Hall	" "	18	49
	15	Box Tree		14	90
	16	Devonshire Arms	Dinner, 4 nights B+B for D.T.	88	64
	17	Cash	Petty Cash	30	00
	"	Marks & Spencer	Pullover	5	99
	18	L. Roche		19	00
	20	Cash	Petty Cash	20	00
	23	O'Flynns Stores		13	15
	24	O'Keefe	Meat	23	71
	"	John Carey Ltd	Carpet	175	00
	25	Cash	Wages & Petty Cash	100	00
	"	C. McAlister	Meat	10	83
	28	O'Flynns Stores		9	29
	"	Mrs O'Buckley	Church subs.	5	00
	"	W.J. Thompson & Son	Stationery	4	00
	31	Cash	Wages & Petty Cash	90	00
AUG	1	Fine Wines	Wines	21	14
	"	Smiths Limerick	Down payment on replacement car	338	00
	2	Camera House	Camera repair	58	00
	7	Cash	Wages & Petty Cash	80	00
	"	Cork C.C.		38	00
	8	M. Roche	Milk	12	15
	9	Longueville House	Dinner, luncheon	23	92
	11	Cash	Petty Cash	20	00
	15	P.&S. Cradock	Fees	116	39
	"	Cash	Wages & Petty Cash	90	00
JUNE	30	W.J. Thompson & Son	Stationery	14	00
JULY	16	A.A. subs		5	50
AUG	20	St Johns Hospital	Ex-Ray fee	2	25
	"	Dowcrak Motor Works	Car repairs & petrol	87	83
	"	E.S.B.	Electricity	13	65
	"	J. Burrowes		72	75
				8954	79

your devotion to the monarchy. You keep alive something which only lives in this funny little island of ours. We thank you for letting us into this happy family and if there is any way we can serve the things you do it will honour us greatly.'

Crème Forestière

'This was the soup we created on the night we won our first Cordon Bleu'

Ingredients

2lb (900g) blanched, unpeeled button mushrooms

8oz (225g) peeled very small shallots

2oz (50g) potato flour (*fécule de pommes de terre*)

2oz (50g) butter

1½fl oz (45ml) pure olive oil

Gros sel

Mignonette (ground black peppercorns)

1pt (600ml) modest Chablis

½pt (300ml) Jersey cream

4pt (2.40 litres) chicken stock reduced by half by simmering

1 flat dessertspoon (1 x 10ml spoon) dry English mustard

Method

Hand-chop the scalded unskinned mushrooms and the shallots very finely. Place the latter in a large thick frying pan with melted butter and olive oil. Cook gently until almost tender, pale yellow and totally unbrowned, otherwise discard and begin again. Add prepared mushrooms, work in with the back of a wooden spoon and then add the mustard, potato flour and a light seasoning of salt and pepper. Continue working until the mixture forms a paste in the pan. Add a quarter of the given wine and work up as before. When smooth and slightly less thick, repeat three more times, adding the small quantity of wine, then working down to a gradually thinning paste until all is absorbed. Stir in 5 fluid oz (150ml) of reduced stock.

When this is blended scrape into a large saucepan and stir in the remainder of the stock. Set over the merest thread of heat to simmer with an occasional stir for at least 30 minutes. Stir in the cream, taste and correct seasoning with salt and pepper.

A Lifetime in the Kitchen, vol. III, 1985

THE DOG'S DINNER

House-hunting visitors to Fanny Cradock's Blackheath home – on the market for £17,000 – have been rather surprised by the contents of this great cookery expert's store cupboards.

There are 60 wholesale-sized packets of cornflakes in one and tins of sardines in another.

Mrs Cradock says: 'The cornflakes are devoured almost exclusively by one of my house-boys, who gets through two-thirds of a packet each breakfast, while I am the one who eats the sardines.'

She explains: 'One of my favourite snacks is made up of crushed sardines, mixed up with crumbled brown bread and soft boiled eggs.' She calls it 'the dog's dinner'.

Daily Mail, 1968

'THERE'LL BE NO WINTER IN OUR GARDEN'

Master plans were a Fanny Cradock speciality, so when she first laid eyes on the 'sad old orchard of long-unpruned fruit trees', the 'cat-ridden front shrubbery', and the 'balding lawn intersected by wasteful pathways' which comprised the garden of the Cradocks' Blackheath home, she saw something more than an intensive care patient.

Garden goddess: Fanny and Johnnie relaxed the dress code when they were outdoors in Blackheath. The mod-cons included a gas-heated greenhouse. *(Planet News)*

Autumn harvest: the
Cradocks made every
season productive.
(Michael Leale/BPC
Publishing)

Gardening was both therapy and pastime for Fanny, who was almost as conversant with flowers, plants and herbs as she was with ingredients. The Shooters Hill Road house gave her the space to grow and experiment that she had lacked in the fourteen years she and Johnnie had spent in South Kensington. They had been able to preserve, pickle and can at South Terrace, but here they could strive for kibbutz-like self-sufficiency. 'From garden to gourmet is our slogan now,' Fanny promised.

The Rolls-Royce, their premier arriviste symbol, was commandeered for tree-felling duty: 'We put chains on the Rolls and drag 'em out by the roots,' Fanny explained – and she didn't even resent the two slipped discs that were a consequence of removing 92ft of concrete. 'We also excavated enough false hair to coat a Yeti from blackened rockeries . . . sank our Christmas ski money in horse manure. We dug the lily pond and nearly lost our three-year-old grandson in the landslide he engendered. It has been such satisfying slave labour.'

Fanny wrote in *The Daily Telegraph*: 'We planned our garden campaign to cock a snook at the seasons. No one can do it without a three-way plan

'We also excavated enough false hair to coat a Yeti from blackened rockeries . . . sank our Christmas ski money in horse manure. We dug the lily pond and nearly lost our three-year-old grandson in the landslide he engendered. It has been such satisfying slave labour.'

based on green house, smoke house and kitchen where quick-freeze, preserving pans and home canner form the bridgehead between gourmet and garden.' She also told the *Sun* and *Empire News* that she wanted 'to reproduce my ancestor's herb garden. A talkative old soul who married Henry the Eighth, you may have heard of her – Catherine Parr was the name.' The smoke-house plans were on their way to the local council, but even Fanny had to concede defeat on one Good Life-style ambition. 'If it were not for the mortal dread of the borough surveyor, we would never have relinquished our first intention to keep a cow,' she wrote.

Two years after moving in the benefits were obvious. The same heating supply that fuelled their terrace illumination – and the much-chuckled-over 'Fanny by gaslight' references – was piped to the greenhouse. The Cradocks now felt they could cheat the seasons. Fanny told the *TV Times*: 'If we had to pay shop prices for all the vegetables we use in the kitchen, we would have to be millionaires. We have saved £10 a week on our greengrocer's bill by growing our own stuff. Just try buying cantaloupe melon, aubergine, asparagus and those delicious foreign gooseberries – all essential for good cooking. We grow all these and lots more.'

T & P: FOR TOP TOMATOES

Fanny Cradock was once asked how she managed to grow such healthy-looking and flavoursome tomatoes. 'T and P,' she replied. 'T and P', her puzzled guest repeated, 'what's that?' 'Tea and pee,' Fanny emphasised. Wendy Colvin, who worked for the Cradocks at the time, confirmed: 'That's exactly what she did. Every night she used to pee in a bucket. I used to wonder what it was for.' The homemade fertiliser was dubbed 'Madam's Tonic' by one member of staff, who saw Fanny at her most relaxed in the garden at both Shooters Hill Road and Dower House. 'It was almost as if they were her children,' recalls Alison Leach. 'She'd be furious if someone had forgotten to water the tomato seedlings. "Poor little things", she'd say.'

Cordon Bleu NIGHT

THE DATE: **4 May 1949**

THE PLACE: **29 South Terrace, SW7**

THE HOSTS: **Major and Mrs John Whitby Cradock**

THE GUESTS: **The Viscountess Chetwynd, Lady Daniel, M and Mme André Simon, John Lehmann, Andrew Dakers, and Captain Dudley Cutbill**

THE FARE:
> **Les Canapés des Gourmets**
> **La Crème Forestière**
> **Les Coquilles St Jacques des Marquises**
> **La Poularde poëlée Massena**
> **Les Petits Pois Lucullus**
> **La Salade verte**
> **La Fondue Gribourgeoise**
> **Le Sabayon Sicilien**
> **Le Bavarois enrubanné**
> **Les Petits Four Parisiens**
> **La Corbeille des Fruits**
> **Le Café Brûlot**

THE WINES:
> **Macharnudo Fino**
> **Meursault Charmes 1942**
> **Wehlener Sonnenuhr Auslese 1943**
> **Château Haut-Brion 1934**
> **Château Haut-Bailly 1929**
> **Château d'Yquem 1937**
> **Taylor's 1924**
> **Roullet & Delamain 1906 Grande Champagne**

The Cordon Bleu: Frances Dale

FANNY THE DOMESTIC DIVA

For all the influence that the Bon Viveur column exerted in the 1950s, nothing pandered to Fanny Cradock's eclectically dogmatic nature more satisfyingly than her four-year stint as woman's editor on the *Sunday Graphic*. She was a bargain-chasing Martha Stewart for post-war Britain, mixing and matching recipes, gardening and beauty tips; short-cutting to style on a shoestring. She even pontificated about the rights and wrongs of parenthood.

Fanny set up the *Sunday Graphic* Court of Inquiry, a 'sensational investigation into glamour': 'Women must learn that fashion is achieved by THOUGHT, not money, and that a tidy mind breeds a tidy appearance . . . they must buy their hats AFTER a "hair do," not before . . . they must develop the poise which comes from right thinking . . . and ABOVE ALL they must educate their menfolk to take a deep interest in their appearance.'

She warned of the evils that were gripping fifties Britain: 'Whatever your way of life, you have only one responsibility. To make sure your daughters never come within shouting distance of dirty little clubs, wide boys, latchkeys, unchaperoned late night careening, or any of the grubby forerunners to 20th century tragedies.'

And she outlined the pitfalls of sexual equality: 'You can't have equal pay and equal privileges without the equal responsibilities and suffering that go with them. Equality to me spells: the dubious privilege of strap-hanging on crowded buses while the wise male clings to his equal seat; the right to stride out with one's own suitcases at the station, instead of having a husband to carry them and heave them on to racks; and the pleasure of going out to work all day and coming home to a dreary round of chores.'

DIY FANNY: BLUE PETER FOR ADULTS

There was an economising fervour in Fanny Cradock which all the minks, Rolls-Royces and luxury hotels in the world could not dampen. In the early fifties she may have been reflecting the do-it-yourself or do-without realities of the time, but she never stopped preaching homegrown virtues.

Johnnie's carpentry skills were exercised on the pelmets that set off the Cradock-inspired curtains. In a single issue of the *Sunday Graphic* in 1952 Fanny showed how to make a lampshade using an old chianti bottle and the

DIY Fanny: a home-made Christmas wreath at the Dower House. *(Michael Leale/BPC Publishing)*

straw covering from a wine bottle, kitchen curtains using an old fishing net, and a coolie hat – the in-style headgear for Continental beaches that summer – using stiff tarlatan. Fanny poured enormous energy into the homemade Christmas decorations, wreaths and flower displays that adorned the Cradock houses. She abhorred unnecessary expense and waste.

Their three-volume retrospective *A Lifetime in the Kitchen*, devoted to beginner cooks, family fare and the ambitious practitioner, appeared in 1985, the same year as Delia Smith's *One is Fun!* The opportunistic optimism of Delia's book contrasted starkly with the comically dark Cradock perspective. Next stop, Samaritans.

> 'If you drink tea, you will need a pan for boiling water but you can even dispense with a teapot if you buy a billy-can, which costs far less.'
> 'Scour the junk shops for an old pre-stainless steel knife. If cleaned up and brazenly sharpened against a stone kerbside, it will serve as a kitchen cutting knife until you can raise the wind for a set of professional ones by Sabatier.'
> 'If from your flatlet or bed-sitting room you can see some healthy looking dandelions flourishing below, cover them with a flower pot to blanch the leaves. Then use and enjoy in your salads.'

They showed how to convert an ordinary glass jug into a measuring jug by marking it with nail varnish, how to make a measuring box using thick typing paper and even how to construct a homemade toasting fork for bed-sitting room toast with the help of a pair of pliers, a scrap of insulating tape and three wire coat hangers.

CHRISTMAS WITH THE CRADOCKS

Christmas was an excuse for year-round planning, and planning was the quick-setting glue that held together Fanny Cradock's world. She had grave doubts about the festive season's distorted values – 'rather pagan, revolting and commercial' was her description in 1961 – but it was still a time to give, receive, show off and entertain.

Less organised revellers might scoff at any mention of the word Christmas before the start of December; Fanny liked to have Christmas puddings safely made and stored away a year in advance. Her idea of 'nonsense' shopping, while basking in 90-degree high-summer heat in the south of France, was to scour markets and alleyway curio shops for unusual Christmas presents, 'coloured soap babies' to adorn the tree and 'spirals' to place on top. Tradition demanded, however, that the Christmas tree itself could not be decorated until the evening of 24 December.

She and Johnnie sent out about 500 cards each year, based on a meticulously maintained index system. They kept three present lists: gifts being sent abroad, gifts for the domestic market, and those to be handed

Puddings à la Cradock: Fanny and Johnnie had an occasional sideline in Christmas puddings, even if the Harrod's batch went mouldy. *(Tolleth)*

Christmas cracker:
Fanny and Johnnie
capture the mood
of the festive season
with cake and
decorations.
*(Michael Leale/BPC
Publishing)*

over on the day. The *TV Times* asked in 1960 what the Cradocks bought for each other. Johnnie: 'I give Fanny one more cookery book' (1,017 and counting). Fanny: 'I give him another bottle of vintage wine to add to his already fantastic cellar.'

Any consideration of Christmas decorations sent Fanny scuttling back to her days of enforced DIY economy. In 1958 she could even get away with the suggestion that children would be willing partners in the enterprise: 'It keeps them absorbed and happy throughout the long winter evenings.' The 'garden to gourmet' mentality ran deep. 'Don't give yourself the added expense of a bought traditional Christmas wreath for hanging on the front door,' she said. 'Hoard the stiff wire from packing cases – or use a narrow strip of chicken wire – twist to shape, pack with moss and stuff with holly sprigs, evergreens and fir cones. Tie up with scarlet ribbon and be justly proud of your front door.'

She regarded Christmas lunch – 'the most monstrous intake of the world's most indigestible food' – as a necessary evil, and one which the Cradocks held back for evening consumption. 'We always have a cold luncheon and eat our Christmas dinner at night. No-one is allowed in the dining room because the table must be a surprise. I spend hours over it, contrary to all my good advice. . . . And we change for dinner because it makes it feel more of an occasion and it's odd how even the family put on party manners with a party dress.' Even then, the resident gourmets found it hard to stomach. 'John and I hardly touch anything,' Fanny told the *Evening News* in 1963. 'Instead, when it's all over, we creep upstairs to the pot of caviare we have waiting by our bed.'

NINE COOKERS AND A MILLSTREAM

The Dower House, cosily cocooned in the smart part of Watford, would have made a suitably prestigious long-stay retirement home for the Cradocks. The work was still pouring in, but they were ready to take their final bow as stage performers. In moving from Blackheath to the outskirts of London in 1968 (they were intensely secretive about the exact location), they left

Home comforts: the Dower House in Watford was the Cradocks' residence from 1968 to 1974.

House proud: Fanny and Johnnie show off their quirky eye for design at Watford.

behind a man-made pond and inherited a millstream. The river Gade – trout and freshwater crayfish on tap – also bordered the elegant Queen Anne mini-mansion. Fanny and Johnnie enjoyed a daily dip in their swimming pool and, though both now in their sixties, limbered up in the morning with a game of table tennis.

For all their earning power, Fanny and Johnnie found themselves in a financial pickle, struggling to repay the £682 they owed the BBC in a laughably protracted dispute over repeat fees for the *Advanced Cookery* series. Fanny explained, in a self-pitying letter to the Corporation in August

Lord and lady of the manor: Fanny and Johnnie, with their Alsatian Orlando,
in the garden of the Dower House.

1968, that they had 'spent to the limit' on the Dower House and had
unwisely agreed to let the buyers of Langton House delay payment for six
months. The result was a £40,000 black hole. The accident that almost cost
them their lives a year earlier in the south of France, when their recently
bought cruiser exploded, was also proving costly: Fanny and Johnnie had
incurred legal costs of £10,000 in preparing a case against the company from
which they bought the cruiser. The BBC agreed to Fanny's proposal that they
receive a £50-a-month bankers' draft and finally agreed to write off a debt of
£2 10s (£2.50) at the end of 1969, four years after the programmes appeared.

The kitchen at the Dower House was like a residence in its own right,
dominated by nine gas cookers. Hygena supplied the fitted units; the
ceramic tiles were by Pilkington and Carter. The rest of the house shrieked
of slightly quirky opulence: a marble table was the centrepiece of a dining
room that also featured a gold ceiling frieze with cherubs in each corner.
'Johnnie and I hate modern furniture,' admitted Fanny soon after moving in.
'We don't believe in spending much money – we are bargain hunters in the

Garden goodies: Fanny and Johnnie show off a sumptuous spread at the Dower House. *(© BBC)*

most vulgar sense.' French windows in the drawing room opened out on to a terrace lit in traditional Cradock fashion by old-fashioned gas street lamps. Fanny declared her determination to turn the garden into 'the finest of its size in the British Isles'.

She also boasted, with more than a hint of exaggeration, of the property's fortress-like security. The *Evening Press* in Dublin reported in 1971: 'The estate is surrounded by an electric fence and there are two guards employed and a couple of Alsatian dogs to snarl at the heels of trespassers.'

MEET THE STAFF

There were distinct up sides and down sides to working for Fanny Cradock. The positives, especially for the student cooks who learned their craft under her tutelage, were a privileged grounding in the culinary art and an influential kick-start for their CV. The negatives centred around a hectoring boss who demanded obedient perfection from dawn to dusk, both in the kitchen at home, and when they popped up as timid aides during her television appearances (pretty assistants who might show up Fanny's garish plainness on screen were restricted to hands-on shots). One critic wrote in 1970: 'The way she treats her helpers would make a worm shrink back into its hole.'

No one who worked for her would forget the wild-eyed charisma, the brain and tongue in permanent fast forward, and the tantrums. Fanny's extraordinary self-centredness made her an asphyxiating employer. When she found staff who matched her standards – no one could match her energy – she also presumed, egotistically, that there could be no more fulfilling mission for them than promoting the Cradock brand. Early signs of dissent or independent thought were ignored, rogue ambitions were laughed off, but once the inner circle was broken the most poisonous, unreasonable side of Fanny's personality surfaced. As Wendy Colvin discovered when she decided to hand in her notice, lurking within the psyche was a slanderous witch:

> I'd seen what she'd done to other people when she'd taken over their lives, devoured them and spat them out and I thought no, this is not going to happen to me: she's trying to own me.
>
> Johnnie rang asking me to reconsider, then I heard from Tenniel [Evans] that she was saying the most dreadful things about me. Tenniel said to me, 'Did you really sleep with her Spanish boy in her bed and leave your knickers there?' And I said of course I didn't. People would ask, 'Where's Wendy?' And she'd say, 'I had to get rid of her. She stole.' There wasn't a scrap of truth in any of it.

Peter Botterill, a star pupil whose hands and (occasionally) face featured in Fanny's television appearances in the mid-sixties, warmed initially to her 'wicked sense of humour', then found that the fun drained away. 'She started to have awful mood swings,' he remembered, 'and she became so vitriolic she would literally make you squirm. "I'm walking out," I said. "Well you're fired," she replied, "and go out the back door." I told her I was leaving by the same way I came in, by the front door.'

LIKELY LAD

'Why do you want our autographs?'

'Because I'm your greatest fan. And I'm very fond of cooking too. I'd like to be a chef.'

'If you're such a fan you can stay and do a bit of weeding, then stay to tea.'

Johnny Harper was a cheeky neighbourhood scamp of 12 when he talked his way into the Cradocks' lives and affections. The autograph-hunter who peered over the garden wall at Blackheath in 1959 had embarked on a five-year adventure that projected him as a bizarre cross between the Artful Dodger and Little Lord Fauntleroy. Fanny and Johnnie were also the winners. At a time when their *Lucky Dip* programmes were wowing 'small fry' everywhere, and attracting record postbags, Johnny Harper gave them a free-flowing conduit to their new audience.

He was a helping hand on more than 100 stage shows and twenty TV programmes; his south-east London accent was cleaned up by a private tutor. He slept at home, but from dawn to dusk he played kitchen dogsbody at Langton House. He filled in as doorman for the Cradocks' frequent evening functions, welcoming artists and aristocrats, and tempting the sultry Hungarian actress Eva Bartok with a plate of winkles at the launch party for *Something's Burning*.

Date magazine was smitten: 'John Harper has a round, beaming face and a sweet nature and lovely manners, and he's just thirteen. In fact, he's every girl's idea of the ideal kid brother.' He was so much part of the family by 1962 – he remembers that the private education came a distant second to the

Johnny, Johnnie and Fanny: Butler-cum-page Johnny Harper gave the Cradocks a youthful image makeover in the early sixties. *(Mirrorpix)*

 'The French Riviera is the one place in Europe where we willingly spend our own hard-earned money with the certainty that we shall have the best possible value and the maximum of casual pleasures.'

'slave labour' – that he joined the Cradocks on their extended summer vacation in the south of France. He was instructed to dine alone, but Fanny joked: 'In the end he was telling US the best places to eat.' The *Daily Mirror* dubbed Johnny 'Britain's youngest butler', reporting: 'Now he gets £5 a week, thirty lessons a day on anything from kitchen French to appreciation of wine, his own fan mail and a high life atmosphere that includes travelling about Britain in the Cradocks' Rolls-Royce.' Forty years on he recalls being 'chased down the aisle by screaming schoolgirls' at the Kelvin Hall in Glasgow.

Put on the spot – 'Go on, pudding face, speak up' was Fanny's no-nonsense exhortation – the fifteen-year-old Johnny admitted: 'Well actually I want to take over from Fanny and Johnnie.' Johnnie Cradock reckoned their protégé had star quality, but his career took some odd twists before he became a professional foodie. John Harper sold potatoes, launched his own record company, and pandered to the seventies sophisticates by starting up the Grapevine wine bar in Greenwich. Most recently he has drawn on the Cradock tradition at Harpers restaurant in Bexhill, East Sussex.

EXILE AND THE RAM-RAIDERS

Fanny and Johnnie Cradock turned their backs on Britain, or more precisely the British tax system, in 1974, and never again experienced the homely bliss they had known in South Kensington, Blackheath and Watford.

Their initial refuge was Doneraile, in County Cork, and a Georgian mansion Fanny had spotted while on a journalistic assignment; but there was no place for them in the bosom of the Irish aristocracy. After an extraordinarily complicated move, which involved transporting three deep-freezers without disturbing the contents, they were soon homesick, retreating to England as often as the regulations permitted. They also discovered that Cork was a hotbed for IRA sympathisers and sensed that it was time to bale out when a 'you're next' threat was daubed on their front door.

Our Christmas Cake

Ingredients

8oz sifted flour

1 flat coffeespoon each of nutmeg, ginger, cloves and cinnamon

grated rind and strained juice of 1 small orange and 1 small lemon

2 oz ground almonds

1 oz shelled, chopped walnuts

4 oz glacé cherries

4 oz mixed diced peel

¼ lb currants

¼ lb sultanas

4 oz seeded raisins

8 oz butter

8 oz soft brown sugar

3 standard eggs

¼ gill each of brandy, madeira or marsala, and port

1 oz black treacle

1 oz golden syrup

1 coffeespoon orange flower water

1 coffeespoon rose water and, if possible, the same of noyau from a miniature bottle

Method

Cream butter thoroughly. Cream in sugar. Mix flour, spices, dried fruits and nuts. Whip eggs with brandy and fortified wines, rose and orange flower waters, fruit juices and rinds. Add to slightly warmed treacle and syrup (mixed).

Add fruit and flour mixture gradually to butter cream with gradual addition of mixed fluids and beat thoroughly with well-scrubbed hand.

Line cake tin or tins (both base and sides) with oiled greaseproof paper, making sure side papers rise a minimum 2in above tin rim. Fill in mixture and level off to two-thirds the depth of tin.

Bake one shelf below centre at 335°F (Gas 3), on a baking sheet covered with four thicknesses brown paper. The cake is cooked when the mixture stops the faint 'singing' sound you will hear if you slide out shelf and put one ear close to the cake. Cooking time from two to six hours depending on tin dimensions. Leave in greaseproof papers for storing in tin or closely wrapped in aluminium foil.

Daily Telegraph, 1964

Fanny and Johnnie were no happier in their next tax-dodging port-of-call, but spent six years in Guernsey before rerouting to Little Bentley, just outside Colchester, in 1984. Fanny, recuperating from a hip operation, wrote to her friends Tony and Yvonne Norris in October of that year: 'As soon as I get walking clearance I can start to clean up this house which is simply a pigsty, exactly as the removal men bunged the stuff in and left it. We cannot even unpack let alone shift furniture and work a hoover and dailies seem as rare as gold dust here too. However, we love it here and know we shall be very happy once this is all over. By comparison with bloody Guernsey it's heaven now.'

Two years later Orchard House was restored to its dishevelled state after being ram-raided twice in the space of six weeks. Burglars, taking advantage of the Cradocks' extended absence – Johnnie was in hospital after being diagnosed with terminal lung cancer – left a trail of destruction. The haul was estimated at £50,000 and though Fanny later received an insurance payout of £80,000 there was no compensation for the trauma. A 100-piece Crown Derby set engraved with the initials BV, for Bon Viveur, was taken, along with one of Fanny's beloved mink coats, Georgian saucepans, a gilt carriage clock and a Chinese cabinet worth £1,200. By the time the court case came up, Johnnie had died and Fanny was bereft and disorientated. Now living in a warden-controlled flat in Stockbridge, Hampshire, she could not initially be traced by the police. When she did turn up to give evidence at Chelmsford Crown Court, there was a familiar Fanny tantrum. 'She was barred from taking her tiny white dog Mia into court,' the *Daily Mail* reported. 'After a brief exchange she agreed to let him go to a nearby police station – and sent along a pound of beef and two pints of skimmed milk to keep him going.'

ROAD RAGING FANNY

Fanny Cradock suffered acutely from uniform phobia, especially where officious police officers and haughty hospital matrons were concerned. Her erratic driving and short-fuse temper made for a combustible combination, and her anger was carried unchecked from the scene of a crime to the ensuing court case. She told *Daily Mail* readers in 1955 that she was 'flushed from acrimonious exchanges with the bluebottles who administer our demoniac parking laws'.

According to Alison Leach, Fanny's long-serving personal assistant: 'Johnnie was a moderately safe driver, but Fanny was most erratic. If she didn't care for a road she just went on the wrong side.' She adopted much the same unilateral approach to driving which her grandmother had demanded of her chauffeur, Francis, during the First World War. 'Keep to the middle of the road, man. Don't rock.'

DAILY MAIL, Friday, July 3, 1964

The day Fanny Cradock boiled over

By Daily Mail Reporter

THE day television cook, Fanny Cradock had a brush with a policeman was described yesterday when she was fined £5 for driving carelessly in her £7,000 Rolls-Royce. Mrs. Cradock, who was charged at West London Court in her r e a l n a m e o f Phyllis Cradock, admitted calling the police "uniformed delinquents."

Not surprisingly, there were some scrapes along the way, and they were *never* Fanny's fault . . .

1957: Oxford. Fined £20 and banned for three months for driving at a dangerous speed. Fanny pleaded not guilty. When police asked for an adjournment, she said: 'It has already cost me a small fortune to come here. Why can't it be heard now?'

Just before being stopped, she told the court, 'I exclaimed to my husband, in my own colloquial language. "There's a policeman."' Her defence: 'The car was heavily laden with luggage and if I had driven at high speeds it would have sent all the luggage toppling over.'

1964: Olympia, London. Fined £5 for careless driving. Fanny parked her Rolls-Royce in a driveway outside Olympia, with the back jutting out into the road. Asked by PC John Sillence to move it, she called the police 'uniformed delinquents'. She then reversed the Rolls into another car and told PC Sillence: 'It's your fault, you told me to back up.' After coming out of court, Fanny said: 'I used to respect the police, but now I have completely lost my trust in them.'

1968: M1, Newport Pagnell. Fined £8 for speeding with a trailer. Fanny said in court: 'I am not mentally defective and only an idiot would pass a police car, knowing they were breaking the law.'

1978: Guernsey. Fined £5 for failing to give way. Fanny was unimpressed when a photograph was produced in court in support of the prosecution case. 'The camera can easily lie,' she said. 'I know that from my experiences as a photographer.' She claimed that the driver with whose car she collided was going at 'maniacal speed'.

1983: Guildford. Fined £110 and banned for three months for careless driving and failing to stop after an accident. She veered across the Guildford bypass, hitting a car driven by Roderick Taylor. When he went to remonstrate Fanny said: 'Shut the bloody door. How dare you hit my car!' She drove off and was pursued for 15 miles and then overtaken by Mr Taylor. He stood in the road and waved her down, but she ran into him.

Fanny's solicitor told the court: 'When she saw Mr Taylor standing in the road with his hand raised, being a television personality she feared for her safety. When the car hit Mr Taylor in the legs it was going very slowly.'

1987: Stockbridge, Hampshire. A careless driving prosecution was dropped after Johnnie's death. Fanny reversed into a tree, running over her dog Mia in the process. Her insurance premium had risen to a prohibitive £1,200 per annum when, mercifully, she stopped driving the following year.

'ARRÊTEZ! VOUS AVEZ TUÉ MA FEMME'

Alison Leach thought that she had broken free of Fanny's inner circle in 1962, but was persuaded to re-enlist the following year, in the oddest of circumstances. 'We met again in court' was the long and short of it.

Alison had been summoned to give evidence in a preliminary hearing to establish whether Johnnie should be prosecuted. He and Fanny had been cruising gently through Cannes (with Alison minding her business in the back of the Rolls-Royce) when they struck a pedestrian. Johnnie's honourable instincts, to face the music, were countered by Fanny's determination to avoid tiresome debate and dispute.

As Johnnie drove off, sheepishly, the injured party's husband shouted out: 'Arrêtez! Vous avez tué ma femme (Stop, you've killed my wife!)' The damage, they discovered later, was more to pride than body, and the case was dismissed.

TAKING ON THE TAXMAN

Fanny and Johnnie Cradock went into tax exile in 1974, finally convinced that the Labour government in general, and Denis Healey, the freshly installed Chancellor of the Exchequer, in particular, had declared wealth off limits. A top income tax band of eighty-three pence in the pound was introduced, kicking in at a level that equated to £75,000 in today's terms.

Her father's descent into bankruptcy and her own breadline existence in the 1930s had given Fanny a natural antipathy to income tax and, as the Cradock riches accumulated in the 1950s and '60s, she lured the instinctively honest Johnnie into creative domestic accounting. Duplicated expenses began to appear in their tax returns.

Their departure for the Republic of Ireland, tax-free for writers, and subsequent move to the Channel Islands, where they just passed the wealth test, failed to deter the Inland Revenue, and the proof was presented, rather publicly, at a launch party for three of her books, all published on the same day in November 1978. The 130 invited guests at the caviar-on-tap Mayfair gathering – Fanny had arranged for goodie-packed freezers to be flown over specially from her home in Guernsey – included her friend and fellow Channel Island resident Alan Whicker. Uninvited was the Inland Revenue interloper.

The *Daily Express* reported: 'As she swept grandly into the proceedings, all fur and velvet, he pulled out the writ, alleging non-payment of taxes, and handed it over with his compliments. A spokesman for W.H. Allen [her publishers], who witnessed the incident, said: "It was difficult to know whether Fanny was surprised or not. She was wearing so much make-up." ' The *Sunday Express* took up the story: 'As the party was breaking up, it was detected that Mrs Cradock's stiff upper lip slightly cracked. She went up to an enormous pedestal of flowers, provided by the publishers, on the grand staircase. Carefully she removed every single bloom one by one – leaving all the greenery behind. Then with fist clenched tightly round the stems, she descended the stairs with great dignity and swept out into the night.'

A letter to diplomat Dugald Malcolm, whose wife Patricia was among the closest and longest-lasting of Fanny's friends, reflects the mood of almost apocalyptic despair which enveloped her in the 1970s:

25 March 1974

I am now in such a state of complete bewilderment that I cannot think straight. The problem is a vital one and calls for a very clearly-thought-through decision and in a sense must I feel colour what you decide to do if only in terms of financial survival however rich you may be. The crux being that the more you have, the more you stand to lose now.

Four financiers have told us in the last few days that in their considered opinions there will be a huge European slump by October and as one man, Moutafian the Armenian who is married to the Russian princess Helena, told us seriously, 'your money will be virtually worthless and the only hope is to put it into gold, diamonds, furniture, objets d'art or paintings'. Now this is all very well, but he did not seem able to tell me where in this country we could find a market for such items if money is to become like the mark was in Germany after the First World War! There is a

kind of quiet panic spreading like locusts through the moneyed people we know. . . .

Of course the shame of what Wilson and Co. are doing, and the savage spending on these miners, about whom I have learned a LOT in the past few weeks, not from hearsay but from a miner who is disgusted with their hypocrisy and duplicity, beggars description. The rape of the country's funds for them and the ensuing Borgia orgies which will inevitably follow, make us all feel faintly sick.

Books to sell: Fanny introduces ex-Goon Michael Bentine to her recipe collection with a difference, *The Sherlock Holmes Cookbook*, at a launch party in 1976. *(Mike Humphrey)*

HOME AWAY FROM HOME

For two months each summer the Cradocks put spending money before making it. When the Rolls slid away from South Kensington or Blackheath in mid-July, weighed down with white suitcases, Fanny was transported back to childhood adventures. Destination: the French Riviera, her favourite spot on the planet. The notebooks were not left behind, but they too were on partial vacation. The badgering, hyperactive Fanny gave way to a mellower version; and when Fanny relaxed, Johnnie's pulse rate and blood pressure fell in concert.

She captured the essence of the appeal in their 1960 Bon Viveur book, *Holiday on the French Riviera*:

> No one who lives a pressurised life can relax fully if time regulations compel any measure of regimentation. But when it does not matter if you sup at seven or midnight, dance at 10 p.m. or 5 a.m., gamble at 4.30 in the afternoon or 7.30 in the morning then relaxation sets in, with wine to iron out the creases of our daily lives and send us back genuinely refreshed. We travel incessantly, mostly free – since one way or another we are on 'expenses'. Yet the French Riviera is the one place in Europe where we willingly spend our own hard-earned money with the certainty that we shall have the best possible value and the maximum of casual pleasures.

Fanny claimed that the family on a strict budget and the jet-setters for whom money was no object could feel equally privileged. She wrote of the Monte Carlo nightclub Tip Top: 'You may see Mr Onassis with a party; a weary figure in jeans drowsing over a beer; a woman wearing a quarter of a million pounds' worth of emeralds and someone you last ran into at a point-to-point in Somerset.'

Short measures: Fanny dressed for the beach in Monte Carlo in 1970.

The Cradocks' entrée to the casino in
Monte Carlo in 1955.

Eating in style: a menu from the renowned
Lasserre restaurant in Paris.

The Cradocks liked to mix with
the well-off and well-bred (five
outfits a day were *de rigueur* for
the trendy). Fanny was still easing
her slim figure into the tightest of
shorts in her sixties, and shedding
all for the Mediterranean dip. 'The
best bathe is by moonlight when
the water turns phosphorescent
and there is nothing immodest in
bathing in the nude – the only
perfect way to swim,' she recom-
mended.

Their haven of seaside lethargy
was Théoule-sur-Mer, even with
the memory of the cruiser explosion which almost cost her and
Johnnie their lives in 1967. Fanny
wrote in 1981:

> There is too on our favourite
> small beach a café where a
> glass of vin rosé costs the
> native, or those who speak
> fluently, the equivalent of 6p;
> the English pay 12p and the
> Americans 20p. This café is our
> base as all our friends know.
> Notes are left for us, telephone
> calls taken, and the proprietors,
> who are darlings, always report
> when the American fleet is in
> the harbour for then we take to
> the hills, mostly to a villa which
> looks out across the valley
> below.

Down the hatch: Fanny and Johnnie tasting in Cognac in the autumn of 1954.

The only down side was the journey back home, by which time the bulging suit-cases would be supple-mented by shoes, cheeses, Picasso-style ceramics and antiques: 'We once spent hours trying to work out how to get a staircase on the roof-rack so as to transport it back to London.' They dubbed the long hike to Calais the Via Dolorosa, and Fanny's melancholy was articulated in her 1950 book *Bon Voyage*. 'That was the last of France for us, as we turn towards the coast, restrictions, meals at set hours or no meals at all, the national loaf, the stew, the rice pudding and the toast which always tastes as if it had been chilled in a refrigerator before serving.'

TROUBLE IN PARADISE

Fanny and Johnnie Cradock were consumed with pride when they took possession of a 38ft cabin cruiser in 1967: the four-berth *Françoise II* was a worthy trinket to sit alongside the succession of Rolls-Royces that had defined their wealth and social standing since the mid-fifties. There were boats to hire and berths to borrow, but only owners were full members of the Riviera élite.

Fanny and Johnnie, who had been joined by Fanny's stage designer friend, Joan Jefferson Farjeon, were moored at Théoule-sur-Mer, the location of their favourite, unspoilt beach, and planned a gentle 5-mile trip into Cannes on 12 August. As soon as Johnnie started the engine there was a massive explosion. The subsequent sequence of events was painfully relived by Fanny in an interview with the Dublin *Evening Press* almost four years later:

'She started to have awful mood swings and she became so vitriolic she would literally make you squirm. "I'm walking out," I said. "Well you're fired," she replied, "and go out the back door." I told her I was leaving by the same way I came in, by the front door.'

Peter Botterill

'I was thrown twenty feet in the air,' Fanny recalled, 'and my face was badly cut. But Johnnie got the impact far worse than I did. He was very badly burned. So badly that when we tottered up the quayside both, by some miracle, still conscious, I could see strips of blackened flesh hanging from the backs of his legs.'

They were taken to hospital in Cannes and placed in adjacent beds by the hospital nuns who believed they were dying. Meanwhile a private plane was hired to take them back to England. They had a nightmare journey, both lying naked on rough blankets on the floor of the plane because they were too badly burned to be covered.

In the London hospital they were separated. 'But we both knew we were dying, so we demanded that they put us together,' said Fanny. 'Johnnie was at death's door for eight days, I for six. But somehow we both survived.

'My face looked awful,' Fanny went on, 'I couldn't bear to glance in the mirror.' 'How is your face unmarked now?' I asked her. 'Nivea,' she said firmly. 'I kept rubbing Nivea into it. I never had plastic surgery. Many people don't believe me, but if I had undergone plastic surgery my face would never be sunburned. But it is, so that proves I didn't.

'While I was lying at death's door a woman journalist rang me up for information on how I felt. Being an experienced journalist myself, I was anxious to co-operate with her, so I gave her an interview from my sick bed. From all I told her the woman knew how ill I was. Yet she closed the conversation with me by saying, "Well now, Mrs Cradock, as you lie there in such pain, tell me what colour negligee you are wearing."

'Such heartlessness is appalling, isn't it?' Fanny said angrily. 'And when Johnnie was being carried out of the plane naked on an improvised stretcher there were rows of cameramen lined up to take pictures. How could they be so cruel?'

Five weeks after the accident, Fanny and Johnnie returned to Théoule: 'The best way to lay ghosts is to walk right through them,' Fanny told the *Sunday Mirror*. They then embarked on legal action against the Bletchley Boat Company, from which they had bought the cruiser, seeking £10,000 in special damages to supplement their general damages claim.

THESE WE DO NOT LIKE: GERMANS AND AMERICANS

Fanny Cradock could find fault with everywhere and everyone (bar France and the French, of course), but she reserved her greatest vitriol for Germany and America. The antipathy to the Germans was a hyperbolic version of the general resentment felt by her contemporaries, but the anti-American feeling was strictly personal.

If Basil Fawlty famously urged his staff not to mention the war, Fanny favoured a more direct approach. Always a hand grenade ready to explode, she shocked friends and a multi-national clientele in a restaurant in the south of France by leaping to her feet and exclaiming loudly, 'The only good German is a dead German.' She carried with her a clichéd parody of Teutonic excess, neatly demonstrated by an angry encounter in the transit lounge at Düsseldorf airport in the mid-fifties:

> A blond, young, jack-booted Hun accoutred with guns suddenly put his booted foot on one of my cases and began flicking off a film of dust from his boot with a silk handkerchief. All my revulsion was concentrated in this ill-mannered gesture.
>
> I snapped in German, 'Take your boot off my case, young man, and behave properly.'
>
> He looked up, amazed. 'What have you got in this bag?' he countered.
>
> 'Stand up straight', said I furiously, 'salute me respectfully, address me as madam, remember to say please and I may consider replying.'

Fanny saw Americans as the benighted half-wits who had deprived her of a Transatlantic fortune and wasted no opportunity to put the boot in. 'She was convinced she could have made millions there,' said Alison Leach, who was ridiculed by her employer for choosing to work in the United States in the 1960s. 'She thought the people were ignorant and the food was filthy, but she also knew that it was difficult for her to go there because of her uncertain marital state.'

A visit to California in the mid-fifties brought no commercial breakthrough for Fanny, who then sneered and sniped from afar. Asked to respond to an American study suggesting that male cooks made for happier families, Fanny told the *Daily Herald* in 1963: 'With Americans I feel as I do when I hear children portentously discussing discoveries of which grown-ups have been aware a long time.'

7

Fanny: the Look

NEW NOSE, NEW HORIZONS

Fanny Cradock's third husband, Greg Holden-Dye, decided early in their relationship that she had an inferiority complex. Her nose was the problem. The BBC came to the same conclusion in 1953, ironically on the damning evidence of publicity shots for radio programmes. 'You look so awful in pictures,' producer Mike Meehan told her bluntly. The observation was restated a year later, when Fanny was auditioned as a would-be compère of BBC fashion programmes by Stephen McCormack. 'My nose was the same as my father's nose, only mercifully smaller,' she wrote. 'My sons' noses are the same. All of us for countless generations have had large long noses with a bump in the middle and a blob on the end.'

She decided to consult Sir Archibald McIndoe, the New Zealand-born plastic surgeon whose experimental grafting techniques had transformed the lives of badly burned and disfigured RAF pilots during the Second World War. In peacetime McIndoe maintained his roster of deserving cases while taking on vanity-driven calls for cosmetic surgery: the actress Ava Gardner

A nose to be proud of: Fanny shows off her
new profile in 1954. (© *National Portrait
Gallery*)

was another of his celebrity clients. Fanny
thought she needed a facelift. McIndoe
suggested otherwise. 'There's nothing to
lift yet,' he told her. 'What's more, it
wouldn't make the slightest bit of difference if there was and I did. It's your nose
that's all wrong, my girl. It throws shadows
all over your face. It brings your eyes too
close together and it makes your whole
face look like a currant bun.'

She took little convincing and employed
a ramshackle identikit method to choose
her new look. She removed the old nose from one of the offending publicity
photographs and replaced it with a selection of features from glossy French
magazines. 'Thank you for the enclosed picture of the nose you have
selected,' wrote McIndoe's secretary. 'He asks me to say he will endeavour
to supply you with exactly what you require and looks forward to seeing
you on July 14th next at 6pm.' McIndoe was by now reshaping about eight
noses a week and charging 170 guineas – 100 for the operation, 20 for the
anaesthetic, 50 for a week in a nursing home.

Fanny noticed an immediate return – financial and emotional – on
her investment. She claimed that her daily fee immediately shot up to
100 guineas; the self-consciousness was shed;
staff and friends were assured that bossy Fanny
would become benign Fanny (any softening on
that score was strictly temporary).

**'This woman was born
last week'**
Sunday Graphic

29 August 1954: 'Let's get rid of all the humbug at the beginning. It's no
good arguing whether this kind of thing is morally right or wrong. The fact
is it is happening every day. And more than ever each month. Women are
coming to London from all over Europe. For new faces.

'It took all my nerve to face him. I couldn't help thinking of the important
work this man had done – the burnt, smashed faces and bodies he had
rebuilt.

'Johnnie had said the night before the operation: "I was thinking this is the last time I'll see you with the face I fell in love with years ago."

'McIndoe said: "You will become an easier person to live with when you lose your inferiority complex. *That* came through always being conscious of your nose."

'How clearly he had seen through me. To keep people from noticing that nose of mine I had become a woman who talked fast and loud. I had become an eccentric in dress and manner . . . defensively.'

5 September 1954: 'I had to stop making up my eyes to try to draw them away from my nose. Next came the hairdresser. I lost my parting I have had all my adult life. I could have curls! Fluffy soft on top, brushed up, instead of sleek!

'I went home to show my husband. He walked all around me in absolute silence. Then he said, "Are you doing anything tonight, Mrs Cradock, or would you dine with me?" I burst into tears.

'When the coffee came [at a restaurant], I automatically helped myself to a cigar. Then I caught sight of myself in a mirror. It looked awful, a woman like that smoking a cigar in public!

'That was when I began to realise the surgeon was right about me getting a new personality. The old eccentric me, the woman who became deliberately flamboyant and outré – *defensively* – was gone. When I was with someone I used to talk my head off – instinctively, I suppose, to draw attention away from my appearance, my nose. Now I'm becoming like those sweet feminine creatures who need only smile when a man talks to them. To a certain extent, anyway!

'The change hits me in all kinds of ways. I can wear simple clothes now. I don't need gimmicks. I have thrown the outsize earrings, the feather bows and parasols, into a drawer.'

FEASTING AND FASTING

The cameras were not there to reveal the bloated truth – Fanny Cradock was an astute and vain censor – but she liked to preface her dietary advice with the admission that she and Johnnie had once been grossly overweight. Both were prone to piling on the pounds, and as rationing regulations eased after the Second World War, the 6ft 1in Johnnie filled out to 17st 9lb and 5ft 5½in

Johnnie recreates the Edwardian look in 1951. His verdict: 'Definitely smarter than the sloppy jacket styles in current favour'. *(Daily Graphic)*

Fanny inflated to 14st 9lb. 'We were quite a lot of boy and girl, believe me,' she later reflected. 'Couldn't see the pavement for years. In those days we wouldn't have both fitted on to the TV screen, let alone got a TV job.'

Drastic solutions were called for and once the stones were shed Fanny felt qualified to attack the obese with the same self-righteous zeal that ex-smokers reserve for the unreformed. 'If men and women are fat and do not suffer from any medical condition which prevents their slimming . . . they are just lazy and greedy!'

Worth getting fat for: centre front, coupe sarou; left, coupe framboise; centre back, coupe aux fraises; right, black plum ice cream. *(Michael Leale/BPC Publishing)*

The battle was never won, just under control. The calorific orgies still took their toll, so Fanny and Johnnie tried to adopt the Duchess of Windsor's principle of six days' careful eating and one day's crazy consumption each week. 'I have to watch my weight all the time,' Fanny admitted. 'People must say, "Gosh, how does she eat all that stuff and still keep her figure?" I think if I lost my waistline our act would fall down flat.'

Alison Leach, Fanny's personal assistant, confronted alluring desserts with the silent query, 'Is it worth getting fat for?' Fanny hijacked the phrase and posed another conundrum. 'Each time you are tempted by a rich, sweet pudding or cake, say to yourself – "A moment in my mouth and a lifetime on my hips".'

THE DRASTIC DIET

The two-part Bon Viveur stratagem for pound-shedding was outlined in *The Daily Telegraph* in 1976 under the banner 'We've done it so our loyal readers can do it too'.

Any healthy person can slim, provided they stick to the rules. First, and by far the most important in this diet, is to obtain a clean bill of health from your doctor. This is essential, as it is also to have a daily medical. Then you must either own a pair of reliable scales or else arrange for weekly visits to a nearby chemist who will check and mark your card.

And do find out if, in fact, your adipose tissue stems from eating too much or the wrong things.

When we faced the fact that we were disgustingly overweight we both agreed, 'no clinics'. Instead, we did our first two weeks of drastic slimming at home.

For the first two days we felt dreadful and both had splitting headaches. On the third morning we felt marvellous and from then on we were never hungry either. After 14 days the male half of this partnership had come down from a shaming 17st to 14st 7lb, while the female half, who clocked 14st 3lb at the onset, had sunk to 11st 8lb. That was when we began Diet No. 2, which the male half finished with when he came down to 13st 9lb. The female half went it alone until she achieved her target: 8st 12lb.

By this time, neither of us could ever face a nice hot cuppa with plenty of white sugar again. Instead we drink China Tea with lemon or, preferably, black coffee with sugar substitute.

DRASTIC DIET UNDER SUPERVISION ————————————————
DAYS 1 AND 2: The strained juice of one lemon in 6fl oz boiling water, sipped on waking; at noon; at 4pm; at 6pm and at bedtime.
DAY 3: On waking, the strained lemon juice and boiling water. For breakfast, the strained juice of one orange; at 11am the same, plus juice of one lemon; luncheon ditto. At teatime, the strained juice of one lemon. For dinner, our Slimming Soup which provides essential roughage. At bedtime, the hot water and strained juice of one lemon.
DAYS 4 TO 14: Same lemon drink on waking, same soup at night and for the rest merely double the intake of strained oranges each day, adding in one grapefruit each day at luncheon.

IN *VOGUE*: DRESSMAKER FANNY

The thrifty side of Fanny Cradock's nature never quite deserted her, even when the budgetary necessity for drawing-room dressmaking had vanished. Mary Hill, the broadcaster and television commentator, told *Vogue Pattern Book* readers in 1958 that she was impressed to find that Fanny's quest for the 'versatile wardrobe that will shine in the constant limelight' helped keep her feet on the ground:

I went to tie up details of the first TV series she and Johnnie were to do for Associated-Rediffusion. When I arrived, Fanny was on her hands and

'I'd just as soon tie a bunch of carrots to my head, or wear a scooped-out cabbage as spend my hard-earned money on the pigmy uglifiers on sale at prices ranging from one to thirty guineas in London today.'

knees – on the floor – fitting geometric patterns of coloured felt over a Vogue Pattern to make a replica of a beach outfit she'd seen in a Knightsbridge store . . . 'because, my dear, you don't think I'd pay fifteen guineas for a bit of nonsense to wear on the beach.'

Fortunately Fanny is as passionately interested in sewing as she is in cooking and, while she no longer has time to make many of her own, more often than not, she has her clothes made rather than buy them off the peg. I've rarely sat down at the long Regency table at which she works

Read all about it: Fanny in trendy newspaper dress at South Terrace in the fifties. (*Associated Newspapers*)

without finding two or three Vogue Patterns with little bits of fabric pinned to them among the piles of papers. And I'm afraid many a script conference has got away to a late start because of the difficulty in deciding which pattern will look better in which fabric.

She has no doubt that the greatest feminine triumphs in practical things are 'to furnish a room with grace and comfort, to cook a dinner that is appreciated, and to make a dress in which she is admired'.

VITAMIN PILLS, NIVEA AND WEEK-OLD EGGS

Fanny Cradock became a firm friend of novelist Barbara Cartland in the late sixties – she longed in vain to be honoured as Dame Barbara was in 1991 – and contributed some typically unconventional beauty tips to *Cartland's Book of Health and Beauty*:

Except for a vast number of vitamin and health pills I use very little in the way of beauty aids. . . . The late Archie McIndoe (Sir Archibald McIndoe) taught me to use my only face cream – Nivea. He said he had pots of it around for his burned patients at East Grinstead, and he told me of many instances when after he had done all he could, Nivea, in the advanced stages of healing, could and did the rest!

For the rest, when I feel especially gloomy at the sight of my own reflection I whip up one week-old egg white (we have our own hens) very stiffly indeed and spread the foam all over my face and neck right down to the collar bones and right around the side of the neck.

Then I lie down with a neck-pillow under my neck so that the face is tilted back and let the egg-white dry out and gradually tighten. Then I sponge it off with warm water. Of course you do not put the foam over the skin directly under the eyes and for safety I put a little Nivea on the area before I begin.

Anything else? Only top-of-the-milk on a pad of cotton wool right over the whole face and neck area whenever I can spare the time to do it before doing my face up in the mornings.

Oh and another thing, I believe in 'resting faces' i.e. going around without a scrap of make-up, especially on the precious days I spend at weekends gardening furiously and with only the family, who refer to this as 'Mum's weekend face'.

Spot on: Fanny and escort John Kyle at the Eton and Harrow cricket match in 1948.

Fanny confessed to taking Poten C tablets and Gev-E-Tabs every day, and had been a dedicated consumer of pills since the 1950s. Wendy Colvin, who assisted Fanny at home and on stage in her *Daily Mail* days, confirms:

She did take an awful lot of pills. I thought they were slimming pills or uppers and downers. Evangeline [Evangeline Evans, Fanny's friend and next-door neighbour in South Terrace] joked: 'If you strung all those together, Fanny, you'd have a very pretty necklace', because they were all different colours. Fanny just looked at her, because she didn't have a great sense of humour where she was concerned herself.

HAGGIS CURE

Fanny Cradock knew how to get a crowd on her side: shower praise on local products, people and places to earn that extra helping of applause. She even ascribed health-giving properties to Scotland's national dish when she and Johnnie played the Palace Theatre, Kilmarnock in 1969.

'I have a soft spot for haggis,' the *Glasgow Evening Citizen* reported her as saying. 'When I was ill with a nervous breakdown some years ago, Johnnie had to make a flying visit to Scotland. He came back with a haggis. I was ill in bed, eating very little. He didn't know how to cook it – I told him and then ate the whole haggis myself. That was the start of my recovery and I've never had nervous trouble since.'

Haggis

'This "great chieftain of the pudding race" really derives from Abruzzi, in Italy. It was brought to Scotland by the Romans.'

Ingredients

1 sheep's stomach bag, pluck and liver
1 lb suet
1 lb onions

½ lb pinhead oatmeal (crisped in oven, but not browned)
salt and pepper to season
a pinch of spice

Method

To make it, first clean the haggis bag thoroughly and boil the pluck and liver, starting with cold water. Cook for 1½ hours at a gentle simmer. Take out and remove all pipes and gristle. Mince half of the liver only, the lights and the heart. Blend with the oatmeal, the minced onion and the minced suet. Season strongly with salt and pepper and moisten with a little of the strongly reduced liquor in which the pluck has simmered. Pack carefully into the well-cleaned paunch and sew up the opening, being sure to allow sufficient space for the swelling which will presently occur. Place either in water or in milk and water and boil for about three hours, being sure to prick with a needle to prevent bursting when the mixture begins to swell out of the bag.

Bon Viveur Recipes, 1956

AN AUDIENCE WITH DIOR

Christian Dior was one of Fanny Cradock's favourite designers. He explained to her and to *Sunday Graphic* readers in 1953 that English women might be the 'most beautiful in the world', but they were failing the style test.

'Madame, their downfall lies in CLASHING COLOURS. You cannot buy a hat . . . gloves . . . a coat . . . a pretty frock . . . some accessories, put them all together and expect to produce a good outfit.

'To be chic,' he said softly, 'a woman must follow five rules.' They are:

1. Learn to know yourself: your worst and your best.
2. Conceal the worst. Try to highlight the best.
3. Be natural, never ashamed, and never proud.

4. Don't be a fashion sheep. Follow fashion only as far as it becomes YOU. There is always some variation in the newest fashion which can be adapted to the individual.

5. Don't buy clothes at random. Always try to make them part of a BASIC WARDROBE.

'UNFASHIONABLE' FANNY

A *Sunday Graphic* reader wrote to the paper in the 1953: 'The photograph of your fashion expert, Frances Dale, interested me. I would like to remind her that plucked, pencilled eyebrows went out of fashion years ago, and lipstick

Our Slimmers' Soup

Ingredients

3 lb (1.5kg) small, meaty beef bones, but *not* marrow bones
5 pt (3 litres) water
6 oz (175g) roughly shredded, tight, white cabbage
3 oz (75g) red cabbage
2 large rough-chopped onions
6 leaves de-stalked spinach
4 large, skinned and de-seeded ripe tomatoes
1 faggot of herbs (*bouquet garni*)
1 peeled garlic clove
6 bacon rinds or 1 strip bacon rind which has *not* been soaked to remove its saltiness
1 peeled, cored, rough-chopped cooking apple
1 large leek, trimmed, washed and sliced thinly
black pepper

Method

Put the bones into a baking tin and bake on second shelf for 45 minutes at Gas Mark 4 (approx 350°F, 180°C). Drain off fat and put bones into a casserole. Cover with cold water and lid. Return to oven on lowest shelf Gas Mark 1 (approx 275°F, 140°C) and leave for 3 hours. Remove bones, skim off any remaining fat. Tumble in all remaining ingredients, cover and simmer in the oven or on a top burner for 1 hour. Remove bacon rinds and herb faggot. Ladle with well-stirred vegetables into a large bowl.

Taken at night at the beginning of a really austere, fatless, starchless, sugarless diet this soup provides the necessary roughage and may be used for several meals if refrigerated in between.

A Lifetime in the Kitchen, vol. I, 1985

carried above the natural outline of the mouth is unfashionable any time.' Says Frances Dale: 'My eyebrows are as God made them. I have used lipstick since the age of 16 simply because my natural lip-line does not exist. Now I'm 44 and Christian Dior tells me I'm making the best of a bad job.'

HARTNELL AND THE 'QUEEN'S DUST SHEET'

Norman Hartnell could claim a significant if expensive assist in the Fanny Cradock glamour parade. If he was good enough for royalty, he automatically added lustre to Fanny's wardrobe, even if the £100 ball gowns (she took some persuading that they were offered on a discount basis rather than as gifts) stretched her spending power in the 1950s.

Fanny the journalist also owed one of her biggest coups to 'Normie', as he was affectionately known. She was granted a *Sunday Graphic* exclusive on the queen's coronation robe, which had been the subject of cloak-and-dagger secrecy before being revealed in all its magnificence on 2 June 1953. The following morning, Fanny and Normie sipped Dom Perignon in his penthouse flat above the Bruton Street salon as the designer gave his impressions of the ceremony in Westminster Abbey and suggested 'Peter Pan of the dress world' as an apt epithet.

The reward for Fanny was a story to delight the 'high-ups', a framed picture of a replica section of the robe, and a more practical addition to her collection. She explained the background to the gift in her food-based memoirs, *A Time to Remember*, in 1981:

> A number of attempts were made to break into the workrooms at No. 27 where eighteen embroiderers worked on the Coronation Robe embroidery for six weeks. The great problem was not to keep burglars out because if they intended getting in, as any police officer will tell you, they do so. It was how best to hide the robe and train. Eventually Norman had a brilliant idea. In his previous collection he had shown a strapless black velvet dress embroidered with broderie anglaise over a white underskirt. He used for it over forty yards of the most exquisite Lyon velvet and it cost a bomb. Every night the Queen's dress was pulled into this costly tent, then thrown down on the floor in one of the workrooms as if it had merely slipped from an adjacent rail of much worn models. Evidence showed later that some of the pirating thieves must have stepped over the

'dust sheet' and its priceless contents. After the Coronation, Norman let Fanny have the dress, which had a little velvet jacket as a dinner-dress cover-up. It fitted her perfectly. From then onwards she has always worn it for Christmas Dinner and she still has it. It is in perfect condition to this day.

HATS FOR ALL SEASONS

Fanny Cradock loved hats; she particularly liked statement hats, toppings which emphasised her style and individuality. She was not so enamoured of British milliners who, she believed, were determined to foist bizarre or inappropriate headgear on the hat-wearing public. She reflected sadly on the 1952 collection: 'We have fairly earned our screwy head-piece reputation, what with domed candlesnuffers (cloches), wind-reversed brolleys (vagabonds), plus lampshades, cabbages, whipped-cream walnuts, egg-cups and pancakes – all star turns in last season's millinery shows.'

The following year, Fanny was digging her claws into the small-hat fashion, 'pimples' she called them. 'I'd just as soon tie a bunch of carrots to my head, or wear a scooped-out cabbage as spend my hard-earned money on the pigmy uglifiers on sale at prices ranging from one to thirty guineas in London today.'

A piece of cake: Fanny, in one of her more distinctive hats, grabs a guilty bite. (Briggs)

FASHION VICTIMS

She had compèred and commented
on fashion shows in London, but
Fanny Cradock expected to find herself in a unique haven of chic when
she attended the Paris collections in
the early fifties. She found instead
that the counterpoint to the poised
beauty of the models, and the startling creations they wore, was a drab
assortment of catwalk habitués.

> I rather thought I knew the kind
> of women who frequented Paris
> couturières. Then I went alone to
> my first premiere for the Press.
> Neither then nor at any other
> seasonal presentation in London
> did I find the galaxy of elegant
> connoisseurs I had envisaged.
> Instead I saw short fat women

I'd put my hat on it: Fanny keeps a dish
under wraps. *(Verity Press Features)*

and tall thin women, old women and spotty girls, all gazing with
absolutely blank faces at streams of fabulous clothes. I saw women who
sat with their fat knees apart and locknit draws sagging down like extra
chins. I saw women who looked like Skye terriers, harassed women,
women with wrinkled stockings, women with muddy shoes, women with
fussy veiled hats and sturdy Glastonburys, but seldom a fashion plate!

FANNY PASSES THE STYLE TEST

Style is neither easily defined nor easily achieved, but the verdict from *The
Daily Telegraph*'s fashion director, Hilary Alexander, is that Fanny passed the
test more often than not during her twenty-five years in the celebrity
limelight.

After surveying a range of stills from wartime to the early eighties, Hilary
said: 'She definitely got it right most of the time. I think she understood the

whole celebrity thing, because you do have to be slightly larger than life on television if you're going to make a career out of being a personality, and I think she absolutely got that right. Towards the end it was a little bit of a parody and there was too much make-up, but she was still very striking: you wouldn't miss her.'

In the early pictures, Hilary sees a movie influence: 'She looks like one of those silent-screen film stars. She obviously modelled herself on Rank studios and Hollywood.' Then there is the touch of Carmen Miranda, with flowers in her hair, the 'overdone' look on her TV debut in 1955 and, in 1959 the sensible hair-do and sombre dress which give her the Margaret Thatcher look for a session in the photographer's studio with Johnnie.

The constants are Fanny's addiction to furs, hats and necklaces, which range from classical pearls to gaudy displays reminiscent of mayoral chains

Keeping it simple: Fanny chooses a simple topee for her visit to the Chelsea Flower Show in 1963. *(J.Wilds/Keystone/ Getty Images)*

High priestess Fanny:
the cook-hostess
prepares for action at
the Dower House in
Watford. *(Mike
Humphrey)*

'We were quite a lot of boy and girl, believe me. Couldn't see the pavement for years. In those days we wouldn't have both fitted on to the TV screen, let alone got a TV job.'

of office. She is always aiming to make an individual statement, while advising herself (and others) against the danger of 'wearing all your costume jewellery at once'. Fanny's friend Phil Bradford estimates that she built up a collection of more than 500 pieces, most of them paste, which she would alter subtly to add an air of exclusivity.

In Fanny's mature years Hilary Alexander glimpses Barbara Cartland, Bette Davis, even Lucille Ball. Her hair is frequently highlighted or dyed every conceivable shade of brown. She opts, riskily, for the girlish flourish: the bow, the ribbon, the scarf.

Fanny ON FASHION . . .

- 'Women depend on their mirrors to tell them what they look like. Men never tell them – except when they propose.'

- 'No woman with a more than 38-inch hip should wear trousers.'

- 'Why do fat girls and matrons hanker for the cruel revelations of the Bikini?

- 'Keep it plain and you will shine far more brilliantly than the over-decorated muddlers.'

. . . AND BEAUTY

- 'Never fear soap and water.'

- 'Silence please while wearing your face mask. No smiling, no smoking, no speaking.'

- 'Wrinkles are nothing to worry about – provided they are the RIGHT SORT of wrinkles . . . the happy sort, the lovable sort.'

- 'On coming home from the office, remove your make-up and rub your skin with a slice of cucumber – it will make you feel wonderfully fresh.'

- 'Soak hair in olive oil, and wrap in scarf for one day – it makes an excellent home treatment.'

Fanny tried to resist the ageing process with nips and tucks, but retreated increasingly behind cloying make-up. It was easy enough for her to write, in her mid-forties, that 'wrinkles are nothing to worry about – provided they are the RIGHT SORT of wrinkles . . . the happy sort, the lovable sort', but it was harder to face up to them herself, twenty years later. She was needlessly self-conscious about her skin, though more secure when sporting a rich, summer tan, and she failed to divert from her slightly mad, staring hazel eyes. The false eyelashes – she always insisted when they were left in bath-room sinks at friends' houses that they were not hers – compounded the prob-lem. The Alexander solution? 'Softer colours would have helped, not that harsh black line. Perhaps more colour on the lips just to draw attention away from the eyes as well.'

'I'm becoming like those sweet feminine creatures who need only smile when a man talks to them. To a certain extent, anyway! The change hits me in all kinds of ways. I can wear simple clothes now. I don't need gimmicks. I have thrown the outsize earrings, the feather bows and parasols, into a drawer.'

Fanny's philosophy, as expressed in the *Sunday Graphic* in 1954, was: 'I'd rather see a woman use too much make-up than lose all interest in herself.' Her own heavy-duty approach, and use of lipstick in particular, attracted considerable criticism. Wendy Colvin, her assistant in the 1950s, said: 'I always thought her make-up was appalling, the way she put her lips up into a bow and the amount of make-up she used. I didn't see her very much without make-up. She normally appeared in the morning fully made-up.' Victor Lewis-Smith, the *Evening Standard*'s TV critic, described Fanny's lipstick as having been 'applied so wildly that she looked as though she'd been sipping from a rough-edged glass'. Hilary Alexander sounds a sympathetic note: 'In those days you didn't have lip pencils. They're much more in use now, so people draw in the line and then fill it in with lipstick so it's not so obvious. The use of make-up has become much more subtle. I think they've understood the rule that it's better to wear less than more because otherwise you just look stupid, as if you're trying to be younger than you are, and there's nothing worse than that.'

8

Triple Challenge

F anny Cradock had a showman's flair for self-promotion. In the 1950s she jousted in the kitchen with one of France's foremost chefs, wrote and starred in the world's first cooking comedy for the stage, and made a record drive from London to Monte Carlo.

DUEL IN THE KITCHEN

CAFE ROYAL, 9 JANUARY 1956 ⎯⎯⎯⎯⎯⎯⎯⎯⎯⎯⎯⎯⎯⎯⎯⎯⎯
RAYMOND OLIVER. 'Women do not know how to cook. They are incapable of inventing a dish.'
FANNY CRADOCK. 'I just could not let M Oliver get away with the statement of his. It's become a question of national honour.'

Raymond Oliver's provocative put-down, first aired in the *News Chronicle* in the autumn of 1955, was quickly followed by a general invitation to prove him wrong. On reflection, he said, make it an Englishwoman. He harboured the cross-Channel prejudice that the English housewife's culinary

Let battle commence: the programme for Fanny's cooking duel with Raymond Oliver at the Café Royal in 1956.

competence began and ended with bacon and eggs. The Cradocks were on one of their frequent European jaunts at the time, but they returned to find that their manager, Reg Gregg, had done what he sensed Fanny would have done: taken the bait.

Under duel conventions, Fanny was given the choice of weapons. 'I chose, because they were three things every chef had apparently flogged to death, a bird, a soufflé and a pancake.' She also stipulated, to the chagrin of friends who saw a perfect opportunity to champion English food, that the dishes must conform to the requirements of *la haute cuisine française*.

She was confident enough of her own ability, and three years of live appearances in front of packed audiences ruled out stage fright, but she was also painfully aware of Oliver's reputation. He was not only the bearded face of *l'art culinaire* on French TV – cue inevitable comparisons with Philip

Out of the pan . . . into the fire: Fanny Cradock and Raymond Oliver meet at the Mirabelle restaurant, two days before their duel in the kitchen. *(Keystone/Hulton Archive/Getty Images)*

Harben – but the master-chef behind Le Grand Vefour in Paris, one of only eleven *Guide Michelin* three-star restaurants in the whole of France.

In December 1955 Fanny paid due homage. Le Grand Vefour, she wrote in the *Daily Mail*, was 'obscurely placed down a narrow street where the down-and-outs still sleep heartbreakingly under tattered copies of *Le Figaro* and *France Soir*.' The 'fabulous' Oliver was described as 'crony of world-famous food and wine savants'. The Cradocks dined on *les ortolans aux raisins Oliver* – 'sparrow-sized buntings of subtle flavour incorrectly thought to be larks by the gastronomically illiterate' – and left with the secrets of Oliver's puff pastry.

He succeeded only in further stirring the pot of female indignation when, a week before the challenge, he told the *Mail*: 'I do not wish to be ungallant but it is a fact of history that women have always been outclassed by the glory of men in the creative arts – in writing, poetry, sculpture, painting, and also in cooking. This is incontestable. Women are capable of very great success. Some women can even cook well. But all have inferiority

Fanny's Oyster Soufflé

The one she created for her contest at the Café Royal against Raymond Oliver of the Grand Vefour in Paris. She subsequently cooked it on Eurovision.

Ingredients

1pt (600ml) dry white wine
½pt (300ml) single cream
7 separated No. 3 egg whites
2 No. 3 egg yolks
3oz (75g) finely grated Parmesan cheese
1 flat eggspoon (1 x 2.5ml spoon) salt
a generous pinch of black pepper, freshly ground
6 transparently thin pancakes
3oz (75g) white *roux*

THE FILLING
1 dozen small bearded oysters and
   their accompanying juices
1oz (25g) butter
1fl oz (30ml) dry white wine
2fl oz (60ml) double cream
a fat pinch of black pepper

Method

Soften the *roux* in a saucepan over a moderate heat. Add quarter of the wine, wait until this bubbles and then stir, increasing to a vigorous beating with a wooden spoon. Add remaining wine in the same way. Add a quarter of the cream, the salt, pepper and a flat dessertspoon (1 x 10ml spoon) of the cheese. Wait until the cream boils, then stir and finally beat until smooth. So continue until all ingredients except the egg are absorbed. Remove from heat and beat a little to cool down slightly before beating in the egg yolks. Finally add the stiffly whipped egg whites.

Put one-third of this mixture into an 8in (20cm) diameter Pyrex glass, heat-resistant, well-buttered soufflé mould. Slip the remainder into the refrigerator while you make the filling for the pancakes.

Bring the wine to boiling point, stir in the butter, then the strained oyster liquor and finally the cream. Work together over a low heat until the cream has bubbled well and reduced. Slide in the oysters for a slow count of fifty. Remove from the heat, add pepper and turn into a Moulinex food processor. Switch on for a 10-second burst and then divide the mixture between the six pancakes.

Roll these up. Lay three on the soufflé mixture already in the mould. Cover with half the refrigerated soufflé mixture, then the remaining pancakes. Cover with remaining soufflé mixture and level the top right across with a metal spatula to lock in sides all around.

Bake one shelf above centre at Gas Mark 7 (approx 425°F, 220°C) for 16½ minutes. By this time the top will be richly browned and risen right up above rim of mould, disclosing about 1in (2.5cm) of creamy, pale risen mixture. Remove and serve with oyster sauce.

A Lifetime in the Kitchen, vol. III, 1985

Royal appointment: Fanny accepting the challenge at the Café Royal in 1956. (© Hulton-Deutsch/Getty Images)

complexes, which make them nervous of failure. From that I deduce that it is impossible for a gastronome to place his entire confidence in a fragile woman.'

Fanny was getting nervous. 'I've never undertaken anything quite so terrifying,' she admitted. 'Frankly I've lain awake at night for the past three weeks worrying about it and working out dishes in my head.'

THE CRADOCK COLLECTION ─────────────────────────

Soufflé aux huitres (with English oysters, of course)
Suprême de volaille à la Florida (colloquially referred to by Fanny as chicken buns; served on wild rice)
Soufflé glacée au citron (surmounted with Sabayon sauce)

THE OLIVER COLLECTION ————————————————————————
Crêpe Melusine (mushroom pancakes, Hollandaise sauce, soufflé potatoes)
Corbeau à la Edgar Allan Poe (breasts of woodcock injected with brandy using hypodermic syringe, laid on beds of fresh goose liver, covered with sauce of goose liver and cream)
Soufflé Eole (cream extracted from old box of chocolates, remaining chocolate melted, sugar and Cointreau or Benedictine added)

Fanny arrived in quasi-regal splendour at the Café Royal, chauffeur-driven in the imposing 1911 Renault which had been loaned to the Cradocks. She was helped from the car by Raymond Oliver, and any doubts the pair may have had about the symbolic importance attached to the contest were dispelled by the forty photographers who snapped madly as they retreated towards the entrance. Fanny wore a diamanté-studded pink satin ball gown, self-designed and cut, embossed with ostrich feathers. Oliver was more functionally attired in dove-grey blazer, open-necked scarlet shirt and blue tea towel at the waist.

Fanny in the 1911 Renault which transported her in style to her challenge with Raymond Oliver in 1956. *(Photo Coverage)*

The Napoleon Suite was packed with 300 celebrities, gourmets and journalists; a BBC television crew was in place to shoot a thirty-minute programme for transmission the following night. Charles Forte, the master of ceremonies, tossed a 5-guinea gold coin dating from Queen Victoria's jubilee. Fanny won, the combatants kissed and Oliver was put into bat.

Fanny wrote in her autobiography: 'We were allotted twenty-five minutes for each dish. Raymond overran by ten minutes and several people slipped out for a drink. This so annoyed me that by the time I stood up I was in a stinking temper, which banished nervousness completely.' She recalled that at every step she had to kick her 3ft train out of the way, but there was the usual Cradock stage banter and slick presentation. Explaining that she had built her dishes around English ingredients, she told the audience: 'English foodstuffs are supreme until they reach the kitchen door.' Johnnie, her second and consultant on the wines which accompanied each dish, philosophised idly: 'A few more bottles of *vin ordinaire* on the table and there would be a lot more happy marriages.'

A patriotic roar went up when Fanny's opening gambit, *soufflé aux huitres*, emerged from the oven as a 'wobbling golden mushroom'. She finished with a stiffening-free lemon soufflé dessert and, by way of a theatrical flourish, handed the judges a basket of chocolate eggs. At the count of three each was instructed to break an egg over his or her portion. Inside was the whole, blown eggshell and inside that a syrup composed of fourteen different liqueurs.

THE VERDICT

Fanny Cradock had what seemed to be a natural ally on the three-strong judges' panel, Constance Spry, who was a regular on *The Daily Telegraph*'s roadshow brains trust. Fanny, however, was taken to one side before the contest and told: 'I am very fond of you and we are friends. So I hope you won't blame me if I am harsher towards you than I might have been.' Fanny expected nothing more or less – 'there is little pleasure playing with loaded dice!' – than a fair hearing from Spry and her fellow sages, Eugene Kaufeler and Jean Dupont, head chefs at the Dorchester and Café Royal.

The verdict was a diplomatic draw. Kaufeler said: 'It was impossible for Mrs Cradock to surpass the cooking of M Oliver. But we congratulate her on proving that one woman at least can show us creative cooking.'

A good judge: Fanny and Johnnie talking tactics with Eugene Kaufeler, head chef at the Dorchester hotel, in the mid-fifties. *(Daily Mail)*

He turned to Oliver. 'Do you agree?'

The Frenchman replied: 'With all my heart.' For the evening, at least, he maintained the façade of contentment. 'Your Mrs Cradock had me worried a little,' he said. 'She is so confident. So sure. So charming.'

Oliver walked off with his prize of a Stilton cheese and a bottle of port; Fanny lit up one of the choice cigars which were her reward. 'Don't all good dinners end like this?' she joked with the audience.

THE AFTERMATH

The bonhomie barely lasted into the following day; and as the BBC television highlights package approached – three hours condensed into half an hour of drama and humour – tempers were fraying. Fanny recounted in *Something's Burning*: 'Half an hour before transmission Monsieur Oliver

The ONES THAT GOT AWAY ─────────

'Fanny: the early years' – film script rejected on both sides of the Atlantic during the Second World War.

Career as a radio commentator – After a test at Lord Mayor's Show in 1952, Fanny admitted: 'It was perfectly clear as soon as I picked up the mike that it was not my métier.'

The Bon Viveur cookery school – It was first mooted in the early fifties and by 1963 they were touting the imminent opening of 'the largest authentic school of cookery Britain has ever known'.

Italian travelogue – Johnnie played 16mm cameraman in 1955; the BBC turned it down after a dispute over editing.

Live and dangerous – Fanny's idea to broadcast live from viewers' kitchens in 1962 was dismissed by the BBC as 'impracticable'.

'More Light Please' – a panel game for children rejected by the BBC in 1963.

'Castle Rising Closes the Circle' – an intended eleventh and final book in the Lormes family saga.

'Paradise Regained' – a novel dedicated to Fanny's sons, Peter and Christopher. Proposed pen name: Peter Christopher . . . or Christopher Peters.

'The Life and Death of Agnes Bertha Marshall' – 'the greatest British cook who ever lived'.

Fanny, fetching in Wellington boots, and cameraman Johnnie on location in Cognac.
(*J. Goguet*)

Cooking up a storm: this Chrys cartoon was carried in the *Daily Mail* the day after Fanny and Raymond Oliver's battle of the pots and pans was declared a diplomatic draw.

THE BEATON TRACK
by CHRYS

"Now I want us all to pretend we are Mrs. Cradock and that we have just been challenged by M. Oliver . . .!"

refused to participate unless the judges said he had won, at which quiet Johnnie exploded! A nightmare followed, till finally, reading from the bit of paper which my husband had insisted Oliver signed before we appeared, poor Monsieur Kaufeler repeated the judgment of the night before, looking dignified, of course, but not precisely merry.'

She also believed that television had proved the point, incontrovertibly, in her favour. 'That little screen is a pitfall to the uninitiated. You cannot use it to deceive. Something about the intimacy of the medium makes it an X-ray form of entertainment. If you do not know, if you do not believe, if you are pretending – you will get copped, sooner or later.' Another person who needed no convincing was Fanny's father. His letter of congratulation was proudly glued into her scrapbook. 'Until they invent some new words in this

'Women are capable of very great success. Some women can even cook well. But all have inferiority complexes, which make them nervous of failure. From that I deduce that it is impossible for a gastronome to place his entire confidence in a fragile woman.'

Raymond Oliver

language of ours,' he wrote, 'I shall never be able to tell you the very wonderful thrill I got when I opened my *Daily Mail* this morning.'

Oliver returned to France later that week in what *France Soir* described as 'an agitated state'. Clutching what he regarded as biased articles from English newspapers, he fumed: 'I won easily, and the jury knew it. Moreover, if I hadn't I'd never have dared set foot in France again.' He said the result was 'fixed', citing the 'ecstatic' response to his dishes from the audience at the Café Royal. He also claimed that Fanny had been working on her dishes for three months and that he had been given 'inferior equipment'; worse still, he had been handicapped by having to use English chocolates for his dessert. 'I was all alone,' he complained, 'while Mrs Cradock turned up with an army of helpers.'

In the final analysis, however, both contestants had reason to be satisfied. Oliver told *France Soir*: 'British television has just offered me a contract.' Fanny, meanwhile, sensed that she had acquired a new credibility when she set foot in France a week after the duel. Four years later she reflected: 'Unbeknown to me the story had leaked out. I was stopped in the street by a very famous chef, who congratulated me. Thereafter kitchen doors swung open to receive me in famous restaurants all over France. The French were furious at what had happened and they have never ceased to give me encouragement, assistance and secrets since that day.'

SOMETHING'S BURNING

Arts Theatre, 3–16 June 1958

A brilliantly improvised rescue act after the gas went out at the Royal Albert Hall in December 1956 was reheated eighteen months later and served up as one of the least distinguished episodes in the Cradocks' professional lives. Ten minutes of frenetic ad-libbing by Fanny, gamely supported by Johnnie, fired the collective imagination of the watching representatives from the Arts Theatre.

Bernard Gillman and Campbell Williams had established a reputation for risk-taking. Here, they thought, was another enticing expedition to the

Comedy or farce? The
programme for Fanny
and Johnnie's theatrical
first in 1958.

THE ARTS THEATRE CLUB

Directors — Campbell Williams, G. E. A. Williams, Toby Rowland
6 & 7 GREAT NEWPORT STREET, W.C.2. (near Leicester Square Tube Station)

THE ARTS THEATRE CLUB, IN ASSOCIATION WITH

BON VIVEUR (PHYLLIS AND JOHN CRADOCK), PRESENT FOR

THE FIRST TIME IN THE HISTORY OF THE THEATRE

SOMETHING'S BURNING

A Cooking Comedy in three Acts

by Bon Viveur

FIRST NIGHT TUESDAY, 3rd JUNE, 1958

theatrical hinterland. They collared the Cradocks as the adrenalin levels
receded and put a proposition to them. 'Turn the last act into a three-act
cooking play and put it on at the Arts,' said Campbell. 'But mind you, Fanny,
I want that French act played exactly as you played it tonight. It doesn't
want a word of alteration anywhere!' Nor were they put off when Fanny
admitted that every last word was delivered off the cuff.

Fast forward to New Year's Day 1957. Fanny and Johnnie are recovering
from the excesses of a starry night at Maxim's restaurant in Paris. Ingrid
Bergman and Yul Brynner have agreed to feature in a travel film to which
they are putting the finishing touches. Johnnie squints through the haze of
euphoria to remind Fanny that they have an imminent one-night stand to
fulfil. 'I don't want to disturb you, madam, but do you realise that we are on
at the Arts in fourteen days and we haven't written a line of the flaming
play, yet?'

They scribbled, rehearsed on the hoof and were rung by Gillman a week before the big night to report a sell-out. He also reminded them that they had, unwisely in his view, rejected the offer of a short season. Fanny reasoned that if the play failed to ignite they could put it down to experience and quietly resume their tried-and-tested roadshow routine. If it was deemed a success they could return for additional helpings. Fanny told the *Evening News* that it was akin to 'crossing the Styx'. Could a cooking demonstration, with a little dramatic tweaking, masquerade as pure entertainment?

The problem, though it did not become apparent in time to save them from a roasting at the hands of cynical critics the following year, was that *Something's Burning* contained too much cooking – Fanny calculated that more than 450 ingredients went into the 22 courses – and not enough plot. The acolytes turned up to look on, awestruck, as Fanny weaved her cooking magic, but the regular theatregoers were left nonplussed and under-nourished.

Even Fanny was forced to admit that it was an exhausting gig, though she assured the *Kensington News*: 'My sweat never gets in my sauce.' She wrote in her autobiography: 'We were on stage throughout the entire play. We had three changes. All this was not at all restful. The stage manager aged ten years in that one evening. Our props list read like something conceived by Emett in closest collaboration with Heath Robinson and compiled by a malevolent poltergeist in a drunken stupor.'

Still, they made a £7 profit and felt so vindicated by the venture that they bought their first Rolls-Royce.

A FORTUNE IN THE MAKING

ACT I: The kitchen of the Cradocks' London house. A Friday morning in early summer.
ACT II: A restaurant in France. The following day at lunch-time.
ACT III: The kitchen of the Cradocks' London house. Late the following evening. Time: the present.

Both the Arts Theatre and the Cradocks were sufficiently encouraged by the dry(ish) run to commit to a fortnight-long season, though prior commitments on both sides delayed the production for almost eighteen months.

Fanny tried, without obvious success, to tighten up the script, but she was now convinced that they had a blockbuster on their hands. She sought, at every turn, to gain her father's hard-won approval; her wartime emergence as a novelist took her to the first rung and she believed that *Something's Burning* gave her something to rub shoulders with his long-running 1920s farce, *Tons of Money*.

Fanny and Johnnie were suddenly gripped with ambition: two weeks before *Something's Burning* opened they took out an advertisement in *The Stage*, announcing their availability for 'acting experience without Frying Pans'. It continued: 'Johnnie (several good toupees available) willing to play

THE STAGE 22/5/58

Two stage struck cooks, intoxicated in "alas, poor Yorick" tradition, desire acting experience without Frying Pans. Anticipating equally traditional query, "What have you done?", Fanny offers three brief appearances, one with Alfred Marks and two with Hughie Green in Jack Hylton's Monday Show. Husband and Partner, Johnnie (several good toupees available) willing to play anything from American concept of upper crust English Public School type (astonishingly lifelike) to barrow boy (trained by own troops on Isle of Dogs during London blitz).

Reason for vaunting ambition coming up!

THEY NEED ACTING EXPERIENCE

Fanny and Johnnie, internationally known stage and TV cooks, journalists, broadcasters and gastronomes (Bon Viveur) with masses of work till June 1959 lead with silly chins and play leads at Arts Theatre Club on June 3rd next in

SOMETHING'S BURNING

the first cooking comedy in theatrical history; a three act modern play written by Bon Viveur. During the action of the play the team will cook 20 dishes and serve same to audience. (No fatalities to date.)

Would-be actors for hire: Fanny and Johnnie placed this advertisement in *The Stage* in 1958.

anything from American concept of upper crust English Public School type
(astonishingly lifelike) to barrow boy (trained by own troops on Isle of Dogs
during London blitz).'

They also tried to communicate the same copper-plated confidence to
their next-door neighbours in South Terrace, Tenniel and Evangeline Evans,
actors and newly-weds who fitted the bill perfectly as the Cradocks' co-stars
at the Arts. The seasoned comedy actress Mollie Hare completed the cast in
a play touted, a trifle pretentiously, as 'bridging the gap between legitimate
theatre and the culinary art'.

Evangeline remembers being 'extremely poor at the time' and desperate
for work. Tenniel recalls being told by Fanny: 'Darling, we're going to do this
all over the world and it's going to make you a fortune.' The Evanses
scented disaster and an indelible blot on their CVs; they also worried how
their stomachs and waistlines would weather the culinary onslaught.

> **EVANGELINE:** There's no two ways about it, it was a dreadful script and a
> terrible play. What's more the Arts Theatre smelt of not terribly good
> cooking for months. At the dress rehearsal Tenniel and I, the director of
> the play and the stage manager went down with food poisoning. We were
> seriously ill. The poor director [Eric Croall] was a Christian Scientist so he
> couldn't admit he was being poisoned.
> **TENNIEL:** Fanny and Johnnie were fine because they didn't eat any of their
> food. They just had a steak.
> **EVANGELINE:** Anyway, they were probably immune to all the germs by that
> time. . . . If you can imagine having had food poisoning the day before
> and then having to perform the play the next night with the same food
> again, warmed up. One of the things was pancakes which had a stuffing
> of prawns.
> **TENNIEL:** Prawns and anchovies. It couldn't be more dangerous.
> **EVANGELINE:** I was just about to take my first mouthful and say, 'Delicious',
> when Tenniel, to be heard by the entire Arts Theatre, said, 'Don't touch it!'
> And it was glowing like a torch and winking at us. How we survived I
> don't know.
> **TENNIEL:** They put the food down on the front of the stage just before the
> curtains down for each interval and all these old ladies who were Fanny's
> fans used to fight their way to the front to have a bit of this food.
> **EVANGELINE:** If they'd known how poisonous it was they would have left it.
>
> *Lifestory*, BBC Radio 4, 1997

Friends, neighbours, co-stars: Tenniel and Evangeline Evans in *Something's Burning* at the Arts Theatre in 1958. *(Michael Boys)*

If you can't stand the heat: Johnnie and Tenniel Evans take charge in *Something's Burning* as Fanny has a breather. *(Michael Boys)*

Café Brûlot

A Cradock crowd-pleaser at home and after their record-breaking Rolls-Royce drive.

Method

As *Café Brûlot* is made either in the drawing-room after dinner or at the table if the guests so wish, it is necessary to have the *mise-en-place* carefully arranged. Have a measured quantity of strong black unsweetened after-dinner coffee standing *au bain-Marie* in the kitchen. Put a measured quantity of very ordinary brandy in a small thick pan. Make sure this is tightly covered with double duty Alcan Foil which must be whipped off when the brandy is warmed otherwise you will have a small explosion when hot. *Achtung*! Allow 16fl oz (480ml) to every 4fl oz (120ml) brandy.

Also assemble the following on a tray: a punch bowl and ladle, the thinly peeled rind of a thin-skinned orange, ortanique or tangerine wrapped in foil, a vanilla pod and one lump of sugar to every cup of coffee.

Begin by using the base of the ladle bowl to bruise the chosen peel with the vanilla pod and sugar lumps in the punch bowl. Do this vigorously so as to crush the sugar lumps and impart the flavour and aroma of the citrus fruit. Have ready a box of Swan Vestas matches. At this point an assistant brings in the brandy, which has been heated only until it just nips a cautious finger, and empties it into the punch bowl. All the lights are turned out and the surface of the brandy is touched with a lighted match. You grab the ladle and begin lifting ladleful after ladleful aloft and pouring it back in a stream of blue flames. In the darkness this is both very effective and performs the essential function of burning in the flavour. The lifting of ladlefuls also creates a draught which keeps the flames burning brightly. Then the very hot coffee is brought in and poured over the burning mixture which gradually dies away. Ladle it into the coffee cups and add *nothing*, please.

A Lifetime in the Kitchen, vol. III, 1985

For dedicated Cradock-watchers there was a double helping to feast on: Fanny and Johnnie both as themselves and as vague variants (John and Françoise Huggins) on the cockney husband and French-accented wife who offered light relief in their Bon Viveur shows and in their early television appearances on Associated-Rediffusion. They gave it their plucky best shot, but *Something's Burning*'s metaphorical soufflé collapsed in a barrage of ham-fisted attempts at lavatory humour – Evangeline Evans returns from a visit to basic facilities at the 'French' restaurant to announce, 'Il n'y a pas de seat' – and shameless name checks for a clutch of sponsors: feather boa by the Ostrich Feather Manufacturing Company; stockings, gloves and socks by

Morley; Virginia cigarettes by Abdulla; lighters by Ronson; electric mixer by Kenwood; refrigerator by Kelvinator; port by Croft; wines and spirits by Gilbey's; frozen fruit and vegetables by Fropax; clocks and ringers by Smiths . . .

WHAT THE CRITICS SAID

THE TIMES. 'As dialogue this is undistinguished, as comedy it tends to be crude.'

THE DAILY TELEGRAPH. 'The sight of Mrs Cradock in full evening dress, with an osprey flung negligently over the sink, hard at work on a four-course dinner

of awful elaboration, sipping champagne between times, while her husband, also suitably attired, looked on was one I will long treasure.'

SUNDAY TIMES. 'While the Moscow Arts Theatre continues to fill Sadler's Wells with its unique warmth, our own Arts Theatre offers a cookery demonstration entitled *Something's Burning . . .*'

EVENING NEWS. 'As theatre, *Something's Burning* at the Arts is pretentious nonsense. Described as a cooking comedy, it is a thin excuse for John and Fanny Cradock to cook a number of exotic dishes while wearing a range of exotic clothes.'

NEWS CHRONICLE. 'As cooks, the Cradocks are passable amateur actors; as actors they are terrible playwrights.'

DAILY SKETCH. 'The flimsiest story I've seen on any stage. . . . How the highbrow theatre club let this performance appear defies comprehension.'

MANCHESTER GUARDIAN. 'The dialogue sounds like a collection of cooking columns from one's favourite women's page strung together with comments which are occasionally whimsical, often bawdy, and never funny.'

DAILY MIRROR. 'Even more unattractive than Mrs Beeton's cookery book.'

CHURCH OF ENGLAND NEWSPAPER. 'A glorified hunk of Ideal Home Exhibitionism.'

JEWISH CHRONICLE. 'Fails through lack of two essential ingredients – acting and a plot.'

THE SPECTATOR. 'Mr Cradock's role consists of screwing and unscrewing a monocle into a beef-pink face and chuckling.'

STOKE NEWINGTON OBSERVER. 'Any one of our local amateur dramatic societies could do better.'

OPERATION BON VIVEUR

London to Monte Carlo, 30 June 1958
> 'Later in 1913 Radley set out to break the existing record from London to Monte Carlo, including the Channel crossing. Twenty-six hours and four minutes after leaving the offices of the A.A. in Coventry Street he pulled up his Continental Silver Ghost in front of the Casino in Monte Carlo: a record still unbroken!'
>
> *Veteran and Vintage magazine*

Fanny Cradock was addicted to planning. She merrily mapped out everything from major strategies to minutiae: one year's summer holiday merged into the check list for the next; Christmas arrived months early in the Cradock household. At best it was an attention to detail that defined Fanny at her professional peak; at worst it was a damagingly obsessive trait that alienated family, friends and employees.

'The dialogue sounds like a collection of cooking columns from one's favourite women's page strung together with comments which are occasionally whimsical, often bawdy, and never funny.'

Manchester Guardian

There was also a quirky, harmless middle ground in which the mundane could assume epic proportions: Operation Bon Viveur fell neatly into this category. The idea was ignited by one of the Cradocks' aristocratic chums, the thirteenth Duke of Bedford, who spotted the reference in *Veteran and Vintage* magazine to an adventurer's ripping run from London to the south of France. He suggested an assault on the record to Fanny and Johnnie, who had invested in the first of their succession of Rolls-Royces the previous year. The fact that motoring was still in its infancy in 1913, and that Radley had to cross the Channel by boat (as opposed to a Silver City Airways flight from Lydd to Le Touquet) were mere details. It *was* a record and, barring major mishap, it was there to obliterate.

Johnnie was given an excuse to supplement his already extensive collection of maps – Fanny never ceased to ridicule him for his diffident suggestions of alternative routes – and the Cradocks were able to accommodate the drive within the meticulous planning for their annual two-month break in the south of France. The British media were largely unmoved by a press release which explained:

God speed: Fanny and Johnnie set out from Leicester Square on their record-breaking drive to Monte Carlo in 1958.

A cake in the shape of a Rolls-Royce greets Fanny and Johnnie at the Carlton Hotel in Cannes as they celebrate their record drive in 1958. *(Traverso)*

For the record and following their own cookery traditions the team will arrive in full evening dress although their four scheduled stops (for oil and petrol) are of only two, and maximum three, minutes' duration. Departure clothes? Slacks and sweaters.

The serious purpose of this trip stems from the fact that Bon Viveur are tired of the denigration of British goods. British natural foodstuffs are the best in the world. They only suffer at British kitchen doors. Britain also produces the finest cars in the world; neither food nor cars are sufficiently extolled abroad. Bon Viveur seek to prove that in a British car such a trip is within the scope of any average motorist – and in no sense of the word an endurance test.

Fanny's attached 'Menu for Car Journey' confirmed that she was applying the same dietary rigour to this jaunt as she might have done to an assault on Everest.

GENERAL ISSUE: Bitter chocolate, sultanas, small raw carrots.
In the Boot for Easy Handling at Speed
A. *Airborne Lydd–Le Touquet:* Fruit, thin brown bread and butter crisp bread, hard-boiled eggs, thermos of hot coffee laced with brandy.
B. *10–10.30 a.m.:* Thermos of hot consommé, smoked salmon sandwiches with brown bread, fruit.
C. *Noon–12.30 p.m.:* ½ pint iced orange juice each, punnet of raspberries or strawberries with ryebread and cream cheese sandwiches.
D. *2–3 p.m.:* Cold turkiette, buttered crisp bread, Wensleydale cheese, black coffee, fruit.
E. *Around 5 p.m.:* Basket of fruit, mineral water.
F. *7–8:* Caviar brown bread sandwiches, hot black coffee laced with brandy.

Rolls-Royce, scenting positive publicity, lent the Cradocks a new Silver Cloud, which eased away from the AA offices at 5.15 a.m. on 30 June. A handful of photographers were on reluctant dawn duty, while an Associated-Rediffusion television crew ensured that their exploits would be immortalised for *Late Extra*.

'The serious purpose of this trip stems from the fact that Bon Viveur are tired of the denigration of British goods. British natural foodstuffs are the best in the world. They only suffer at British kitchen doors. Britain also produces the finest cars in the world; neither food nor cars are sufficiently extolled abroad.'

Johnnie (adequate driver) and Fanny (multi-prosecuted menace on the road) operated an hour-on, hour-off rota, making such good time that they passed Auxerre, in the Burgundy region, at 12.15, sped past Aix-en-Provence at 18.40 and stopped for about 20 seconds outside the Carlton Hotel in Cannes at 20.40 – sufficient time for a brief stamp on their passports – before arriving in Monte Carlo at 21.34. Travel time: 16 hours 19 minutes, almost 10 hours quicker than the Radley run.

Then it was back to the Carlton, a rapturous reception and a celebratory cake in the predictable shape of a Rolls-Royce. The only sour taste was left by faulty brakes which imperilled the final stages of their trip and brought the threat of legal action when they returned home.

9

Fanny on Food, Wine and Cooking

ESCOFFIER AND FRIENDS

You could just about detect the reverential quiver in Fanny Cradock's voice whenever she mentioned the words Georges Auguste Escoffier. If he had received a posthumous franc (Fanny would not have approved of the euro) for every Cradock name check the master chef would have been dining out nightly in style in culinary heaven. Fanny described her devotion as 'hitching our culinary and gastronomic wagons to that very great star'.

She was also fond of quoting Escoffier's principle that 'in the matter of provisions the cheapest is the dearest in the end'. She accepted this challenge to her natural thrift and reasoned, in the best-selling *Daily Telegraph Cook's Book*: 'If, in Britain, you buy a pound of those large, overblown little cabbages which masquerade as Brussels sprouts, you will find that the discarded trimmings weigh about one-third of the total weight of your purchase. If instead, you buy (at a one-third higher price) a pound of the more costly baby Brussels sprouts, you will find there is no waste. This is a perfect example of spending to save, with the advantage of obtaining considerable increase in

The king of cooks:
Georges Auguste
Escoffier was Fanny's
greatest inspiration
(*Mary Evans Picture
Library*)

flavour and nutriment value.' Warming to her theme, Fanny urged *Telegraph* readers to shout and bawl their way to satisfaction. 'Roar at barrow boys. . . . Tear a strip off the tradesmen who deliver inferior brands of a product when you have specified the ones you want.'

Escoffier, who crossed the Channel in 1890 to revolutionise hotel catering at Richard D'Oyly Carte's newly opened Savoy, was both innovator and organiser. He argued that haute cuisine should be light and healthy and its sauces less rich and more subtle. He also, according to the *Oxford Dictionary of National Biography*, 'insisted that a sense of occasion and

Basic White Sauce

Ingredients

1½ oz flour
1½ oz butter or other fat

½ pt milk or stock for thick sauces,
(¼ pt for medium and 1pt for thin)

Method

Dissolve butter and add flour. Stir until mixture forms a smooth paste which leaves sides and base of pan cleanly. Cook for a minimum two minutes to cook out the taste of the flour. This is the roux. Pour in approximately one-fifth of the quantity of chosen fluid. Allow to boil without stirring. Stir until mixture blends smoothly, beat vigorously and add remaining quantity of fluid as described, beating well after each addition. For Sweet White Sauce add sugar and vanilla pod to chosen liquids in a separate saucepan, bring to the boil slowly and allow to cool to blood heat. Then remove pod, wipe it and store in a glass jar for future use.

Home Cooking (BBC), 1965

luxury should come from flowers, fine china and glass, and specially designed serving dishes and containers (including sculpted ice)'.

Fanny recognised an almost mystical element to the creation of the finest sauces. 'Think of the approach of the great masters,' she wrote in *The Daily Telegraph* in 1954. 'When doing a sauce they don't just use butter – they run it lovingly and gently through their fingers so that it actually imparts on the sauce at a certain temperature by the warmth of the hand.' Escoffier was also speaking the language of presentation which she understood and endorsed.

She was not a natural devotee of the minimalism of nouvelle cuisine, though she placed great and time-consuming emphasis on the appearance of a dish. Fanny favoured a full plate (Johnnie was a confirmed trencherman), and even the 1970 part-work series, *Fanny and Johnnie Cradock Cookery Programme*, featured alluring dishes bobbing in an unbroken sea of garnish-free garden peas. Modern critics who claim that the dishes did not work would have been assailed by Fanny with the nearest rolling pin. She stressed endlessly that what set her apart from Isabelle Beeton and many of her contemporaries was that her published recipes *were* tested *ad nauseam*. She even appended the 'F' seal of approval to dishes featured in the *Cookery Programme*.

BEETON BASHING: GOOD COOK, BAD COOK

Like any aspiring British cook of the early twentieth century, Fanny Cradock looked to Mrs Beeton for guidance. The discovery in 1962 that Isabella Beeton had been in her early twenties when she wrote the *Book of Household Management* sent Fanny into forensic overdrive.

The *Sunday Times* commissioned 2,000 words: a ruthless debunking exercise in which Fanny disparaged Mrs Beeton as a shameless charlatan. She wrote: 'I always regarded this famous cook as a comfortable, starch-aproned, well-upholstered, middle-aged Victorian wife and mother. I had

Hate figure: Isabella Beeton was derided by Fanny for her untested recipes (© Hulton-Deutsch Collection/ Corbis)

always pictured her working away in a great kitchen with a vast scrubbed table and even vaster kitchen range.' On the strength of her research, Fanny concluded: 'It seemed to me that Mrs Beeton had perpetrated a wildly funny joke on the world. Whatever the merits of today's revised versions, which are bought and loved by millions, when Mrs Beeton wrote her famous book she had little or no experience of cooking. It seemed to me that Mrs Beeton never had the time to cook!'

Fanny argued that the majority of the recipes in the *Book of Household Management* were effectively donated to Mrs Beeton on the strength of an appeal from her husband, Sam. Isabella was 'a prolific journalist' and Sam 'devilishly clever', but there the Cradock well of praise dried up. 'I am equally convinced that Mrs Beeton herself never fried an egg, and if she did I find it hard to believe that it could ever have been worth eating.'

The flip side of this Beeton-bashing enterprise was Fanny's adoption of a true cooking heroine, the much less well-known Agnes Bertha Marshall who, she decided (in a heavily implied act of self-congratulation), was the Fanny Cradock of the second half of the nineteenth century. Impressed by the 'faultless' French sub-titles in *Mrs Marshall's Book of Extra Recipes*, Fanny made notes for an intended article pointing to a kindred career pattern: 'She not only cooked every published recipe, but created many, and also cooked on stage both in Britain and America in exactly the same way as we do today. Her notices from *The Times*, the *Morning Post*, the *Manchester Guardian* and many other newspapers are identical in content with our own. She even dressed as I do, wore diamonds on stage, had similar fans, commercial sponsors and reclame.' Fanny voted her another two plus marks over her rival: 'She wrote of "table napkins" when that little journalist wrote of "serviettes"; she was bi-lingual.'

Detective Cradock also formed the theory that Mrs Marshall had met a gruesome end. 'I am now hoping to establish that A.W. Marshall poisoned his wife in order to marry his mistress Miss Walsh and that the dismissal was because Agnes Bertha caught them *in flagrante delicto*. That he subsequently murdered his brother-in-law Jack Osborne Wells because he knew too much.'

Fanny refused to let Mrs Beeton off the hook, though she did manage to joke: 'If ever I meet her when I quit this life I shall doubtless be facing a charge of spiritual murder!' She had no doubt what the answer would be when she said in 1964: 'Today people may take their pick: Mrs Beeton – or Fanny Cradock?'

Ice work: an 1898 advertisement for Mrs Marshall's quick-freezing equipment.

TO MOP OR NOT TO MOP?

Fanny and Johnnie were faced with an agonising social dilemma while dining with Countess Lupe in Nuits St Georges in the early sixties. To mop or not to mop was the burning question. They took the plunge. '"Please may we mop?" we asked. "This sauce is so wonderful," which pleased everyone. So, with bits of French crust, we mopped and sucked, as the finger-bowls were placed at the top left of each one of us. We mention this mop-problem simply to indicate that once you know what is correct, you can afford to be slightly incorrect.'

The Cradocks' booklet *Giving a Dinner Party*, based on the BBC TV series, steered hostesses – 'the perfect hostess, like the perfect gentlewoman, is one who always remembers others and never forgets herself' – round the minefield of social indiscretion.

Italian job: pasta shells with Italian veal sauce, as featured in in the part-work *Cookery Programme*. (Michael Leale/BPC Publishing)

THE WINE EXPERT

Wine was the special subject that earned Johnnie Cradock his prince regent's place beside the queen of cuisine. Friends enthuse about his deep knowledge of the subject and unite in endorsement of his sobriety. 'I never saw him drunk' is the recurring tone of the defence; the rollicking caricature of a drunk was a convenient, made-for-TV device.

Johnnie himself showed characteristic diffidence when bringing Fanny into the equation: 'Where wine is concerned my wife bows to me slightly and where food is concerned I bow to my wife deeply.' Johnnie was the one with 300 wine books, but Fanny too was a well-read oenophile. Her relative reticence on the subject was more out of social convention than anything else.

She boasted that she had never set foot in Johnnie's wine cellar (not *the* wine cellar) in the fourteen years they spent at South Terrace, and ridiculed wine snobs. She told the *Sunday Times* in 1960 that one of her pet hates was 'phoneys who try to tell me whether a bottle of claret comes from the left bank of a river or the right'. Fanny accepted, unthinkingly, that wine-serving was a man's domain; she also believed that their drinking comfort took automatic precedence. 'A hostess has no business serving a good bottle of wine if she reeks with perfume that spoils the bouquet. When I go to a big wine-tasting I use scentless powder, scentless soap, and my clothes are either brand-new or carefully cleaned for the occasion. If I go there smelling like a chemist shop I simply ruin the wine for every man present.'

Both Fanny and Johnnie could go misty-eyed when discussing great vintages and dishes lifted up to a plane of orgasmic ecstasy by perfectly matched partner wines. Their favourite line was: 'Wine irons out the creases

Grape expectations: Fanny and Johnnie sample the local produce in Cognac.

Uncorked: Johnnie does the honours
at South Terrace in the fifties.
(Associated-Rediffusion)

in our daily lives, and softens the
sharp corners of our personalities
into benevolent curves. Your wine's
home should be chosen with the
same care as your dog's basket.'

Wine was the one subject which
Fanny trusted Johnnie to write about
under his own name, though the
petty prejudices and sniping sarcasm
were clearly seconded. They blamed
American 'fashionables' for turning
'the dinner table into a smoking
room and ruining the wine for
everyone else'. Johnnie went further
in a philosophical contribution to
their part-work *Cookery Programme*
in the early seventies: 'Frankly I have
always felt that the reason why
America had such dreadful tasteless
food – eighty per cent of which is
ersatz – is because they are not capable of recognising the finer nuances of
taste because of their excessive national consumption of hard liquor before
meals.'

The Cradocks detested 'pernicious' cocktails and cocktail parties; they
were not very fond of the hard stuff either. Fanny had a weakness for a pre-
prandial schooner of Tio Pepe sherry, but their elixir was red or white (they
were a touch sniffy about rosé). Johnnie claimed that doctors prescribed
wine for the very young, while the professorial Fanny told a Wine Fair
gathering in 1963: 'Take it from me that all wine drinkers live much longer
than anyone else.'

Though long dead in 2002, both would have enjoyed a *Daily Mail*
reference to the findings of researchers from the University of Tennessee,
who had proved that the taste of wine was affected by the shape of the glass

Cooks,
COOKING AND COOKERY ————

- I have never found a good cook divorced, deserted or even widowed.
- No cook is a good cook until she can make a number of appetising soups.
- A steamer is to a good cook what a pressure cooker is to an ignorant one.
- Better an electric mixer than a fur coat if you are a wise cook.
- Women spend time to make themselves look attractive, so they should spend time to make the food they cook attractive.
- A kitchen is place to cook in, not perform surgical operations.
- Cookery is a cleanly and creative art and not a grubby chore.
- There is a lot of sloshing and bungling in good cooking.
- There is no such thing as English cookery.

in which it was drunk. It was pointed out that the Cradocks had reached the same conclusion thirty-two years earlier. In the *Cook Hostess' Book,* 'without a research grant, they revealed the effect of a glass's shape on the quaffing experience'.

THE GREAT BRITISH VEGETABLE SCANDAL

Few things set off the Cradock spleen-venting alarm more consistently than the use and unimaginative abuse of vegetables. 'What has become of

What goes up . . . doesn't come down: Fanny demonstrates how the mix defies gravity. (© *National Portrait Gallery*)

cabbage?' Fanny lamented in 1956. 'Once the National Vegetable Poultice, it is now rarer than the Olley Olley bird and entirely superseded by *those* peas, which range from lurid, emerald pellets best swallowed with a glass of water to a grey pulp not unlike the Helford Estuary at low tide.'

She elaborated on the theme for the Gas Council-published book *Cabbages and Things* three years later:

> It is a curious paradox that when Britain is in the throes of a genuine renaissance of interest in both food and wine, as today, British vegetables, which are the best in the world, are the worst cooked of anything in our islands.
>
> The best is automatically discarded when a good fresh vegetable is first peeled, then boiled, and finally strained over the plug hole down which the liquor flows into the sewers. There is first-class value in those vegetable fluids. When they are discarded away with them go the majority of vitamins, and the calories, the aids to good digestion, clear skins, bright eyes and contentment.

Was the lesson digested? Not judging by Fanny's cynicism in 1964: 'Carping about the way cabbage is cooked in Britain is like shooting a sitting bird with a gun that isn't licensed, on a Sunday out of season.'

SAY IT WITH GARLIC

The name was a trifle long-winded – Fanny called it the 'Garlic Sleep Well Late Night Fortifier' – but she was adamant that the benefits outweighed the nocturnal complications: 'Crush four garlic cloves, place in a small pan with half-pint of fresh milk, season with vegetable salt, bring to the boil, strain, and drink in bed. N.B.: As the health-giving properties in this drink are somewhat anti-social, you are advised to share beverage with partner'.

CLEAN COOK, DIRTY COOK

The *haute couture* and coiffeured precision of the Cradocks' television shows contrasted dramatically with their slumming-down lifestyle at home. In Fanny's book obsessive cleanliness was just another 'American fad'.

In the mid-sixties the BBC auditioned for a series of educational programmes and gave Fanny her most lucrative television work to date (a 2,000-strong petition from school teachers who claimed that she was unqualified for the job was pointedly ignored). Alison Leach, her personal assistant, recalls:

> Suddenly she had to be very hygiene conscious. She had to be fussy about washing her hands, using a clean towel, and she couldn't wipe her nose on it. She wasn't allowed to wear rings, she couldn't have nail polish and she couldn't puff a cigarette and shake it in the food. She really had to pull herself together. It was a different sort of Fanny, very correct and careful and compliant. Quite entertaining in a modest way, and it went down a bomb.

A dyeing art: Fanny pipes her way to a butter carnation in a Pathe short in 1957. *(British Pathe/ITN Source)*

She couldn't always avoid reverting to type: *Nationwide* viewers in 1971 were shocked to see Fanny wipe her nose with the back of her hand and then carry on cooking.

In South Terrace, and later at Blackheath, the grubby instincts also went unchecked. 'They were the dirtiest people I've ever met,' admitted Alison, who became used to finding knives and forks, allegedly clean, sticky with the residue of dog meat. 'I would generally have to wash any implement before using it and I'm not that fussy.'

Fanny and Johnnie were also willing to eat food in an advanced state of decay, as Wendy Colvin discovered to her alarm. 'When we were in the south of France once I remember taking a ham out of the fridge and I said, "It's crawling with maggots, you've got to throw it away." And Fanny said, "Nonsense darling, nobody ever died from eating maggots. Boil it up and it'll be delicious." I wouldn't eat it, but she and Johnnie did.'

> 'Frankly I have always felt that the reason why America had such dreadful tasteless food – eighty per cent of which is ersatz – is because they are not capable of recognising the finer nuances of taste because of their excessive national consumption of hard liquor before meals.'
>
> *Johnnie Cradock*

Tenniel and Evangeline Evans also witnessed the Cradocks' antipathy towards cleaning duties at South Terrace. Fanny believed that cooks should be spared washing-up, but she was equally allergic to bed-making, vacuum-cleaning and dusting. Nor was Johnnie prepared to fill the void; so only when occasional home helps intervened, or when soirées loomed, was the grime confronted. 'She made this gougère, which is like a huge Yorkshire pudding with cheese on it,' said Tenniel. 'And it went wrong and went wrong and after about the third one had gone wrong – while she was rehearsing – she picked it up and threw it across the room and it landed on the side of the sink and sank down to the floor. And there it stayed.' Fanny and Johnnie's solution, according to Evangeline Evans, was just to put down another layer of newspaper as the kitchen debris accumulated.

Predictably, Fanny thought that the French were the one nationality to get their priorities right. She told the *Radio Times* in 1968 that the British were pre-occupied with hygiene. 'They are far more interested in the facilities for flushing the "toilet" (put that in quotes and then they'll know I'm laughing). Whereas we will happily go down the gardens to the privy as long as Madam is cooking a superb meal.'

Prime cut: Fanny and Johnnie make their selection at the butcher's.

FANNY'S FOOD FOR THOUGHT

'In the first half of the century we had tinned foods which revolutionised the kitchen. Now, in 1951, comes Frood (frozen food).'

Sunday Graphic, 1951

'The very characteristics which are most laudable in Englishmen make them find difficult the mixture of slave labour and invisibility which Continental waiters achieve with grace.'

Daily Mail, 1955

'For the love of good eating never stoop to canned rice pudding, which we learn with horror is now on sale. We only await canned porridge to know our country is irretrievably degraded.'

Daily Mail, 1955

'Cod is a simple word associated with cheapness, so folks cock a snook at it. Rechristen it pterodactyl and some would still offer sales resistance because they could not pronounce the name easily.'

Daily Mail, 1955

'Anyone can have the new menace which is seeping into the little restaurant life of London: the Cult of the Dirty Fingernails and Unbrushed Hair, where slatterns slop food on to squalid tables while wise-cracking with kids.'

Daily Mail, 1956

'In a few short weeks our cooking has been completely revolutionised. We are now refrigerated cooks.'

Daily Mail, 1957

'It is just as flabby as the average soufflé, as limp as the average hors d'oeuvre, and as dull as the average boiled potato.'

Sunday Express, 1957 (on the standard of professional catering in Britain)

'In less time than it takes to boil an egg – it was cooked! What a saving of time! But what a criminal waste of a good steak! It looked ravaged. As if it had been boiled all night.'

Sunday Express, 1957 (after watching steak being cooked in a 'radar oven' on a cruise ship)

'It is an astonishing national frailty that anyone who can achieve a lukewarm poultice in a non-stick frying pan, or dig a wodge of scrambled egg off the bottom of a pan which sticks, will at the drop of an egg rush headlong into rash statements about their sometimes rather pathetic versions of omelettes.'

Daily Telegraph, 1966

'When there's a really efficient way of freezing meat *instantly*, then I will stop my war on the stuff. But the delay in freezing can cause cancer.'

Irish Times, 1971

'Alas, the time has come for us to declare two meatless, main-course meals each week.'

Daily Telegraph, 1973

'The enormous increase in Italian restaurants since the war has given pasta a head start, and although a considerable incursion has been brought about by the pizza, I do not think this will be permanently ensconced.'

Daily Telegraph, 1974

'Never keep a soufflé waiting? What rubbish, of course you can. All over France soufflés are taken from ovens in their richly browned, wobbling magnificence and put on shelves over hot cooking ranges to wait, because the restaurant customer is not yet ready.'

Daily Telegraph, 1975

'When it comes to cooking, the best friends of a working woman with a family are a three-tiered steamer and a casserole.'

Daily Telegraph, 1976

'We approached our new microwave oven with the trepidation of two people returning to a reactor station after a leak.'

Daily Telegraph, 1979

'If people really want to be conned into paying out two and three hundred pounds for a restaurant dinner party, then prices will continue escalating until there is one monumental explosion.'

Daily Telegraph, 1980

'There's only one convenience in convenience food: profit for the manufacturers. It's a load of muck.'

Wogan (BBC TV), 1986

'Those evil microwaves give you rashes and diseases.'

Breakfast Time (BBC TV), 1986

CRANKS AND SUPER CRANKS

The meat-loving Cradocks found themselves sharing a campaigning soapbox with meat-avoiding trailblazers in the 1960s. David and Kay Canter had teamed up with Daphne Swann in 1961 to open the first Cranks restaurant in Carnaby Street, and though another ten years would pass before Fanny and Johnnie embraced vegetarianism, their distaste for the artificial was also deeply rooted.

By 1970 Bon Viveur were beginning to feel vindicated:

For several years now we two have been picking our way between the Scylla of 'perilous' foodstuffs and the Charybdis of being dubbed 'cranks'.

And until recently we have been eyed with suspicion mixed with semi-tolerant amusement every time we launched diatribes against artificial fertilisers, flavourings, pesticides, and that beastly gamut which runs from frozen raw flesh to Substitutes for Real Food.

The ultimate decline for Fanny was being invited to use 'meat tenderisers' instead of buying tender meat.

For Johnnie, it was being given bleached white meringue topping made from bottled egg-white fluid (which we suspect is a by-product of nylon) as part of his first meal after a major abdominal operation.

We will not eat raw, frozen meat after a report given to us by the late, great Swiss, Dr Spahlinger, who wouldn't even feed it to animals, after his researches – not until the super-fast quick freezing which is virtually instant becomes low enough in price for every housewife to afford it.

In our last garden, as in this one, we would as soon stock the shrubberies with boa constrictors as use artificial fertilisers.

Once we had neighbours from whose garden some of these phoneys drifted. That summer we spent burning obscene, two-headed, back-to-back dahlias; courgettes like Siamese twins and bloated tomatoes with baby ones like blisters bursting out all over.

'We would as soon stock the shrubberies with boa constrictors as use artificial fer-tilisers. Once we had neighbours from whose garden some of these phoneys drifted. That summer we spent burning obscene, two-headed, back-to-back dahlias; courgettes like Siamese twins and bloated tomatoes with baby ones like blisters bursting out all over.'

Mrs Marshall's Potato Pudding

Ingredients

1 tablespoon flour
1 teaspoon baking powder
1lb cooked sieved potatoes
grated rind of 1 lemon and its juice
2 tablespoons golden syrup
1 egg
3oz butter, melted

SAUCE
4 dessertspoons golden syrup
1 dessertspoon chocolate powder
1–2 tablespoons water

Method

Add melted butter to potatoes. Beat in whisked egg, lemon rind and juice. Add golden syrup, flour and baking powder. Bake in a well-buttered, straight-sided, heat-resistant container or charlotte mould between 6in and 7in in diameter, on middle shelf, Gas Mark 5 or 375°F for 1 hour. Pour on sauce and turn up to Gas Mark 6 or 400°F for 10 minutes. Serve hot.

SAUCE
Mix chocolate powder and syrup in saucepan with water. Heat till dissolved.

Fanny and Johnnie Cradock Cookery Programme, 1970

AVOID SPLASH-BACK (AND BACKACHE): ADOPT THE THIRD BALLET POSITION

Fanny Cradock preached the gospel of apronless cooking with staggering and stubborn persistence, and showed much the same evangelical zeal when urging housewives to adopt the most ergonomically efficient stance at their cookers.

She warmed to the subject for Esme Scott's and *TV Times* readers' benefit in 1955:

'How,' demanded Fanny Cradock, 'does the average cook stand at a cooker? Look! Feet apart, facing it, fatal! If anything splashes, you jerk back – get it full on the tummy – wham!'

Instinctively I tightened my tummy muscles. So did Johnnie, watching his wife with expert interest. He already knew the correct drill.

'Third ballet position,' Fanny explained (she learnt ballet as a child because she was 'too fat'). 'Poised forward on the right foot. See? Now you can sway back on to the right foot, gracefully. You won't get splashed – and never get tired.'

She elaborated on the theme for *Daily Telegraph* readers in 1966: 'This automatically straightens her shoulders, tightens her shoulders and arches her back, making her immune to backache.'

WHAT MAKES A COOK

'The nose of the really good cook must be as perceptive as a Geiger-counter, picking up unerringly the merest nuance of staleness in fish, flesh and fowl.

The fingertips of a really good cook can read; they do the braille work of fine cookery.

The eyes of a really good cook can spot the absurdities in written recipes which have obviously never been tested, and thus avoid the waste of ingredients on pre-destined failures.

Daily Telegraph, 1966

Help yourself: Homard la Parisienne, the lobster flesh cut into medallions and then replaced for easy buffet service. *(Michael Leale/BPC Publishing)*

IF OYSTERS BE THE FOOD OF LOVE . . .

Even in her pre-teen innocence Fanny Cradock had a taste for the exotic. Winters in the south of France meant Portuguese oysters at *6d* a dozen, and when she and her brother Charles had all but exhausted their pocket money they would head for the casino and try to recoup their expenditure at boule.

'I don't care how much people eat, but I hate waste. To see good food going down the sink drives me mad.'

Fanny recalled that only once had her taste for the bivalve molluscs been sated, which was when she polished off 8½ dozen at the opening of an oyster bar. She came to associate September with the start of the lamentably restricted oyster season in Britain. While Johnnie did not share her addiction he did agree that their aphrodisiac properties were exaggerated.

Knighted: Johnnie becomes a chevalier of the French chapter of the Chaîne des Rôtisseurs. *(P. Bourdin)*

A proud day: Fanny is admitted to the prestigious Société des Arts, Sciences et Lettres. *(Actualités Mondial)*

'We do, however, know one meal which qualifies,' she wrote:

Begin with at least one dozen oysters, follow with pigeons cooked in Burgundy with green olives, then with ripe and not too salty Roquefort cheese and plenty of celery. Drink real Chablis with the oysters, Burgundy with the pigeons and cheese – hence the old ruling, 'claret for longevity, Burgundy for *l'amour*'.

Finally you drink strong, sweet black coffee with, as a digestive, a mixture of equal parts curaçao and cognac. To this menu we add our family punch which was originally a brew Fanny's ancestor Catherine Parr gave to Henry VIII in his dotage with quite remarkable results. In our family it is currently known as 'nine months to the day'.

FROZEN ASSET: A £50,000 'TRAGEDY'

Birds Eye wanted to expand their repertoire in the early 1970s so they asked the Cradocks to create an exclusive range of gourmet meals, intended to sell at between 50p and 75p a serving. Market research had shown that two-thirds of the British public regarded Fanny and Johnnie as the last words in culinary clout.

Fishy business: Fanny and Johnnie at a launch party for Fish Fingers in 1955.

They warmed to the task of concocting the definitive sole florentine and the perfect beef goulash; and warmed even more to the prospect of the most lucrative work in their entire careers, a tasty earner with retirement age (if not actually retirement) beckoning. Fanny recalled, in a rueful foreword to *Fanny and Johnnie Cradock's Freezer Book*, how the lottery-style pay-day from 'a very famous frozen foods firm' fell victim to inflation:

After months of developing the items, setting up tastings for a most awesome panel, and thereafter teaching the cooking of our dishes to the company's professionals – and we may add that nothing was spared either in time, labour, cost or quality – just as we were in the early stages of the first experimental test-launching, the price escalation hit us all and the project simply died or, to be more accurate, was priced right out of existence. This was the end of what we had come to expect would eventually yield us a revenue of £50,000 per annum.

Fanny <u>in</u> Print

FACT OR FICTION: A NOVEL APPROACH

Fanny Cradock adopted her grandmother's middle name to take on the persona of Frances Dale the novelist, her primary calling long before cooking took centre stage. 'Exile in Elba', as the Cradocks described their three years of wartime resettlement in the Warwickshire village of Snitterfield, heralded a two-fingered assault on the typewriter. Four novels rolled off the literary production line as Fanny's income crept past £200 a year. She was said to have a better grasp of plot than punctuation and drew heavily on her tangled romantic CV.

Scorpion's Suicide (1942): Heroine Mary Grey, not very attractive (Fanny's view of herself), finds only misery in two ill-matched marriages. 'Then,' as the *Times Literary Supplement* described it, 'When war is about to overshadow the whole of human happiness, Mary Grey

'The eight wonders of the world can be eight mouldy old backyards as far as we are concerned if our tummies are rumbling.'

meets the man [echoes of Johnnie, of course] who had always been intended for her.'

Women Must Wait (1944): Gabrielle de Trevennes puts career (Fanny-style Knightsbridge dressmaking business) before the assumed destiny of marriage and baby-making.

The Rags of Time (1944): 'A picaresque period piece depicting theatrical life in the nineteenth century and in its character-drawing has something of the gusto and vividness of Dickens in his Crummies vein.' *Manchester Guardian*

The Land is in Good Heart (1945): A plea for farmers everywhere (the message resonated as far as the *Sydney Sun*), but perhaps the detailed description of calving was an authentic touch too much.

Fanny's novelist father, Archibald Pechey, praised and teased her in a letter: 'So you have made another step and will soon no doubt make many more and outstrip your old father. May it be so. But you do hop about, don't you? What's the next book going to deal with – bimetallism, body-line bowling, banshees, Bolshevism, or birth control?'

BIG WORDS FOR LITTLUNS

Under a psychiatrist's promptings Fanny Cradock might have confessed that her crop of children's books were a guilt-ridden cry for forgiveness to the sons she neglected. Johnnie formed the more perverse theory that they were written for her mother.

When Michael Was Three, Fanny's first attempt at the genre, was ostensibly designed to please Michael Sutcliffe, the doctor's grandson in the Warwickshire village where she and Johnnie lived during the war. Fanny admitted: 'No one was more surprised than I that it sold.' A reader's report from the book's eventual publishers, Hutchinson, said: 'Personally, I like the idea of James the young buck-rabbit dancing "intimately" with a lady chinchilla, but perhaps this is slightly sophisticated for the very young readers.'

The sequel, *When Michael Was Six*, 'was partly written for Michael but more for my mother, as at last we had found a book that she could read. She was responsible for the third – *Always*. Indeed Johnnie insists that the remaining eight were all written for her and the publication was incidental.'

After the war Fanny flitted between darker adult themes – the *Birmingham Mail* noted that *A Daughter of Babylon* contained 'sordid scenes which make anything but "family reading"' – *The Story of Joseph and Pharaoh* (the Bible story adapted for children), and fluffy fantasies. Gus Gooseyplum, Claude Kittenpillar, Riki Rabbit and Tommy Tortoise joined forces in the Gooseyplum trilogy, and *The Dryad and the Toad* was 'seasoned by the astringent comments of an elderly snail'.

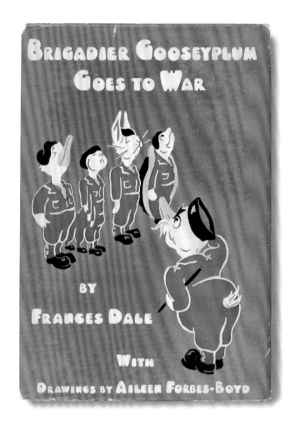

The Practical Cook

'For the moment, the days of easy meals are over. The uses of the tin-opener are restricted by the limited number of points available. There are few joints, fewer steaks, an irregular supply of fish, and only few things available in the cooked meat shops and confectioners. A number of the short cuts are closed to us, and it will be some time before they are all re-opened; therefore all cooking, everyday cooking, takes longer, and involves more work, eking out supplies.'

Fanny Cradock's introduction to her first cookery book, *The Practical Cook*, painted a sombre picture of the dietary pall which hung over the rationing-conscious British housewife in 1949. Her agent had written it off as a daft addition to an overpopulated market. Fanny instinctively dissented, promising that she would return to the novel trade if six publishers rejected it. In the event, the first, John Lehmann, took the bait, though in hindsight Fanny regarded *The Practical Cook* as 'a makeshift affair geared to dried eggs and general shortages'.

One of Fanny's earliest royalty statements.

For all the restrained language (barely an exclamation mark in sight) and sprinkling of rudimentary diagrams, there lurked a flamboyant entertainer of a cook, one counting the days before the full palate of flavours was achievable once more. In the meantime she promoted baked hedgehog (a wartime refuge) and offered some queasy advice:

DO remember that dirty, burnt-end-littered dripping is not useless. Place in a heat-proof container, cover with boiling water. When cold cut out the dripping, pour off the dirty water, scrape any remaining impurities from the underside of the dripping.

DON'T throw away stale sandwiches. Dip them in batter and fry. They're excellent.

DON'T throw cold tea away when using prunes or dried apricots. Soak the fruit in the tea, and cook in this; it makes a lovely syrup with sugar or golden syrup and brings out the flavour.

JOURNEYS TO ATLANTIS

The given author was Phyllis Cradock – for once she employed the name which appeared on her passport – but Fanny claimed more complicated attribution for her voyages to the lost continent of Atlantis. They were written 'through her, not by her. She being incapable of writing the superb prose or originating the lofty thoughts and philosophy they contain.' She even won some offbeat publicity for *Gateway to Remembrance* by refusing to accept royalties, claiming that the book had been dedicated to her by a priest who died 9 million years ago.

The sniggering scepticism would have been a lot louder if *Gateway to Remembrance* and *The Eternal Echo* had surfaced at the height of Fanny's fame, but they were received with indifference in 1949 and 1950. No one had then heard of Fanny Cradock or Phyllis Cradock; the only name which resonated gently was that of her novelist alter ego, Frances Dale.

Fanny found herself implicated in an apocalyptic double act with Aldous Huxley, whose novel *Ape and Essence* appeared while *Gateway to Remembrance* was in production. He predicted Satanic chaos after a Third World War; she chronicled the spiritual decadence which sent Atlantis hurtling towards self-construction. 'Both', according to publisher Andrew Dakers, 'sound a note of dreadful warning to a race either unaware of or indifferent to the doom that threatens it.'

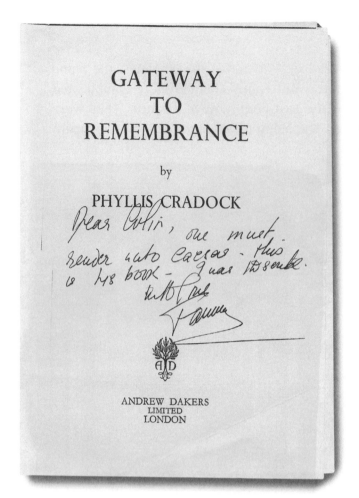

GATEWAY
TO
REMEMBRANCE

by

PHYLLIS CRADOCK

ANDREW DAKERS
LIMITED
LONDON

Credit where credit's due: Fanny's handwritten note on the proofs for *Gateway to Remembrance* reads, 'One must render unto Caesar – this is his book – I was the scribe.'

BON VOYAGE

As a travel writer Fanny Cradock insisted on covering every compass point, from patronising pre-departure tips – cancel the milk, bread and newspapers – to dreamy dissertations about the state of 'blissfully amoebic lethargy' which holidaymakers could aspire to on serene Continental beaches. In her book, food and travel were indivisibly linked, summed up by her contention that 'the eight wonders of the world can be eight mouldy old backyards as far as we are concerned if our tummies are rumbling'.

Bon Voyage, written in 1950, was both soberly informative and wildly discursive. In one breath Fanny was warning that 'flogging a car is a vice, upon which the wise frown most severely'; in the next she was throttling back to list hotel prices; and then she was tearing along in the judgmental fast lane: 'A man in a one-piece bathing suit looks absurd and conspicuous. He must wear bathing trunks, whatever his shape.'

Women were also under strict orders: 'There should be a rule about shorts for women. Never wear them if your hip measurement is more than thirty-eight, your waist more than twenty-eight and your thighs at the fattest part more than nine. If, however, you are slim, let yourselves rip.' Furthermore, 'You can discard your stockings once you have acquired a tan or if you use sun-tan cream, but do not parade a pair of bleached legs to the public eye. They look horrible.'

Luggage louts. 'Ignore the rather ostentatious way in which pedestrians swerve into the road to avoid the mounting mass. Gather together suitcases, bags, coats, open all the car doors, and the lid of the boot. Make perfectly sure that the car is quite clear of any ordinary day-to-day litter, take a deep breath, light a cigarette and begin.'

An English disease. 'There is nothing more shaming than the spectacle of four of one's nationals squabbling in a restaurant in foreign parts, with a

Home away from home: Fanny and Johnnie relaxing in Monte Carlo in 1957.

heap of notes and small coinage before them, catching in the butter, sliding under the plates and generally causing confusion. . . . The resulting post-mortem, if held in public, is at the best undignified and at the worst vulgar beyond belief. It provides for the remainder of the restaurant entertainment of a nature which adds little to the stature of English people abroad.'

THE STORY SO FAR: *SOMETHING'S BURNING*

Something's Burning the unique theatrical event became *Something's Burning* the life story so far in 1960. Mischievous good humour sprung from every page; reviewers who knew nothing of Fanny's darker side warmed to the kaleidoscopic snapshot.

> **'It was centuries since the desire to be ravaged by the monarch was the fulfilment of every woman's dream. He had made it so again.'**
>
> The Windsor Secret

This was about as good as it got for the Cradocks: Rolls-Royce in the garage, diplomas on the kitchen wall, and more television and journalistic work than they could handle. Fanny had even been given a final shot at unravelling the mysteries of motherhood. She had driven off one son, Peter, but been reunited with the other, Christopher. The bonus was a charmer of a grandson, Julian, four when the book was published, around whom she shaped her elaborate visions of the future.

'The Autobiography of Two Cooks', as *Something's Burning* was sub-titled, was, inevitably, the work of one credited author: even the brisk account of Johnnie's formative years was transposed by Fanny. She set about proving direct lineage to high-ranking French aristocracy at the time of the Norman Conquest, met with non-definitive success and wrote it anyway. One letter of inquiry to a distant relation brought a severe, stonewalling reply. Fanny promptly complained to an aunt who had been rather more cooperative: 'I regret exposing myself to a patronising snob. Madame writes as if I were an unsatisfactory parlour maid applying for a post and being found inadequate.'

The vitality of *Something's Burning* was in Fanny's entertaining portraits of her grandmother, mother and father, and her anecdotal insights into life at home, abroad and on location. The half-invented dialogue was of Booker Prize quality by comparison with the laughably ponderous exchanges which

The Lormes' Stirrup Cup

'We use it at our traditional Christmas Party when the drive is spattered with glowing braziers, all is lit by old Victorian street lamps and the entrance is dressed overall with bay, laurel and scarlet ribbons. Guests on arrival are served with this heartening beverage while being serenaded by Carol Singers carrying swinging lanterns. A lit Christmas tree stands in the central drive bed and welcoming candles are set in all the front windows of our Queen Anne house. We adore this.'

Ingredients

2 bottles white rum from Jamaica

2 bottles brandy

4pt water

4 lemons

4 oranges

1 flat teaspoon mixed spices

3 torn bay leaves

4½oz green tea (obtainable still from Mr Laity, The Tea Shop, St Ives, Cornwall, or substitute the best only Orange Pekoe tea)

¾lb unrefined (beige) loaf sugar (substitute soft, brown dark pieces sugar)

1 small stick cinnamon

1 split vanilla pod

generous eggspoon of nutmeg from the nut

Method

Make, rest for 30 minutes, then strain the tea. Sweeten to taste. Add cinnamon, nutmeg and leave until quite cold. Then place in a very thick pan to heat to, but not reach, boiling point. At the moment of service rub loaf sugar pieces on oranges and lemons until these crumble and turn yellow/orange. Do this into a large silver punch bowl or make into two half batches in smaller punch bowls. Strain in the juice of both citrus fruits. Heat rum and brandy together *without* boiling. Set alight to mixture, ladle up and down high to cause spirits to burn well for one minute. Douse flames with very hot infused tea, stir and serve into heated glass or silver goblets. If the former add a silver spoon to each glass to avoid any risk of cracking.

The Lormes of Castle Rising, 1975

populated her later, snob-ridden fiction. Fanny's bumpiest romantic interludes were either bypassed or shrugged off in cryptic asides, but she took a stoic's pleasure in recalling the poverty-line grafting of her early adult years. The good times were described with coy smugness and when Fanny catalogued the dishes and vintages of the Cradocks' most memorable feasts she became plain indulgent.

After reading *Something's Burning*, the *Daily Mirror*'s Alan Fairclough was moved through secondhand familiarity to describe Fanny as 'one of the goofiest, zaniest, fizziest, nicest characters I've ever met'. The professional bandwagon rolled on happily enough, but the book's fantasy sequences, set in the Cradocks' recently acquired Garden of Eden in Blackheath, were soon ridiculed by reality. Christopher's marriage disintegrated and Julian was whisked away by his mother to start a new life in Australia.

ELIZA DOOLITTLE THROWS A COCKNEY PARTY

Shooters Hill Road had never seen anything quite like it. The *Pathe Pictorial* cameras rolled as Fanny and Johnnie Cradock hosted a cockney-themed party to celebrate the publication of their autobiography *Something's Burning*.

It was a grand night for star-gazing: the Duke of Bedford, actor Ronald Shiner, comedian Jimmy Hanley, husband-and-wife TV celebrities Bernard Braden and Barbara Kelly, and singer Cy Grant all descended on Chez Cradock. Actress Eva Bartok added a touch of Hollywood glamour and glitter, Fanny reinvented herself as Eliza Doolittle and Johnnie donned a cloth cap. *Daily Mirror* columnist Noel Whitcomb, posing as Madame Clara, commandeered the cat shed to tell guests' fortunes, while thirteen-year-old Johnny Harper (the Cradocks' page/protégé) found that there were few takers for winkles. The kitchen became a fish and chip shop, and the downstairs study was 'Cradock Café, a good pull-in for a blow-out'. The last guest staggered away at five o'clock the following morning.

At home with the Cradocks: Fanny, as Eliza Doolittle, and wide boy Johnnie set the standard in their cockney-themed launch for their autobiography, *Something's Burning*, in 1960. *(British Pathe/ITN Source)*

Fanny reflected happily: 'Many children gathered outside the house to see the guests arrive, but they cheered loudest of all when a barrow-load of ice cream was headed their way. It was delightful to see the way they disposed of it.' A couple of months later she and Johnnie were guests of honour at the Roxy Cinema in Blackheath for the first showing of Pathe's short from the book launch.

DEADLINE FIRST, SURGERY LATER

It was bad enough for Fanny to discover, just before Christmas 1966, that she was suffering from bowel cancer. Her added anxiety was that even if she beat the disease the stigma would destroy her career. Intense media interest was deflected with her surgeon's evasive explanation that the 'operation was for the removal of a sinus lying over the base of the spine'.

As spooked as Fanny could be by illness, she was also a trooper by nature. Alison Leach, recalls: 'She was very brave about it. I remember a few hours before she was going into hospital she finished an article for the *Telegraph*, and there was a discreet acknowledgement Evelyn Garrett made when that column was published, saying that she was a true professional. She was about to go into hospital for an operation and she'd met her deadline first. Which pleased Fanny very much, of course.'

The press suspected that the illness was more serious – Fanny said, with unintended humour, 'It's disgustingly unattractive to have lumps dug out of one's behind and I hoped to keep it a secret' – but the full facts were not known until later. Fanny convalesced at one of their favourite hotels, the Gazelle d'Or in Taroudant, behind the Atlas mountains of Morocco. Fanny reminisced in the third person: 'When she was ready each morning her great bearded Arab reappeared, picked her up and carried her to the chaise longue in the garden where she spent the first few days.'

'There is nothing more shaming than the spectacle of four of one's nationals squabbling in a restaurant in foreign parts, with a heap of notes and small coinage before them, catching in the butter, sliding under the plates and generally causing confusion.'

Bon Voyage

COOKING THE BOOKS

Today's buyer of cookery books is seduced by razor-sharp colour images of dishes hailing from every corner of the globe. The accompanying words are almost incidental. The publishing world which Fanny Cradock entered in the late forties was relentlessly monochrome, picture-free and parochial. The onus was on the aspiring cook to transform the bland instructions of the recipe into radiant reality.

Fanny's forty-plus cookery books were snapped up in impressive numbers – the Bon Viveur *Daily Telegraph Cook's Book* outsold John Lennon's *In His Own Write* as it soared to the top of the best-sellers' chart in 1964 – but the exotica stemmed solely from the gastronomic travelogue. Fanny and Johnnie fed and foraged in thousands of cafés, bistros and restaurants all over Western Europe. They took copious notes, recycled recipes (the best, in Fanny's book, were those with blue-blooded antecedents) and reported their findings to Bon Viveur acolytes for whom even a day-trip to Calais would have seemed cavalier.

Casual analysts of Fanny's contribution to the catering landscape have decided, without much evidence, that she was élitist; that she pandered exclusively to the well-off dinner-party set, the ones who could sub-contract

the time-consuming bits to paid helpers. Fanny's deep-set snobbery and obsessive regard for dinner table etiquette helped to feed the cynics, but she had always been and would always be thrifty by nature. She abhorred the waste of good food (believing that plates should be cleared of lesser-quality fare out of respect for the hostess), and preached the merits of batch cooking.

Fanny also demonstrated that she could move with the times. She produced the humble *Cooking With Can and Pack* in 1962, pleaded for greater imagination in the preparation of vegetables in *Cabbages and Things*, and catered for the growing live-alone generation with dishes which could be prepared in no more than fifteen minutes.

Top of the charts: Bon Viveur head the best-sellers in 1964.

It was not until Purnell approached her and Johnnie to produce an ambitious part-work in 1970 that their food was shown, in print form anyway, in glorious technicolour. The publishers plunged £250,000 into promoting the *Fanny and Johnnie Cradock Cookery Programme*, but sales dwindled so badly that they pulled the plug after eighty of the scheduled ninety-six weeks. In her initial burst of pioneering enthusiasm Fanny had likened it to having a set of 'Culinary Keys', each a gateway to culinary success. She wrote: 'We shall explode old fallacies and share culinary facts so that, once and for all, you can be as scornful as we are about such ridiculous fables as needing a light hand or your pastry will never succeed.'

Inspired by their own collection of gastronomic awards, Fanny and Johnnie created the Golden Diploma of Home Cookery (Le Diplôme d'Or) to 'bestow upon every one of our subscriber/members who is able to produce an endorsement by their family and/or friends that they have eaten and enjoyed at least one dish (this must be named) from each successive part'. They also offered (on a commission basis, of course) cut-price equipment in each issue. An 'original Roman pot', reduced from £3 19s 6d to £2 19s 6d, set the ball rolling in issue one.

Fanny ensured that the programme was eclectic and inclusive. She championed home produce, devoted issues to Italian, Chinese and Indian food, and showed her gift for presentation in a wedding-day special. There was even a return to her DIY roots in the home-made 'receiving arch', constructed from 'rustic poles, cut from saplings in our own spinney'.

Books :

1. **Daily Telegraph Cook Book,** by Fanny Cradock (Daily Telegraph 15s.). Advice from a noted expert (3)

2. **The Shell & B.P. Guide to Great Britain** (Ebury Press 30s.). Tour in prose and pictures (2)

3. **This Rough Magic,** by Mary Stewart (Hodder & Stoughton 18s.). Violence and mystery in Corfu (1)

4. **A Song of Sixpence,** by A. J. Cronin (Heinemann 21s.). Growing up in a Scottish town (4)

5. **The Lonely Sea and the Sky,** by Francis Chichester (Hodder & Stoughton 30s.). The Atlantic sailor's life-story (5)

6. **Louis XIV,** by Vincent Cronin (Collins 36s.). Biography of France's Sun King (6)

7. **In His Own Write,** by John Lennon (Cape 9s. 6d.). Surrealist humour (plus drawings) by a Beatle (7)

8. **Loud Halo,** by Lilian Beckwith (Hutchinsons 21s.). More about life in the Hebrides (—)

9. **Up the Line to Death,** selected by Brian Gardner (Methuen 18s.). World War I poetry (9)

10. **Wild Eden,** by June Kay (Hutchinsons 25s.). Journeying among Africa's fascinating wild life (—)

(*By arrangement with* Smith's Trade News. *Last week's positions in brackets.*)

Flower POWER ———————

- Next time you forget to feed the goldfish, inter them, throw away the water and give the bowl over to flowers.

- Do burn the stems of poppies before arranging them. This seals in the sap and doubles their life.

- Do turn violets head down in water at night. They drink through their faces.

- Do give hothouse flowers luke-warm water to drink and not icy-cold.

- Water begonias upside down so that the other end will produce foliage sooner.

- Do revive tired flowers by dropping a copper coin or half an aspirin into the water.

- Do preserve the colours of autumn leaves by standing in glycerine. They will then last for months.

- Do remember nasturtiums, flowers and leaves make perfect summer (edible) garnishes.

THE SHERLOCK HOLMES COOKBOOK

The Japanese liked *The Sherlock Holmes Cookbook*'s farrago of fiction, fantasy and fact so much that Tokyo bookshops were still raking in the royalties for Fanny Cradock's literary estate five years after her death. Not so much a case of who done it, as who wrote it?

Mrs Hudson, housekeeper-provider for Holmes and Dr Watson, was the given author; Fanny was the medium between imaginary dinner plate and print; Agnes Bertha Marshall, Fanny's heroine of a real-life English cook, was spiritual adviser. (An intended book on her life, recipes and suspicious death, *The Great Marshall Mystery*, floundered for want of reliable archive material.) Fanny both 'borrowed from her writings and associated her in the most tenuous terms with Mrs Hudson'. She also drew from her own family recipes and turned the Cradock kitchen into a culinary laboratory. 'It has driven my little cookery team to the brink of Total Exhaustion, checking every single published recipe, since I will never, in any circumstances, depart from my husband's and my chosen slogan, "nothing published which has not been tested, tasted and found worthy of inclusion".'

Mrs Hudson's household hints were an education in themselves: she could sweeten rancid butter, banish flies from summer windows with paraffin, get the bowels moving with Fowler Lee's Black Treacle and draw an abscess with a parsnip.

FANNY LOSES THE PLOT, PART I

The lengthy gestation period for *The Lormes of Castle Rising*, Fanny's descent into the literary nether world, failed to convince her that abortion might be the most humane solution. She had churned out 25,000 words in

In exile: newly moved to County Cork, Fanny and Johnnie admire her first book in the Lormes saga while relaxing in their garden at Doneraile.

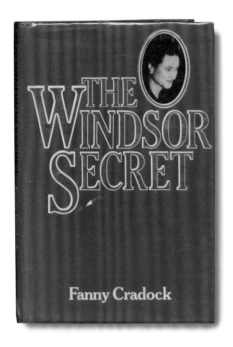

1966, and resumed brooding duties in 1972. She also found a fresh excuse to explore her own past and was so impressed by the sin count that she resolved to 'plagiarise certain aspects of my own family for certain Lorme characteristics'.

This was not just a story, Fanny decided; it was a money-spinning saga, one which, in blurb-speak, 'charts the rise, decline and ultimately the fall of a great family once powerful but in the end unable to survive the social and economic forces which transformed society in the twentieth century'. She was also convinced that the book, and its descendants, would be triumphantly adapted for television, so she and Johnnie left for tax-friendly Ireland in anticipation of a windfall.

There was no TV spin-off, but Fanny wrote on and on. They were the kind of books (Catherine Cookson meets Barbara Cartland) which few admitted to reading but still sold in numbers that kept publishers on side. The intention, on the part of both author and publishers, was that the resilient Anglo-Norman clan would be buried in the late eighties with *Castle Rising Closes the Circle*, the eleventh book in the series, but it never appeared.

W.H. Allen was presented with a manuscript more in need of transplant surgery than a nip and a tuck. The discrepancies were canyon-wide, and it was also pointed out to a disgruntled Fanny that – given the plot span of 1948 to 1953 – references to the Beatles and Princess Margaret's marriage to Lord Snowdon would look anomalous.

FANNY LOSES THE PLOT, PART II

For sheer bad taste and professional misjudgment nothing could compete with *The Windsor Secret*, Fanny's factional flambé of a final novel. She had been puffing it cryptically for years – the laws of libel and personal intrusion kept the manuscript in the vaults of W.H. Allen until the Duchess of Windsor died – and rejoiced in the ripple of controversy it set off when published in 1986.

The story is predicated on the risible fiction that the duchess becomes pregnant with the duke's child, and proceeds with a multi-national cover-up operation as the boy is adopted and brought up in Australia. Fanny embroidered the fiction with trivial insights which she had gleaned from genuine interviews with the exiled couple in the 1950s. The unpalatable cocktail of truth, half-truth and plain invention seemed to summarise Fanny's own life, and she compounded the felony with dialogue that was too dire to be digested without a smirk.

She writes of the Duke of Windsor, in his brief spell as king: 'It was centuries since the desire to be ravaged by the monarch was the fulfilment of every woman's dream. He had made it so again.' The son talks like a teenaged automaton. When he sees the table on which Edward VIII signed the instrument of abdication he laments to his equally stilted chum: 'What a shattering reminder of a world well lost for love.' Fanny's powers of description have also vanished: 'Now he and his old friend, the Diana Kincale who was to adopt the unborn baby, sat beside the lake on the outskirts of Geneva under the dominating plume of water which spurted incessantly, a jet whose sole purpose was to spout as futilely as the leaning Tower of Pisa leaned, looking like the sugar work of some demented pastry cook.'

Chicken Pish-Pash

A speciality of Fanny's mother which sent Johnnie back 'not for seconds but for fives'

Ingredients

1 leg and thigh chicken portion
4oz (100g) rice
¾pt (450ml) milk
1 large peeled onion
salt
pepper

Method

Divide the chicken portion into four. Sprinkle a little of the raw rice over base of a small, lidded casserole. Slice onion finely and scatter about a quarter over the rice. Lay in one piece of chicken, season with salt and pepper and repeat until all dry ingredients are used. Pour on the milk and if this does not fully cover casserole's contents, then add a little more until it does. Cover with lid or piece of Alcan Foil and bake in the oven at Gas Mark 4 (350°F, 180°C), middle shelf for 30 minutes. Check it and continue to cook if rice has not just become moist, but with surplus fluid absorbed. Taste and if not fully cooked to *al dente*, continue for another 15 minutes.

A Lifetime in the Kitchen, vol. I, 1985

FANNY LOSES THE PLOT, PART III

The title, *Paradise Regained*, was unwisely familiar. The author – Fanny couldn't decide between Peter Christopher or Christopher Peters – was a too-obvious sop to her sons. She set the scene, took stock and considered her options for a book which, unsurprisingly, never saw the light of day.

COMMENT
There are half a dozen ways the story can go from here. All are from my standpoint governed by whether there is a TV serial or soap opera in it. If it has to be written as a novel first in order to sell it for what I want, then so be it. I will submit a series of alternative novel endings, just stipulating that the strongest romance element must be American and for this purpose I have created Gary with his old plantation house, Southern background and family history.

As I see it, Jamie manages to get wind of the Elixir, he confides in Danny and the pair plan to obtain the formula. A character, ostensibly Jamie's friend, is brought to the island and he eventually finds out two things for them. The rejuvenation is achieved from an injection of what they call the Elixir based on an extract of a hitherto unknown seaweed. All is elaborately guarded in an underground cavern on what was originally called Ile de Rien. Danny finds a professional to steal the formula only to learn that a supply of the actual fluid is kept in small bomb-like capsules in underground refrigeration. Danny then obtains a suitable oldie on which to experiment, finds the experiment works and proceeds to sell it to a Russian doctor for a huge sum. At this point British Intelligence picks up the trail and after some really tough cloak and dagger stuff the Russian is shot dead and the remaining little bombs of the Elixir are recovered by British Intelligence.

Totally disbelieving its properties, but wide awake to the concomitant dangers if it is a rejuvenation, a series of photographs are shown to the small quiet man who is the only contact in this drama. They are of Mamie, who has regained her figure and is becoming younger every day. The small quiet man asks point blank if the Guardians and Otto will agree to injecting an oldie of their choice. After some debating this is agreed upon and the results are so staggering that all doubt is stilled and this is only one of a dozen ways in which the series could be extended.

Fanny: The Legacy

LIFE AFTER JOHNNIE

The media apathy which marked Johnnie Cradock's death in 1987 – barely a paragraph of recognition – told its own silent story. Fanny, on the other hand, felt his loss acutely, retreating into an ever more irascible shell as she waited impatiently for her own call from the grim reaper.

She was also an old woman in pain. In 1985, aged seventy-six, she wrote in a letter to friends Tony and Yvonne Norris: 'We are plunged into a hideous slough of despond.' She had just learned that a failed and expensive hip operation would have to be repeated on the NHS. 'The very thought of the lack of privacy, filthy food and curious people drowns me in misery,' she said.

Three years later, when she gave her last full-scale interview to the royal biographer Douglas Keay for *Woman's Own*, she was walking with a stick which doubled as a deterrent to public harassers. Keay, who had remained on friendly terms after working with Fanny on *Late Extra* in 1960, cited the widely held belief that she had inflicted forty-eight years of misery on

Acting the part:
Johnnie in relaxed
mood with brandy
and cigar. *(Behn)*

Johnnie. 'But it was all an act, darling,' she said, her eyes misting over. 'We used to practise beforehand. We were devoted to each other. And now that he's gone, I don't want to live. I walk with memories and they're so painful. Everybody thinks I ran Johnnie. But it's just not true. I did every single thing I wanted to do, but when it came to the really major things Johnnie put his foot down. Otherwise I wouldn't have loved him. We had terrible, flaming rows and then we'd go to bed and that was the lovely part.'

She said she was 'keeping my covenant with the Almighty. I've had my cake and I've eaten it. And I mustn't grumble.' She was convinced that Johnnie's and her celestial paths would cross again. 'But I do talk to Johnnie every night,' she admitted. 'I have one particular photograph of him, in uniform, in an old leather frame. And one day I put on his glasses, because they're stronger than mine, and I looked at the photograph and it was alive. So now I look at it every morning and it gets me going for the day.'

Fanny came as close as she ever had to acknowledging that her growl first, think later brand of snob-tinged honesty had claimed too many casualties. 'I think I should have been more dignified and I would have more friends now if I had been more restrained,' she told Douglas Keay.

FANNY AND FAMOUS FRIENDS

The adjective irascible attached itself indelibly to Fanny Cradock, and the same could certainly be said of Gilbert Harding. Their friendship began, appropriately, with a rip-roaring row in a restaurant in the early fifties, but as their professional paths crossed weekly in the Paris Cinema recording studios – Gilbert's *Twenty Questions* preceded Fanny's *The Name's the Same*

A meeting of minds: Fanny and Johnnie in animated conversation with their friend and cantankerous TV personality, Gilbert Harding. *(Dorchester Hotel Photographic Service)*

– reconciliation was imminent. Fanny turned her back on Gilbert. He responded: 'Madam, I am weary of your back view. Will you not turn around and let me say that I am sorry?'

They clashed in another restaurant. 'I have been told,' Fanny wrote, 'that once we had warmed up, service ceased for three-quarters of an hour while we rampaged.' But the skirmishes coexisted with periods of lively truce, and they became firm friends. The tempers ran parallel, but the counter to Fanny's unshakable self-confidence was Gilbert's self-loathing, a characteristic which surfaced all too painfully on *Face to Face* with John Freeman.

When Gilbert Harding died in 1960, Fanny and Johnnie organised a book of reminiscences from friends. More than one described him as the unhappiest person they had ever met. To Fanny he was a 'twentieth century Johnson who lacked a Boswell' and a 'fat man with a thin man's temperament'. She also recalled the polarised mood swings: 'Take the occasion when Harding Benevolent turned in a flash to Harding Snarling, simply because Johnnie and I broke up a drinking session to go dancing together. "Go and be damned to you," roared Gilbert, his face purple with fury, "prancing like frenzied aborigines in a jungle clearing! Faugh!"'

The home hostess: Fanny helps herself at a party at the Dower House in Watford. (© 2001 Topham Picturepoint)

Dining in style: the Cradocks' Blackheath kitchen awaits the guests for a typical sixties dinner party.

Fanny also enjoyed the company of celebrities from varying backgrounds, and stored away scurrilous personal snippets (real and imagined). Her long-time personal assistant Alison Leach observed: 'It was just as well she was never offered a gossip column – she'd have ended up in prison.' Comedian Alfred Marks (Fanny warmed to Jewish humour), game show host Hughie Green, TV personalities and husband and wife team Bernard Braden and Barbara Kelly, and *Just a Minute* quizmaster Nicholas Parsons were all on the approved list. She entertained Robert Carrier, one of the new generation

Cold Lemon Soufflé

'This was created for us by the late Gilbert Harding'

Ingredients

5 eggs and 4 extra separated egg yolks
½ pt double cream
the strained juice of 3 fairly large lemons

the carefully grated zest of 1½ lemons
1 rounded tablespoon of powdered gelatine
7oz sifted icing sugar

Method

Stir gelatine into lemon juice in a small pan over a low heat until clear and slightly syrupy. Whip eggs, extra yolks, lemon zest and sugar together until very risen and foamy. We always use the large bowl of an electric mixer for this and at one stage it almost reaches the top. With beaters still at full speed, pour on gelatine in a fine, thin stream and do not be startled that mixture then subsides considerably. Pour on double cream, still whipping and only switch off when beaters show streaks of basin base through as mixture thickens. Then turn into a 6in diameter soufflé mould. When set, wrap securely in double-duty foil, label and freeze. Just thaw for service. Alternatively the mixture – which is extremely rich – may be poured into little dariole or madeleine moulds to serve as individual portions.

Fanny and Johnnie Cradock's Freezer Book, 1978

of TV cooks, at Blackheath, and readily forgave the actor Douglas Fairbanks Jnr for being American. Fanny considered his wife Mary Lee to be a hostess *par excellence* (it helped that the Queen and Prince Philip had dined chez Fairbanks). The Conservative MP John Gummer was a more heavyweight addition to the Cradock circle of friends. Their move to Watford in 1968 brought them into closer contact with romantic novelist Barbara Cartland, and one of the sunnier aspects of their unhappy stay in Guernsey was a burgeoning friendship with another Channel Islands resident, the TV documentary maker Alan Whicker.

Fanny also used her contacts to engineer the occasional journalistic coup. She was given exclusive access to the Duke and Duchess of Windsor when she worked for the *Daily Mail* in the mid-fifties and also featured them in a short 'Dining with the Famous' series for the *Sunday Express* in 1959 (she neglected to repeat an earlier claim that the duke had approached her, drunkenly, at an inter-war party, and slurred, 'You've got beautiful eyes. . .').

The duchess nominated a restaurant 'used by truck drivers' as one of her favourite Parisian eateries, adding: 'I can assure you I'm not at all a three-star Duchess.' Fanny reported: 'She has the figure and the effortless swiftness of a pony-tailed teenager.' Next stop the writer Somerset Maugham, 'the man with a face like the top of an ivory totem pole'. And finally the Fairbanks family. 'He would eat stewed knitting,' said Mary Lee of her husband.

A DIGNIFIED END

The Fanny Cradock found by Phil Bradford when he called at her nondescript Chichester flat in 1991 was dirty, disorientated and desperate. A batch of pills on the table beside her left him in no doubt that she was contemplating suicide. Johnnie's death in 1987 had, as friends predicted it would, left Fanny bereft and rudderless. She sank into an ocean of self-pity and bitterness, unfailingly rude and irrational in her rare dealings with the outside world.

Phil sought power of attorney and immediately arranged to have Fanny admitted to the Ersham House nursing home in Hailsham, East Sussex, close to where he and Terry Hibbert lived. She reacquired dignity, if not equanimity, passed on the odd culinary tip to the kitchen staff, and died of a stroke on 27 December 1994. A teddy bear which Johnnie had given her just before he died was perched on her bedside table. A week later, on a bitter, depressingly damp day, she was cremated in

Rest in peace: A simple memorial plaque and rose bush mark Fanny and Johnnie's resting place in Bed 42 at Eastbourne Cemetery.

Eastbourne, her ashes scattered next to Johnnie's. Her friend Tenniel Evans, a lay preacher, conducted both her and Johnnie's funeral services and was struck by the contrast. 'The difference was quite marked,' he remembered. 'Because his was rather a sweet funeral, quite beautiful. Hers, one felt, was jagged.'

A household name and instantly recognisable face for the last forty years of her life, Fanny was now shunned. There were fewer than twenty mourners – Fanny's granddaughter Karen Chapman joked that it was the first time she had met her – and the only media interest was from Meridian Television. Fanny's daughter-in-law Jane Chapman noted with disgust that Cradock had been spelt with two 'd's on the cemetery's bookings list for the day – 'Fanny would have turned in her grave' – and borrowed a pen to repair the damage.

> 'We got in a bunch of footage of international TV chefs and some offbeat movie clips. There was a final choice between some Godzilla-style monster and Fanny. In the end, Fanny just bowled us over.'
>
> *Rubin Postaer Advertising Agency*

Even in her last will and testament Fanny chose the unconventional approach. She left £50,000 to Phil Bradford and Terry Hibbert, due reward for their devotion and loyalty in this last, flawed chapter of her life, and the rest, £150,000, to the charity Help a Child to See. The furs had been promised to various friends, but they too passed to Phil Bradford.

FANNY: THE VERDICT

The half-truths and errors which appeared in every obituary of Fanny Cradock were unfailingly traced to source. She exaggerated her Frenchness, understated her spouses and regarded any mention of the word age as gross impertinence.

The Daily Telegraph's obituary on 29 December 1994, later included in a compendium of rogues' retrospectives, said: 'It was easy to make fun of Fanny Cradock and the much-put-upon Johnnie . . . but she did much to awaken British regard for cooking after the war and to improve the standards of commercial catering.' Paul Levy, the food and wine critic, pulled no punches in the *Independent*, describing her as 'preposterous'. He went further in the *Oxford Dictionary of National Biography*, where his entry on Philip Harben read: 'Harben was not a fraud, like Fanny Cradock.'

Open all hours: Fanny cuts the ribbon in Amersham, Buckinghamshire. *(Robert Glover Gallery)*

The late John Diamond, who was married to domestic goddess Nigella Lawson, also made the comparison between Harben and Fanny in *The Times*, but piled on less vitriol. 'We watched the Cradocks because they were glamorous. They dressed in velvet frock and dinner jacket, and showed us plebs the tasty little treats that the other half ate. If Harben was cooking for the family table, then Fanny was catering for small ambassadorial dinners where there was never any excuse for running out of canapés before the gong sounded for the first course. Like a generation of TV cooks, she assumed that people had far more time and were willing to put much more effort into their cooking than was generally the case.' Her 'gentle snobbery', Diamond reckoned, appealed to the re-enfranchised dinner party socialites.

Victor Lewis-Smith, the *Evening Standard*'s TV critic, responded to the reshowing of Fanny's Christmas-themed series for the BBC by saying: 'I learned more useful information from her in each of those 15-minute programmes than from a dozen self-obsessed Jamie Oliver shows.'

FANNY: THE CHEFS' IMPRESSION

Fanny Cradock's death brought the inevitable polite platitudes from the next generation of TV chefs. To Keith Floyd she was 'compulsive. She changed the whole nation's cooking attitudes.' To Antony Worrall Thompson, she 'was like a Godfather figure, frightening and strict. But she was really as soft as butter when you got to know her.' They were persuaded to elaborate for TV nostalgia trips, the BBC's *The Way We Cooked* and Channel 5's *TV Makeovers That Changed The World*.

THE WAY WE COOKED, BBC, 2002 ———————————————

■ DELIA SMITH. 'Nobody could get up and switch that television off when Fanny Cradock was on. You were just mesmerised. The way she was cross with the people who worked for her was very, very funny. I think I did learn things from watching Fanny Cradock.'

■ MICHAEL BARRY. 'I think Fanny worked very well on television in the same way that *Two Fat Ladies* did. Wonderfully eccentric, hugely opinionated and really quite talented.'

■ CLARISSA DICKSON WRIGHT. 'It's quite clear that she could cook.'

■ RICK STEIN. 'She had this very haughty presentation. And you just think, why would anybody watch this stuff? What is it in our psyche that we need to be bullied by bossy women like Fanny Cradock?'

■ BRIAN TURNER. 'I was a great fan of Fanny Cradock. Techniques in kitchens and techniques in recording were so different from today that she was climbing uphill all the time. I think she was a great communicator. I think her reputation should be bigger.'

TV MAKEOVERS THAT CHANGED THE WORLD, FIVE, 2005 ——————————

■ ANTONY WORRALL THOMPSON. 'Fanny put a bit of colour back in our lives after the very dour times of the war and rationing, when food was definitely something you lived on rather than to be enjoyed. However, you'd have to have a cast of thousands at home to produce some of her dishes.'

■ LOYD GROSSMAN. 'She was the middle-class omni-competent *über* housewife par excellence.'

TV CHEFS: THE NEXT GENERATION

As the swinging sixties gave way to the inflationary seventies, Fanny Cradock was losing her grip on the nation. For fifteen years she had held sway on both sides of the box and it took a brash London-born New Zealander to show that there were new ways to sell an omelette.

Fanny Cradock had always been a uniquely British phenomenon, known and respected by the French establishment but never marketable in Calais, Cannes or Carcassonne. She was forced to watch with understandable envy as Graham Kerr, the Galloping Gourmet, charmed his way round the world and banked his first million. America, which had never granted Fanny an entrée, welcomed him with open arms.

Johnnie Cradock's surreptitious sips on set gave way to Kerr's unashamed quick slurps. He drank a bit, tossed the rest in the pot and gave the impression that he was cooking on the hoof, improvising like a free-form jazz musician. In 1957 Fanny had told a stage crowd in Nottingham: 'Do not be afraid to slosh around in the kitchen – unless you are making something very delicate, of course.' She said it but it was hard to be convinced that she meant it. Kerr carried the philosophy through and for three years (before he and his business-minded wife set out on a world cruise and found religion) his easy manner and *laissez-faire* teaching method enticed a new generation of cooks. There was also the first hint of sex in the kitchen: Kerr would commandeer a

'She had this very haughty presentation. And you just think, why would anybody watch this stuff? What is it in our psyche that we need to be bullied by bossy women like Fanny Cradock?'

Rick Stein

Captured by pencil: Fanny was one of almost a thousand TV personalities caricatured by the photographer Cecil Beaton in the sixties and seventies. (© *National Portrait Gallery*)

member of the studio audience, preferably the prettiest, to share in the fruits of his labour.

Viewers would have to wait another ten years for Keith Floyd, a more dissolute, decadent version of Kerr, to pick up the wine glass. By then Delia Smith was soberly entrenched, proving that as long as television offers something seemingly new it can take a hysterical leap forward or step back in time. The Delia who addressed the TV camera with diffident unease in 1973 knew that she could not perform, so she just imparted sensible advice. People watched in their millions, her books sold in their millions and her popularity barely waned in thirty years as Fanny's successor as the queen of cuisine. She was pretension-free, addressed the nuts and bolts of cooking as no one had before, and showed the genius of simplicity.

The *Two Fat Ladies*, Jennifer Paterson and Clarissa Dickson Wright, brought an eccentric maturity to the genre in 1996, but there was no true rival to Fanny or Delia on the man-in-the-street recognition meter until Jamie Oliver emerged in 1999. In the same way that Nigel Kennedy had sold classical violin to a mass audience, the lad-cook introduced street cred to the kitchen. Oliver told the Cheltenham Literary Festival in 2004 that the social conscience of *Jamie's Dinners* was Fanny-inspired. 'I wanted to write a book that would be helpful to the public, kind of like a modern-day Fanny Cradock. I know that's a hard act to follow.' His interviewer at the festival, food writer Matthew Fort, joked: 'You don't look like Fanny Cradock for a start.' Oliver retorted: 'Well, you should see me in a dress mate.'

Nigella Lawson inadvertently brought sex back on to the menu when her programmes were interpreted as 'gastroporn' in 2002, and Gordon Ramsay has made a foul-mouthed fortune out of the fiercest TV cook temper since Fanny Cradock. In 2006 the Scot signed a four-year deal with Channel 4 reputedly worth £8.5 million, and earlier this year he launched a 'Find me a Fanny' competition to identify a modern-day Fanny Cradock.

Doughnuts (like Fanny's)

Ingredients

8oz flour
½ level teaspoon mixed spice
1½oz butter
3oz castor sugar
2 very slightly rounded teaspoons baking
    powder

1 egg
a little milk
hot lard in a deep frier for frying
extra castor sugar for turning
chosen jam – ideally raspberry

Method

Sift flour, baking powder and mixed spice together in a roomy bowl. Rub in the butter until it is extremely finely grained. Dredge in the castor sugar and work with your fingers until well blended. Make a well in centre, beat up egg, pour into well and add a very little milk. Then work up with a small table knife, adding milk very sparingly to make a dough of the same consistency as pastry paste ready for rolling. Then roll into 2oz balls, make a hole in the centre of each with a very clean finger, being careful not to go right through base. Drop chosen jam into made cavity with handle of teaspoon. Work dough over until jam is completely covered. Re-shape a little more on the table between your hands held vertically and drop into deep frier. The temperature of the lard is all important. If it is at peak heat as for second frying of good chips, the insides will still be raw by the time the outsides are a rich golden brown. If the lard is too cool, the doughnuts will be soggy. Test with a strip of raw peeled potato. If, when you drop this in, the bubbles are very sluggish, increase heat and test again with a fresh piece. If the bubbles seethe fiercely it will be too hot. When doughnuts are brown and swollen, drop each one into a bowl of castor sugar.

Fanny and Johnnie Cradock Cookery Programme, 1970

OMELETTE PANTOMIME

When Delia Smith began her apprenticeship at the trendy West End restaurant, The Singing Chef, in 1962, she discovered first-hand that Fanny Cradock could be tempestuous . . . and occasionally tamed.

Chef Leo Evans told Delia's biographer, Alison Bowyer, that Fanny was a 'poseur par excellence':

> I had several run-ins with her but she wasn't too tricky after I had one spat with her. She had been on television a couple of nights before, really selling silver-plated copper omelette pans. We got talking and she said, 'You can't make omelettes decently without the right sort of pan, it's got to be silver-plated copper.' I told her that if you know how to make an omelette you can make one in a biscuit-tin lid. She said, 'Oh no you can't', and I said, 'Oh yes you can' – It was like a pantomime.
>
> Anyway, I went away and cooked her an omelette in a biscuit-tin lid and we had no more trouble from Fanny Cradock after that.

Fanny also played the dissenting diner at Raymond Blanc's Quat' Saisons restaurant in Oxford after discovering that she could not pay by American Express. 'She's one of the three persons that I've thrown out,' he said. 'She was so unpleasant, she had so little grace, she was demanding. She started to insult me, "You don't know what you're doing you people, I know better." So I said I'm sorry you better go now.'

FANNY 1, GODZILLA 0

America largely ignored Fanny Cradock while she was alive and would doubtless have maintained its distance if her snobbish contempt for its people and practices had been widely aired. Americans finally learned what they had been missing in 2001.

A Californian advertising agency was chasing after arresting material to feature in a commercial for the new Honda Acura RSX. 'We were looking for a scary image,' a spokesperson for the agency explained. 'We got in a bunch of footage of international TV chefs and some offbeat movie clips. There was a final choice between some Godzilla-style monster and Fanny. In the end, Fanny just bowled us over.'

Celebrity SNIPING

- *DUCHESS OF YORK* 'She's just a trollop.'

- *MARGARET THATCHER* 'She doesn't only wear cheap shoes, she wears cheap clothes as well.'

- *EAMONN ANDREWS* 'He is the eternal blundering amateur.'

- *GLORIA HUNNIFORD* 'She looks like one of those Barbie dolls.'

- *LES DAWSON* 'He's an awful lump of lard who pulls faces.'

- *CILLA BLACK* 'I hate that quack-quack singing of hers.'

- *ANITA DOBSON AND LESLIE GRANTHAM (in EastEnders)* 'There's something ghastly about her and that Dirty Den. He looks as though he needs a bath. There's something about him that doesn't smell right.'

- *TV COMEDIANS* 'The lot of them are a dead bore. The great unwashed may love them but I don't. These people represent vulgarism.'

  NEWS OF THE WORLD, 1987

- *Readers were invited to have their say about Fanny the following week. One wrote that her 'face seems to be encased in Polyfilla'. Another described her as 'Liberace in drag'.*

Equally bowled over were viewers who wrote in to demand more exposure for the 'crazy, eccentric English lady'.

THE LEGEND LIVES ON

Fanny Cradock has remained a natural reference point for every TV cooking retrospective, picking up fresh devotees along the way. She was as much a part of the language as Delia Smith became in the eighties and nineties. The ridicule of mad-cap motorists – 'Who do you think you are, Stirling Moss?' – persisted long after Moss had hung up his crash helmet; and Fanny was honoured with similar longevity.

The theatre of her working life, coupled with her oddball existence away from the limelight, made Fanny a natural subject for dramatic appraisal. Brian Fillis and the late Julia Darling both produced plays which were well received in the provinces in 2002. Darling married music to comedy in *Doughnuts like Fanny's*, referencing Bill Tennant's memorable continuity link in the days of Scottish Television, though it was later renamed *The Life and Loves of a Kitchen Devil*. Fillis opted for a male lead in *Fear of Fanny*, but reverted to conventional casting when Julia Davis played the title role in his adaptation for BBC 4 in 2006.

She was very forceful and she could be very autocratic and domineering, but in private and with people she liked she could also be very human and gentle. She had a caring side.

Nicholas Parsons

Fanny was also the inspiration for Stephanie Theobald's 2001 novel *Sucking Shrimp*, in which the heroine finds a weekly fix of Fanny Cradock is her romantic release from a drab seaside upbringing.

LASTING IMPRESSIONS

As challenges for impressionists go, Fanny Cradock was an androgynous pushover. Female impersonators played her as low-register, loud and overbearing. The men just put on a frock. The subtler allusions may have caught the sizable blind spot in Fanny's sense of humour, but she loved the second-hand attention and the implication that true fame was rewarded with (preferably affectionate) parody.

Fear of Fanny: Alan French took on the leading role in Brian Fillis's stage play in 2001, later adapted for television.
(Courtesy of Neale Myers)

She gave Benny Hill high marks as outrageous Fanny to Bob Todd's permanently paralytic Johnnie. Morecambe and Wise weighed in, as did the Scottish impressionist Stanley Baxter, but no one made more of a career out of taking off Fanny Cradock than Betty Marsden. In the fifties she was Fanny Haddock in *Beyond My Ken*, evolving into the trendy columnist Daphne Whitethigh in *Round the Horne*. In 1968 the *Radio Times* summed up Fanny's attitude to the imitators: 'Her assistant once told a friend who asked if "poor Mrs Cradock was going to sue", "Mrs Cradock is trying to work out a way to pay Betty Marsden." '

First, with a few new wrinkles on cookery and a great many old wrinkles elsewhere . . . here is Daphne Whitethigh . . .

Top: A tasty role: Julia Davis as Fanny Cradock in the BBC's *Fear of Fanny*. (© BBC)

Centre: *The Life and Loves of a Kitchen Devil*: Sandra Hunt donned the pencilled eyebrows for the late Julia Darling's play about Fanny Cradock. (*Courtesy of Sandra Hunt/Doug Currie*)

Bottom: Fanny familiar: Betty Marsden caught the Cradock hauteur to perfection (*PA/Empics*)

Good news for all housewives: rhino is down in the shops this week and you can give hubby his favourite cut. My suggestion: best end of rhino. The difficulty, of course, is to know which is the best end. Rhinos know, but their cause is not ours. And the good buys are escalope of vole, water buffalo chestnuts and hippo in its shell. For those of you who fancy something a little more *exotique* in the way of poultry, why not try duck-billed platypus . . . flambé.

Round the Horne, 1967

A PERSONAL TRIBUTE: NICHOLAS PARSONS

'I felt huge rapport with her. We got on well from the moment we met, she liked me and there was great affection on both sides.

'She had a larger than life personality. She was very forceful and she could be very autocratic and domineering, but in private and with people she liked she could also be very human and gentle. She had a caring side.

'I was used to big personalities, but I know some found her intimidating. She was open and honest and some people found that difficult to cope with. She could be very rude, but she just had this natural desire to express her view.

'Under pressure her personality could become abrasive; a lot of it was down to adrenalin when she was performing. It appeared on TV that Johnnie was henpecked and under the thumb, but in private life she was very respectful towards him. Johnnie was an old-style English gentleman, utterly devoted to Fanny. She drew strength from Johnnie and drained him on occasions. After Johnnie died she psychologically retreated back into herself. She became her own worst enemy and alienated the people closest to her.

'She was a wonderful hostess who always showed interest in her guests. Her dishes were very unusual, very elaborate and very enjoyable. She had this deep love of and knowledge of food and she wanted to communicate it. Her one desire was to give pleasure with her food.

'She was highly talented and intelligent, but she was a complex type of personality. You have to know them to love them, accept all the peculiarities and see them for what they are. A distorted view of her, the grumpy person she became towards the end, has been presented in recent years. She deserves to be remembered for the things she achieved. She was the first of the cooking stars on TV. Unique.'

WHITE WITCH, BLACK WITCH?

Fanny Cradock found herself dumped in a rogues' gallery of murderers and psychopaths in 2002, named and shamed in Esther Rantzen's Top 10 of Worst Britons. The *Daily Mail* had asked celebrities to nominate their antithesis to the BBC's 100 Great Britons initiative and Esther found a home for dress designer Vivienne Westwood, along with Fanny, Harold Shipman, Henry VIII, Fred West, Rosemary West, Ian Brady, Myra Hindley, Oswald Mosley and the British Town Planner. By way of citation, Esther wrote of Fanny: 'I worked with her, and in a notoriously bad-tempered profession, her rages were legendary. And she created the cult of the TV chef.'

The Esther Rantzen who penned an appreciation of Fanny for the *Daily Express* a week after her death was a more sympathetic creature. There was no forgiveness for her ritual dismembering of housewife Gwen Troake's self-esteem on *The Big Time* in 1976, but a slightly guilty admiration shone through:

> But I remain a Fanny fan. That glorious unpredictable burst of rage was genuine – in a world of retakes and fakery, she burst into flame and lit up the screen. She was worth the tantrums, the bullying, the pretentious spun sugar and couverture.
>
> I've never eaten a crumb she's cooked, never followed a single one of her recipes. But I remember her as a television genius, a personality who could take some pretty dull ingredients, and turn them into a hot, bubbling brandy sauce.

Notes and Sources

Quoted material, apart from where indicated otherwise, is from Fanny Cradock's 1960 autobiography, *Something's Burning*. Unless otherwise stated, the books listed in the notes are by the Cradocks. The following are quoted, except where indicated otherwise, on the basis of conversations with the author: Peter and Pam Vernon Evans, Christopher and Jane Chapman, Helen Davison, Alison Leach, Wendy Colvin, Win Frizell, Tenniel and Evangeline Evans, Phil Bradford, Terry Hibbert, John Harper, Tony and Yvonne Norris, Michael Parkinson, Nicholas Parsons, Hilary Alexander, Val Biro, Douglas Keay.

INTRODUCTION
p.1 'Ah, Fanny . . .': *Evening Standard*, 5 February 2002. Fay Maschler is restaurant critic for the *Evening Standard*.
p.4 'enough energy . . .': *Birmingham Gazette*, 1 April 1954.

1. BEGINNINGS
p.13 'drain imposed . . .': *Eastern Evening News*, 12 February 1930.
p.13 'Oh she's just as mad . . .': *Daily Mail*, 30 October 1976.

2. FANNY AND FAMILY
p.21 'I married . . .': Douglas Keay, *The Real Fanny Cradock*, Channel 4, 17 October 1998.

p.29 'Everything went swimmingly . . .': Pam Vernon Evans, *Daily Mail*, 3 October 1998.

p.30 'conceived in hatred . . .': *The Real Fanny Cradock.*

3. FANNY AND JOHNNIE: A LOVE AFFAIR

p.37 'I'll tell you what . . .': *Daily Mail*, 30 October 1976.

p.38 'I had the reputation . . .': *Reveille*, 21 May 1964.

p.45 'Domineering female . . .': *Lifestory*, BBC Radio 4, 19 June 1997.

p.46 'being dull . . .': *Woman's Own*, 11 January 1988.

p.47 'six months to live . . .': *Will the Real Fanny Cradock Please Stand Up*, BBC Radio 4, 2 July 1975.

p.47 'Johnnie is a superb healer . . .': *Will the Real Fanny Cradock Please Stand Up.*

p.48 'She saw me walk . . .': *Lifestory.*

4. BON VIVEUR

p.57 'There is the delicious . . .': *Around Britain with Bon Viveur.*

p.60 'In a seaside place . . .': *Daily Telegraph*, 28 January 1955.

p.61 'It sounds too much . . .': *Evening Post*, Jersey, 11 January 1960.

p.61 'Demonstration is . . .': *Evening Press*, Dublin, 19 June 1971.

p.64 'Cooking is a cleanly . . .': *Daily Telegraph*, 13 October 1954.

p.64 'Only a slut . . .': *Eastern Daily Press*, 16 October 1957.

p.64 'The great importance . . .': *Western Daily Press*, 11 November 1953.

p.64 'There is a lot . . .': *Nottingham Journal*, 5 December 1957.

p.64 'We've never lost . . .': *Evening Post*, Jersey, 13 January 1960.

p.65 'This Balenciaga dress . . .': *Reading Mercury*, November 1956.

p.66 'On one occasion . . .': *The Real Fanny Cradock.*

p.68 'One day all these people . . .': Wendy Colvin.

p.70 'I think it is only . . .': *Daily Herald*, 10 October 1955.

5. ON THE BOX

p.79 'We feuded . . .': *Daily Telegraph*, 29 April 1970.

p.79 'making the best . . .': *Lifestory.*

p.81 'As Mr Hitler . . .': letter to BBC.

p.84 'I think the highly-strung . . .': BBC internal memo.

p.85: 'What are you going . . .': *Success Story*, Associated-Rediffusion, 16 March 1959.

pp.87 'no dangling earrings . . .': *TV Times*, 22 April 1960.

p.89 'My hands do . . .': *Weekend*, 18 February 1970.

p.99 'About cooking . . .': *Radio Times*, 26 September 1968.

pp.101 'It's all so gloriously . . .'; 'Men are responsible . . .'; 'It isn't easy . . .': *Fanny Cradock Cooks for Christmas*, BBC 2, 15–19 December 1975.

p.102 'Biggest mistake . . .': Tony and Yvonne Norris.

p.102 'Viewers watched . . .': *Daily Express*, 2 January 1995.

p.103 'I could forgive . . .': *Daily Express*, 14 December 1976.

p.104 'You can never be . . .': *Parkinson*, BBC 1, 10 June 1972.

p.104 'That's a very rude . . .': *Wogan*, BBC 1, 11 August 1986.

p.105 'You take this . . .': *Bruce Forsyth and the Generation Game*, BBC 1, 15 December 1973.

p.105 'I sit there enthralled . . .': *What's My Line*, BBC 1, 26 January 1974.

6. AT HOME . . . AND ABROAD

p.106 'the most burgled . . .': *Yorkshire Observer*, 19 October 1955.

p.109 'glad the carriage folk . . .': Alison Leach.

p.110 'Whenever the host . . .': *Sunday Telegraph*, 3 May 1984.

p.110 'My fellow villagers . . .': *Kentish Independent*, 18 November 1960.

p.113 'sad old orchard . . .': *Daily Telegraph*, 9 April 1959.

p.114 'We put chains . . .': *Sun, Empire News*, 14 December 1958.

p.114 'We also excavated . . .': *Daily Telegraph*, 9 April 1959.

p.115 'If it were not . . .': *Daily Telegraph*, 9 April 1959.

p.115 'T and P . . .': Wendy Colvin.

p.119 'rather pagan . . .': *Doncaster Chronicle*, October 1961.

p.119 'coloured soap babies . . .': *Bon Voyage*.

p.121 'the most monstrous intake . . .': *Daily Mail*, 23 December 1955.

p.122 'John and I . . .': *Television Weekly*, 5 September 1968.

p.125 'the finest . . .': *Fanny and Johnnie Cradock Cookery Programme*.

p.125 'The way she . . .': *Birmingham Post*, 8 October 1970.

p.126 'wicked sense . . .': *Daily Mail*, 3 October 1998.

p.126 'Why do you want . . .': *Date,* 21 May 1960.

p.128 'In the end . . .': *Daily Mirror,* 12 November 1962.

p.131 'uniformed delinquents . . .': *Daily Mail*, 8 July 1964.

p.132 'The camera can . . .': Sun, 24 August 1978.

p.132 'Shut the bloody door . . .': Daily Mail, 8 February 1983.

p.136 'There is too . . .': *Time to Remember.*

p.137 'We once spent . . .': *Holiday on the French Riviera.*

p.139 'The only good . . .': *Phil Bradford and Terry Hibbert.*

7. FANNY: THE LOOK

p.143. 'We were quite . . .': *Star Johannesburg*, 13 June 1957.

p.143 'If men and women . . .': *Cabbages and Things.*

p.144 'I have to watch . . .': *Star Johannesburg.*

p.144 'Each time . . .': *Cabbages and Things.*

pp.147 'Except for a vast . . .': *Cartland's Book of Health and Beauty.*

pp.149–50 'Madame, their downfall . . .': *Sunday Graphic*, 1 March 1953.

p.152 'We have fairly earned . . .': *Sunday Graphic*, 21 September 1952.

p.157 'wrinkles are nothing . . .': *Sunday Graphic,* 5 January 1954.

p.157 'applied so wildly . . .': *Evening Standard*, 21 January 2005.

8. TRIPLE CHALLENGE

p.162 'I've never undertaken . . .': *Daily Mail*, 2 January 1956.

9. FANNY ON FOOD, WINE AND COOKING

p.183 'hitching our culinary . . .': *Fanny and Johnnie Cradock Cookery Programme.*

p.186 'If ever I meet . . .': *Lincolnshire Standard*, 13 October 1961.

p.186 'Today people may . . .': *Reading and Berkshire Chronicle*, 24 January 1964.

p.187 'Please may we . . .': *Home*, January 1962.

p.188 'Where wine is concerned . . .': *Stratford Herald*, 3 December 1957.

p.189 'A hostess has no business . . .': *Star Johannesburg*, 13 June 1957.

p.189 'Wine irons out . . .': *Daily Mail*, 28 September 1955.

p.190 'Take it from me . . .': *Evening News*, 22 October 1963.

p.191 'What has become . . .': *Daily Mail*, 16 May 1956.

p.193: 'Carping about the way . . .': *Daily Telegraph*, 23 April 1964.

p.193 'Crush four garlic cloves . . .': *Cabbages and Things.*

p.195 'She made this . . .': *The Real Fanny Cradock.*

p.199 'For several years . . .': *Daily Telegraph*, 8 January 1970.

p.203 'We do, however . . .': *Time to Remember.*

10. FANNY IN PRINT

p.209 'through her . . .': *The Eternal Echo.*

p.209 'Both sound a note . . .': *Gateway to Remembrance.*

p.210 'blissfully amoebic . . .': *Holiday on the French Riviera.*

p.210 'the eight wonders . . .': *Home*, July 1961.

p.215 'Many children gathered . . .': *Kentish Independent*, 29 April 1960.

p.215 'operation was for . . .': from press bulletin.

p.215 'It's disgustingly unattractive . . .': from press bulletin.

p.215 'When she was ready . . .': *Time to Remember.*

p.220 'plagiarise certain aspects . . .': foreword to *The Lormes of Castle Rising.*

11. FANNY: THE LEGACY

p.226 'twentieth century Johnson . . .': *Liverpool Echo*, 28 November 1961.

p.230 'The difference was . . .': *The Real Fanny Cradock.*

p.232 'I learned more . . .': *Evening Standard*, 23 December 2002.

p.232 'compulsive . . .': *Daily Mirror*, 29 December 1994.

p.232 'was like a Godfather figure . . .': *Daily Express*, 29 December 1994.

p.233 'Do not be afraid . . .': *Nottingham Journal*, 5 December 1957.

p.234 'I wanted to write . . .': Cheltenham Literary Festival, 12 October 2004.

p.236 'poseur par excellence . . .': *Delia Smith: The Biography.*

p.236 'She's one of the . . .': *The Way We Cooked*, BBC 2, 14 August 2002.

p.236 'We were looking . . .': *Sunday Times, Style* magazine, 21 October 2001.

Bibliography

The following books by Fanny and Johnnie Cradock, written under their own names and aliases, were consulted:

Bon Viveur, *Bon Voyage*, John Lehmann, 1949

——, *Holiday in Barcelona and the Balearics*, Frederick Muller, 1954

——, *Bon Viveur's London and the British Isles*, Andrew Dakers, 1955

——, *Cabbages and Things*, Gas Council, 1959

——, *Happy Cooking Children: The Young Chef with Fanny and Johnnie*, Putnam, 1959

——, *Holiday on the French Riviera*, Frederick Muller, 1960

——, *Daily Telegraph Cook's Book*, Daily Telegraph, 1964

——, *Sociable Cook's Book*, Daily Telegraph, 1967

——, *365 Soups*, Daily Telegraph, 1977

Cradock, Fanny, *Something's Burning*, Putnam, 1960

——, *Home Cooking*, BBC, 1965

——, *Ten Classic Dishes*, BBC, 1967

——, *Colourful Cookery*, BBC, 1968

——, *Common Market Cookery*, BBC, 1973

——, *The Lormes of Castle Rising*, W.H. Allen, 1975

——, *The Windsor Secret*, W.H. Allen, 1986

Cradock, Fanny and Johnnie, *Bon Viveur Recipes*, Associated Newspapers, 1956

——, *Fun with Cookery*, Edmund Ward, 1965

——, *Giving a Dinner Party*, BBC, 1969

——, *Fanny and Johnnie Cradock's Freezer Book*, W.H. Allen, 1978

——, *Time to Remember: A Cook for all Seasons*, Webb & Bower, 1981

——, *A Lifetime in the Kitchen: Family Cooking*, W.H. Allen, 1985

——, *A Lifetime in the Kitchen: For Beginner Cooks*, W.H. Allen, 1985

——, *A Lifetime in the Kitchen: The Ambitious Cook*, W.H. Allen, 1985

Cradock, Phyllis, *The Gateway to Remembrance*, Andrew Dakers, 1950

Dale, Frances, *The Practical Cook*, John Lehmann, 1949

——, *Brigadier Gooseyplum Goes to War*, Hodder and Stoughton, 1950

Dale, Frances and Cradock, John, *Around Britain with Bon Viveur*, John Lehmann, 1952

Hudson, Mrs (compiled by Fanny Cradock), *The Sherlock Holmes Cookbook*, W.H. Allen, 1976

Also consulted was *Fanny and Johnnie Cradock Cookery Programme*, the 96-issue part-work published by Purnell between 1970 and 1972.

OTHER BOOKS:

Cartland, Barbara, *Barbara Cartland's Book of Beauty and Health*, Hodder and Stoughton, 1972

Troake, Gwen, *Gwen Troake's Country Cookbook*, Macdonald and Jane's, 1977

Bowyer, Alison, *Delia Smith: The Biography*, Andre Deutsch, 1999

Hamilton, Christine, *The Book of British Battleaxes*, Robson, 2003

NEWSPAPERS AND MAGAZINES

Hundreds of copies of *The Daily Telegraph*, home to the Cradocks' Bon Viveur columns for more than thirty years, were pored over in the course of research. The other newspapers which Fanny and Johnnie worked for, the *Daily Mail*, *Sunday Graphic*, *Daily Express* and *Sunday Express*, were also consulted at length. The *Radio Times* and *TV Times* were also useful sources of information. Other papers quoted are referred to in the main text.

Acknowledgements

The author thanks the following for their assistance in piecing together Fanny Cradock's life and career: Peter and Pam Vernon Evans, Christopher and Jane Chapman, Helen Davison (formerly Holden-Dye), Alison Leach, Wendy Colvin, Tenniel and Evangeline Evans, Phil Bradford and Terry Hibbert, Win Frizell, Michael Parkinson, Nicholas Parsons, Douglas Keay, Tony and Yvonne Norris, John Harper, Val Biro, Elsa Waters and Rosemary Bromley. Hilary Alexander, fashion director on *The Daily Telegraph*, generously delivered her style verdict, and I am particularly grateful to Phil Bradford and Terry Hibbert for making it possible for me to acquire the archive of books, photographs and memorabilia which Fanny Cradock gave to them towards the end of her life.

Jeff Walden greatly assisted my research at the BBC Written Archives; the BFI Archive allowed me to spend a day of unalloyed pleasure viewing Fanny's TV programmes; and the staff at the Newspapers' Library in Colindale were efficiency itself over the course of various visits.

Every effort has been made to trace copyright holders, but in some cases this has not proved possible. The author and publisher apologise for any such omissions and will be happy to add an appropriate acknowledgement in future editions of the book.

I would like to offer special thanks to Sutton Publishing, and in particular Jaqueline Mitchell, for their belief that the story was worth telling, and to my sister Vivien Hunot, whose encouragement and support saw me through the occasional bout of self-doubt during the book's lengthy gestation period.

Clive Ellis, London

Index